An Introduction to the Sources of European Economic History 1500–1800

World Economic History
General Editor: Charles Wilson

THE RISE OF THE ATLANTIC ECONOMIES
Ralph Davis

ECONOMICS AND EMPIRE 1830–1914
D. K. Fieldhouse

THE EARLY GROWTH OF THE EUROPEAN ECONOMY
Georges Duby

An Introduction to the Sources of European Economic History 1500–1800

Edited by Charles Wilson
and Geoffrey Parker

CORNELL UNIVERSITY PRESS
ITHACA, NEW YORK

R 330.9402)
Introduction...

First published in 1977

International Standard Book Number 0–8014–1109–2
Library of Congress Catalog Card Number 76–55851

Printed in Great Britain

Library of Congress Cataloging in Publication Data
Main entry under title:
An Introduction to the sources of European economic
   history, 1500–1800.
   (World economic history)
   Bibliography: p.
   Includes index.
   1. Europe—Economic conditions—Sources. I. Wilson, Charles Henry. II. Parker,
Geoffrey, 1933–
HC240.I68   330.9′4′02   76–55851
ISBN 0–8014–1109–2

CIAD

Contributors

Preface

Charles Wilson *Professor of History and Civilization at the European University Institute at Florence*
and Geoffrey Parker *Lecturer in Modern History, University of St Andrews*

Chapter 1: Italy

Giuseppe Felloni *Professor of Economic History, University of Genoa*

Chapter 2: Spain

Frédéric Mauro *Professor of Latin American History, University of Paris*
and Geoffrey Parker

Chapter 3: Portugal

Frédéric Mauro and Geoffrey Parker

Chapter 4: the Low Countries

Jan A. van Houtte *Professor of Economic History, Catholic University of Louvain*
and Léon van Buyten *Lecturer in Economic History, Catholic University of Louvain*

Chapter 5: the British Isles

Charles Wilson (on England and Ireland)
and Bruce Lenman (on Scotland) *Lecturer in Scottish and Modern History, University of St Andrews*

Chapter 6: France

Michel Morineau *Professor at the Institute of History, University of Clermont-Ferrand*

Chapter 7: Germany

Hermann Kellenbenz *Director of the Seminar fur Sozial- und Wirtschaftsgeschichte, Friedrich-Alexander-University, Erlangen*
with the assistance of J. Schawacht, J. Schneider and L. Peters, members of the Seminar

v

Acknowledgements

The Editors acknowledge with gratitude the cooperation of their European colleagues who have made available the specialized knowledge without which this volume would not have been possible. It is not their fault, nor that of the editors or publishers, that economic pressures necessitated the curtailment and sometimes the elimination of illustrative material which we should all have liked to see included.

The editors also thank Angela Parker, Patrick Rayner and Patricia Richardson for their assistance in preparing the typescript of this book for publication. Most of the figures were prepared, from data submitted by the contributors, by Geoffrey Parker, with the assistance of Neil Price and Noel Thompson. Chapter 1 was translated by Mrs R. Maltby and Geoffrey Parker, chapter 6 by Geoffrey Parker and chapter 7 by Philip Broadhead.

C.W.
G.P.

Contents

Tables

Chapter 5 **the British Isles**

Chapter 6   France

Chapter 7   Germany

Figures

FIGURES

Chapter 3 Portugal

Chapter 4 the Low Countries

Chapter 5 the British Isles

Chapter 6   France

Chapter 7   Germany

Preface

During the planning of the series of volumes on *World Economic History*[1] it was decided to add to the studies of particular periods, areas and topics one or more volumes dealing with the source material – especially quantitative – in different regions. This is the first volume to appear. It covers Italy, Spain, Portugal, the Low Countries, the British Isles, France and Germany. A second volume will appear later dealing with northern, central and eastern Europe.

Although originally conceived as a work of reference related to the plan of the *World Economic History* series, it is hoped that this book will provide an introduction, for both students and general readers interested in economic and social history, to the kind of material available for the study of the subject – an *introduction*, not a comprehensive *manual*. Indeed, at present no manual could be compiled for the economic history of early modern Europe because too much of the basic spade-work remains to be done, and it takes time. To give a single example: it has been claimed that to produce a full study of the population of one city of 80,000 people for a century would take 20,000 working hours, or eight years of toil by a single researcher. By the year 1700, Europe contained more than twenty cities of this size and above, including London, Paris and Istanbul with over 400,000 inhabitants.

This volume presents as many as possible of the major known sources concerning western Europe's economic activities (statistics on Dutch trade to the Baltic, on Spanish commerce with America, on English and Italian textile production and the like). But it also offers a selection from less familiar material, both to indicate noteworthy trends and developments and to suggest areas where further research would be both possible and fruitful.

Because of the selective, perhaps idiosyncratic, selection of economic material for the seven countries covered here, the information has been divided up in a special way. The chapters have been organized in an order that reflects the economic shift from the Mediterranean states in the sixteenth century to those bordering the North Sea in the eighteenth century. During the early modern period, the 'core' of the European 'world system' moved from south to north.[2] Then within each chapter, wherever possible, the data have been grouped into the same broad categories: population, agriculture, industry, trade and transport, currency and finance, prices and wages, social structure. This format naturally encourages comparison between the differing economic records of the seven countries and at the same time emphasizes certain overall similarities of the western economies. In all of them, even in Holland, agriculture remained the principal occupation of the population and agricultural goods remained the principal products. In all of them, even in the backward, peripheral areas like Scotland and Portugal, there was some industry and considerable trade. In all of them the outstanding social characteristic was widespread poverty and under- or unemployment.

Recent years have seen a growing volume of criticism of the older, 'institutional', type of economic history which consisted to a large extent of the description of economic institutions and supposed systems, *dirigiste* or *non-dirigiste*. A new generation of socio-economic historians in Europe and America has demanded a type of history more securely, precisely and dynamically based on quantitative material. The demand is not new: economic historians of an earlier generation – Labrousse in France, Clapham in Britain, Posthumus in the Netherlands etc. – themselves criticized contemporary economic history (and even economic theory) for its lack of understanding of the potentialities of statistics and of 'the statistical sense' (as Clapham called it).[3]

Yet, like today's protagonists of the 'New Economic History' in the United States, these critics were only realizing and developing arguments that had been voiced repeatedly at a much earlier date. The philosophers of the Enlightenment did not think highly of history as a branch of thought, learning or science. Voltaire and Dr Johnson spoke on this point with a single voice. 'We require of modern historians more details, precise dates, more attention to population,' wrote Voltaire in his *Dictionnaire Philosophique* of 1764. Scattered through the recorded *dicta* of Johnson, in the *Life* of Boswell and elsewhere, are many observations on history and historians; almost without exception they are unflattering. For

Johnson, the historian was on the level of the lexicographer – 'a harmless drudge' – a peddler of facts, often inaccurate facts, often in false chronological order. History as it was understood demanded only a modicum of application and imagination – about as much as 'the lower kinds of poetry'; certainly no genius was needed. To such views Gibbon added his classic denigration of the *material* of the subject; this was but a chronicle of 'the crimes and follies of mankind.'

The *philosophes* criticized. They proposed reforms. They praised statistics. Yet their contribution was, in the event, disappointing. In Britain, a few valuable exercises in the use of statistical series for historical purposes were performed. An outstanding example was *The statistical account of Scotland* compiled from returns solicited from parish clergymen and published in the 1790s by Sir John Sinclair, an improving landowner of Caithness who built the town of Thurso and became secretary of the Board of Agriculture. His many publications on agriculture, trade, population and public finance combined a devotion to scientific accuracy with a real sense of historical development (see pp. 131 and 144–5 below for some fruits of his endeavours).

Yet on the whole the scientific techniques of history, so conspicuous by their absence in the minds of many thinkers of the Enlightenment, were to be developed during the nineteenth century by the historians of politics and diplomacy and by the exploration and organization of the great archives of *political* documents rather than the further collective exploitation of the materials of social and economic development in the past: one says 'further collection and exploitation' because in practice the men of the Enlightenment, whose sense of history itself was often extremely defective, largely overlooked the existence of great masses of material on the historical development of phenomena (such as population, economic fluctuations, poverty, employment, national wealth etc.) which were not intellectually and socially *à la mode*.

It was only dimly remembered that in the wake of the Renaissance, with its feats of exploration, new firearms, the printing press, bigger navies and merchant fleets, had come the cultural revolution of the seventeenth century, the wide development of experimental methods in science (and even technology) and especially the application of mathematics to the problems of reality, social reality in particular. This was the age of Copernicus, Galileo, Newton, Descartes

Huyghens and Leeuwenhoek; of the Royal Society and other scientific societies public and private in Italy and France; the age when God himself could be conceived as 'the perfect clockmaker'. Throughout the century the battle between medieval superstition, occultism and magic and newer scientific modes of inquiry into natural phenomena went on. There was as yet no final victory for 'sciences' in the modern sense: most of the great mathematicians and astronomers continued to blend their calculating talents and scientific curiosity with purely traditional concepts of religious belief and primitive superstition. Yet the growth of interest in mathematics (and the number of those interested in mathematics revealed, e.g., in the gossip of John Aubrey, the English antiquarian of the Restoration) was to leave a vital residue of information of a quantitative, statistical kind. Not the least important development in this growth of mathematical usage was the appearance and labours of those who called themselves 'political arithmeticians' and who would today be called social statisticians.

In the hands of this new generation of thinkers, speculation moved away from fantasy to rational calculation. In the 1580s the Italian Giovan Marcia Bonardo busied himself with calculations of the distance of Heaven and Hell from the earth, carefully concluding that 'Hell is $3758\frac{1}{4}$ miles from us' (and was $2505\frac{1}{2}$ miles wide) while the Empire of Heaven ('where the blessed rest in the greatest happiness') was 1,799,995,500 miles away. A century later, Graunt, Pétty, Davenant, Vossius, Roccioli, Halley, Gregory King and many others had transferred their attention from the heavens, literal and metaphorical, to more mundane targets – the numbers of persons inhabiting the world, or parts of the world, their wealth, collectively and *per capita*, its sources, the volume and types of employment, fruitful and otherwise, the balances of trade between the nations and so on.[4]

Among those who attempted such 'social' calculations were some whose aims included a genuine ambition to 'quantify' such concepts as production, consumption, population growth or decline and so on: they included men like Froumenteau in sixteenth-century France, Hermann Conring and Ludwig von Seckendorff in seventeenth-century Germany, Jerónimo de Uztariz and the Marquess of la Enseñada in eighteenth-century Spain. The incidence of such studies varied from country to country. It was sometimes related to the desire of governments or individuals to understand or try to control a particular socio-economic crisis; in England in the 1610s and 1620s, for example, a number of estimates of the national trade balance was made because of the critical condition of the contemporary economy; towards the end of the century, the famous surveys of Gregory King were part of an attempt to calculate the natural resources of England and its potential for carrying on a prolonged war against France. King, like a few others, was attempting a genuine statistical exercise for socio-political reasons of state. More usually, the collections of quantities and data which historians later came to regard as 'statistics' were in reality a residue of inquiries made for quite different reasons. The most common motive that caused public authorities to set such inquiries afoot was the desire to find out the most efficacious and economical ways of raising taxes. This caused them to look into such matters as the yield of farming production, the distribution of private wealth, the flow of domestic or foreign trade – all these were possible locations for a 'taxpoint'.

The need or desire to tax was not the only reason for busybodying. There was also the desire to assess military preparedness by counting the number of people who could be called upon to defend the state. Beyond that, government officials and even private citizens might simply be curious to know the total number of inhabitants in a given town, province or country. Surviving population estimates therefore come from many sources, and these vary widely from country to country. Venice took regular censuses of her population from at least 1338. The Grand Duke of Tuscany ordered counts in 1551, 1558, 1622, 1642 and 1672. England had no full-blown census until 1801, though numerous estimates appeared from the mid-seventeenth century. Gregory King's own national estimate seems to have been based on a quite sophisticated piece of fieldwork in his native town of Lichfield. Eighteenth-century estimates were based on calculations of birth and death rates and the residual balance resulting from their interaction. Parish priests were ordered to register births, marriages and deaths in many countries from the middle of the sixteenth century, and these registers form the foundation of most demographic calculations for early modern times, including the still-novel efforts at 'family reconstitution' and studies not only of how people lived or died but also how they moved from place to place and at what ages, to what extent, over what distances and in what numbers. Marriage registrations have been widely used as a guide to calculate the literacy of people in town and country; how many men or women could write their names? How many could only put a cross? (It is worth noting that, despite its innocuous nature, at the time Henry VIII's order of 1538 for the keeping of parish registers in England and Wales was widely regarded as just another tax-gathering device.)

One of the most renowned sources of demographic information in seventeenth-century England was the so-called 'Bills of Mortality' which were authority's response to the recurrent attacks of plague which terrified London and provided a new and urgent motive for attempting to check the growth of the City. The Bills were published regularly, notifying the numbers and causes of death – first of all in the old City, later in suburban areas. By 1660, the arrangements covered 130 parishes. Deaths were attested by two searchers ('ancient women') in each parish, notified to the parish clerks and published weekly, by the Company of Parish Clerks. In 1662 John Graunt and William Petty published their *Observations on the London Bills of Mortality*. Petty thus made one of his many marks on English history: surveyor, geographer, social statistician – and entrepreneur – he was driven on by a passionate conviction that quantitative measurement was the key to the understanding of social movements. Such correct understanding was the only true basis for a sound political system, the only way to obtain 'good, certain and easy government'. At the end of the disastrous third Anglo-Dutch War in 1674 he wrote his *Verbum Sapienti* in an attempt to prove the need to reduce property taxes and increase indirect taxation at large. From such calculations emerged not merely *soi-disant* statistical calculations of national and *per capita* income but also comparative estimates of the value, in terms of wealth produced, of different types of investment and occupation – agricultural, commercial, manufacturing. Petty's pioneering work was refined and enlarged by his scientific heir, Gregory King.

Simultaneously, many minds were busy with the information on *policy* which could be obtained from the customs houses and the port books recording the flow of trade and money in and out of the country. These preoccupations reached their peak in the appointment of a national 'Inspector General of Exports and Imports' to calculate and report regularly on the returns of the local customs houses. The object was 'to present a faire and exacte Scheme of the Ballance of Trade ... between England and any other part of the world'.[5]

This is not the place to attempt a general tally of the sources that are available to historians in search of 'quantitative' data. It is enough to say that, in all the countries surveyed in this volume, there exist, besides some limited and conscious attempts at 'measurement', large reservoirs of records which are the byproduct of other, more mundane, less mathematical, less socially conscious processes. Almost any activity could have an economic aspect, and every economic activity was, in theory, taxable. In Italy prostitutes were taxed: they formed an important source of income for the dukes of Tuscany, and when Pope Pius v attempted in 1566 to expel them, his attempt at pious reform failed because the financial disruption was too great to be contemplated. This was the Pope's problem; for us, this dubious form of taxation has left a residue of valuable evidence which helps us to build up some detail of the social structure of some of the great Italian cities in early modern times.[6]

Thus in many ways and in many places the records kept for reasons of hygiene, health, religion and greed – as well as the ratiocinations of educated people about economic and social policies deriving from such figures – may be used by historians to widen and deepen knowledge of the nature of early modern societies. The information is vast and varied, particularly for the eighteenth century. Yet it exhibits one consistent feature to the very end: it is never easy to interpret or to convert into 'pure' measures of quantity. Sometimes such conversion is impossible because of gaps in our evidence or in our knowledge of the meaning of the evidence. Always, the greatest care as well as expert knowledge of the economic, social and technical processes of the past are needed if the risk of serious error is to be avoided. Never is the problem of conversion easy or straight-forward.[7]

It is improbable that the results of even the most skilled manipulation of evidence such as that presented here can ever be wholly free of error. But the continuous use, confrontation and interaction of different sources – which will continuously be added to and elaborated – will, over time, modify and correct individual mistakes. For example, comparison and reflection have made scholars sceptical about the precision of the statistics of imports of gold and silver from Mexico and Peru set out by E.J.Hamilton in his pioneer work of 1934.[8] *A fortiori*, they have modified some of the general conclusions drawn by Hamilton and his contemporaries regarding the economic significance of the mining, distribution and use of the

American treasure. Yet as an indication of the order of magnitude of the inflow of American treasure to Europe, Hamilton's work remains as valuable as ever. In similar fashion the explorations by Nina Bang of the records of the Danish Sound tolls, the largest single'tax point' in the early modern world, affecting the trade of a dozen nations in and out of the Baltic, have been subjected to trenchant criticism by later scholars. The sources of Scandinavia fall outside the scope of this volume, but since they affect closely the economic development of countries included in it (the Netherlands, England and Scotland especially) it is worth pointing out that here too the student of history must strike a course that avoids both a gullible reliance on figures as such and a destructive scepticism which would reject the possibility of a greater approximation to accuracy. The fact is that our ideas of economic development inside and outside Europe have been powerfully modified during the last fifty years (in some cases over a much longer period) by scholars who have used evidence of the type presented here to give precision to ideas of size and movement formerly vague, general and sometimes quite inaccurate. Our ideas of European agricultural–social development have been permanently modified by B.H.Slicher van Bath and members of the Wageningen group using yield–ratio evidence and combining agricultural and demographic evidence in a new analysis. The school of French historians that has assumed a dominant role in European economic and social historiography – Braudel, Goubert, Le Roy Lodurie, Henry and many others – have led the way in demonstrating how a multiplicity of sources can be combined to produce a type of *histoire totale* that is at once general yet highly particular, encapsulating over very long periods the results of profound, multiple investigations of detailed problems within broad new syntheses. In Italy and the United States Professor Cipolla has performed in his own person a similar function, contributing both a series of highly specialized articles and monographs on monetary, demographic and technological problems and larger syntheses of the socio-economic development of Europe, utilizing the traditional techniques of the historian in close combination with those of the social-statistician.

The results have been of two kinds: theoretical or methodological, and practical. The older, often acrid and generally unfruitful debate (which occupied historians for many years) over the relationship of economic history and economic theory, has – in its old form at least – faded into the background. Modern historians are less concerned with theory, more concerned with the more detailed and practical issues of how to *use* quantitative evidence; how to apply mathematical techniques to its interpretation. But these very applications have already modified our ideas of the 'shape of history'. The importance of colonial trade, of American silver, of the supposed role of Calvinism and other forms of Protestantism, of the 'price revolution', of scientific applications in manufacturing industry and agriculture, of supposed medical advance, of economic 'policies' such as 'mercantilism' etc. – all these trends, concepts, and institutions are seen in a different light as the result of the use and application (especially by post-war scholars) of the sort of quantitative evidence presented in this volume. Some sacred cows have fallen victim in the process: some Aunt Sallies seem less easy targets than formerly. In point of style, the results vary; some of the process of adjusting, deepening and sophisticating received, but very partial, truths has produced results admittedly dull and merely technical. But this is not the only or necessary consequence. Other historians using essentially the same type of quantitative evidence have had an immediate impact on general history and even on the reading public at large.

For the early modern period, 'quantitative' sources are not so plentiful or so precise as to enable us to form clear, well-defined images of European societies and economics. Some general trends are nevertheless beyond doubt, and they are reflected in most of the data assembled in this book. First, the demographic picture: it is plain from all our sources that, until well into the eighteenth century, the forces checking any large growth in population were stronger than the remarkably high birth rates which also prevailed. The towns, in particular, regularly suffered from an excess of deaths over births, an imbalance that was only corrected by large-scale immigration from the countryside. Plague and a hundred other diseases (some of which elude scientific analysis at this distance) struck again and again. Infant mortality was especially high. In general, malnutrition, cold, and ignorance of the perils of dirt and contagion kept mortality at rates that prevented anything more than modest, intermittent increases in numbers. It was significant that the response in England to prevalent poverty often took the form of charitable trusts to provide bread, blankets and coal for the poor: malnutrition and cold at least could be alleviated, even if medicine could help little with other causes of mortality.

Second, if *population* had to fight a desperate battle against mortality, *productivity* – in trade and manufacture – faced similar problems. *Rates* of manufacturing output remained pretty steady between the fifteenth and sixteenth centuries. The ratios of crops raised to seed sown rose in some areas, notably in the Low Countries and later (partly by process of direct imitation of agricultural techniques) in England. Here in the west yields were spectacularly higher than in central and eastern Europe (see p. 121 below), yet later in the seventeenth and early eighteenth centuries the advance paused as adverse demographic circumstances reduced effective demand and perhaps as the high early yields of new lands fell away. Everywhere the lynchpin of the economy remained the harvest, and the seventeenth-century climate was not on the whole kind towards harvest in Europe (or, indeed, elsewhere).[9]

If disaster was always just around the corner for the small peasant farmer, it was also an ever-present risk for merchants and manufacturers. The bankruptcies and shipwrecks that feature so prominently in Elizabethan drama were not simply an ingenious theatrical contrivance. They were drawn from real life and show through repeatedly in the records of the time: seven per cent of all ships sailing from Spain to America in the sixteenth century and fifteen per cent of all Portuguese ships sailing for Asia sank before reaching their destination.

Yet though the problems remained obstinate and were nowhere wholly surmounted, western Europe (as represented by the countries covered in this volume) did not remain passive in the face of the challenge.

It was in an effort to avoid or minimize the impact of impending disaster that those engaged in economic activities experimented with new methods and new techniques. In agriculture, 'hard times' led to the spread of maize cultivation in southern Europe (in Spain from the sixteenth century and in Italy and Southern France from the mid-seventeenth century) and the potato further north (in Ireland from the early seventeenth century, Scotland from the mid-eighteenth, and Scandinavia from the early nineteenth century). Both crops were of critical importance, first because they could be grown on fields after grain, thus eliminating the need to fallow, second because they were less easily destroyed by wet summers than traditional cereals. That was why their cultivation spread. The same was true, on a smaller scale, of the expanding consumption of market gardening around the European cities: vegetables helped to relieve overdependence on the fickle grain crops. By 1800 over ten per cent of all cultivated land in Germany was producing vegetables, compared with sixty-one per cent under cereals (cf. p. 198 below). The evidence seems clear that these new crops were introduced during or immediately following periods of disastrous grain harvests which demonstrated, in the words of Sebastian Mercier, that 'The corn which feeds man has also been his executioner.'

But these reactions to crisis differed from one area of Europe to another. The potato was cultivated in Germany far earlier than in France, in Ireland far earlier than in Scotland, although there is no evidence to suggest that France and Scotland were any less prey to famine. In the industrial sphere the falling demand for heavy woollen garments after 1550 led in England and the Low Countries to the production of an entire new range of lighter clothes, made with worsted yarn and more brightly coloured. In Italy and Spain, however, no 'new draperies' appeared to compensate for the slump in woollens; instead there was a growth in silk manufacture. In commerce the expansion of maritime trade led shipbuilders everywhere to find ways of reducing unit costs: in Spain this led to ever larger galleons, in Holland to mass-produced ships of traditional size with simplified rigging requiring a smaller crew. A phenomenon common to the whole of Europe like the sharp rise of prices between 1450 and 1650 proved deleterious to the economically backward areas of Europe, like Spain, Scotland and Poland, producing mainly raw materials or cheap manufactures; these areas were unable to absorb such an acute rate of inflation. Advanced economies, however, such as the Dutch Republic, found some inflation favourable to profit accumulation and economic growth.

The Dutch Republic presents a remarkable example of economic progress based on the application of empirical observation in agriculture, trading and maritime techniques and manufacturing technology. Her urban growth and agrarian specialization interacted to produce a precocious example of modern economic growth: England followed, overtaking the Dutch in those respects that enabled her to inaugurate a new kind of economic specialization we have come to call 'the Industrial Revolution'. In France too, agrarian monoculture (with its concomitant: repetitive crises of famine and death) gave way to more varied and specialized agrarian and urban economies. Slowly and painfully, Europe by the eighteenth century was casting off its shackles. So much the figures have made clear: they do not themselves by any means show us how the change came about nor give us all the reasons why. The sources given in this volume provide no instant or final answers to any problems at all. Indeed, they often seem to provide more extra questions: the work of interpretation remains. All that 'quantities' such as those provided here do, is to give us some indication of the scale and scope of economic activity and a wider range of evidence with which to search for a greater measure of truth and avoid at least the grosser kinds of error.

1 Italy

1.1 Population

Italy in early modern times was both larger and smaller than today: larger because it covered an area of some 310,500 square kilometres (about ten per cent larger than its present size and including Corsica, Savoy and other territories later swallowed up by France and Austria); smaller because this considerable area was politically fragmented to an extraordinary degree. In 1559, although almost half the peninsula was subject to foreign powers (Spain controlled 144,000 square kilometres, France 5000 and the Empire 2700), the rest was split up among over a score of independent sovereign states. However, in the course of time, there was some unification. By 1790 there were only eleven sovereign states covering 287,000 square kilometres (headed by the House of Bourbon with 102,800). Spain's dominion had disappeared, the Empire now controlled about 11,000 square kilometres and France about 17,000 square kilometres (including the isle of Corsica).

This political fragmentation is of fundamental importance for the economic historian, because the multiplicity of political divisions has caused both the dispersal of statistical records and a lack of concordance in the periods to which they refer. The problems this creates are particularly evident in the estimates of the population of Italy during the early modern period: data are seldom available for all political units at the same time. However, a general picture emerges from Table 1.1.[1] It would seem from that data and from Figure 1.1 that the total population of Italy almost doubled between 1550 and 1790, from 11 million to over 19 million, while the population density increased from 35.5 to almost 62 people per square kilometre.

Italy was one of the most highly urbanized areas of Europe, possibly of the world, in early modern times. In 1550 there were 30 cities with over 10,000 inhabitants; at that time the Low Countries had 20 or more cities of this size, the entire Holy Roman Empire had

TABLE 1.1: Italian population 1550–1790 by states (boundaries of 1790)

State	c. 1550	c. 1600	c. 1650	c. 1700	c. 1750	c. 1790
STATE OF THE HOUSE OF SAVOY	?	?	?	?	2,643,341	3,350,859
Principality of Piedmont	700,000	800,000	750,000	920,000	1,084,593	⎫
Duchy of Savoy	280,000	300,000	?	?	351,032	⎬ 3,006,344
Duchy of Monferrat	200,000	230,000	150,000	191,120	219,638	⎪
Other territories of Terra-firma	?	?	?	?	627,686	⎭
Kingdom of Sardinia	200,000	266,444	285,000	260,486	360,392	344,515
REPUBLIC OF VENICE (without Istria)	1,590,040	1,820,000	1,340,000	1,700,000	2,060,000	2,354,066
REPUBLIC OF GENOA	290,700	355,800	400,900	?	451,100	491,300
DUCHY OF MODENA AND REGGIO	222,000	244,000	?	277,005	283,680	341,668
DUCHY OF PARMA AND PIACENZA	283,590	314,500	?	418,000	413,425	442,351
REPUBLIC OF LUCCA	100,000	?	110,000	?	118,000	123,000
DUCHY OF MASSA AND CARRARA	12,500	15,000	13,000	16,000	?	21,156
GRAND DUCHY OF TUSCANY	729,781	?	754,837	?	901,149	983,522
PAPAL STATE	1,150,000	?	1,810,216	1,997,340	?	2,385,596
Territories of central Italy	?	1,360,000	1,260,782	1,419,474	1,500,000	1,688,236
State of Bologna	?	207,795	225,434	228,779	?	280,832
Duchy of Ferrara	?	?	165,000	184,711	206,780	223,485
Duchy of Urbino	?	150,000	140,000	144,376	?	166,575
Other territories (Castro and Ronciglione)	?	?	19,000	20,000	?	26,468

State	c. 1550	c. 1600	c. 1650	c. 1700	c. 1750	c. 1790
PRINCIPALITY OF PIOMBINO	6,000	6,000	5,000	6,500	6,515	8,000
STATE OF THE HOUSE OF BOURBON OF NAPLES	3,226,253	4,148,326	3,937,013	3,670,588	4,786,021	6,617,937
Kingdom of Naples	2,373,253	3,045,326	2,813,013	2,521,588	3,461,021	4,954,770
Kingdom of Sicily	850,000	1,100,000	1,121,000	1,143,000	1,319,000	1,660,267
State of Presidi	3,000	3,000	3,000	6,000	6,000	2,900
IMPERIAL FIEFS	105,000	125,000	130,000	?	140,000	155,000
FRENCH DOMINIONS (Isle of Corsica)	?	?	118,510	?	120,389	152,342
DOMINIONS OF THE HOUSE OF AUSTRIA					1,145,914	1,384,279
Duchy of Milan	271,000	?	?	?	582,223	?
Principality of Pavia	?	?	?	?	74,567	?
County of Cremona	120,000	148,000	?	?	145,769	?
Duchy of Mantua	116,502	130,000	106,000	130,000	156,732	?
Other territories	?	?	?	?	176,623	?
STATE OF MALTA	30,000	35,000	?	60,000	65,000	95,000

only 19 and the British Isles had 4. The rest of Europe only overtook Italy in the eighteenth century (cf. the first sections of the other contributions in this book). At the same time, the large towns gradually declined in relation to the total population: between 1550 and 1790 the population of the 36 largest towns (that is, those which attained a size of 20,000 inhabitants at least once during the period) rose by an average of 60 per cent, but the population of the rest of the country rose by an average of 80 per cent.

Tables 1.1 and 1.2 are based on census data which are extremely numerous in Italy and contain a wealth of detail on the ages, sex, and sometimes also the property of the population surveyed. To take two examples – the town of Carpi in 1591 and the town and countryside of Pesaro in 1689. Both censuses show the enormous number of children in each community, compared with the number of adults: 28 per cent of all males and 26 per cent of all females at Carpi were under 10, and

FIGURE 1.1: The demographic evolution of Italy, 1550–1790 (population in millions)

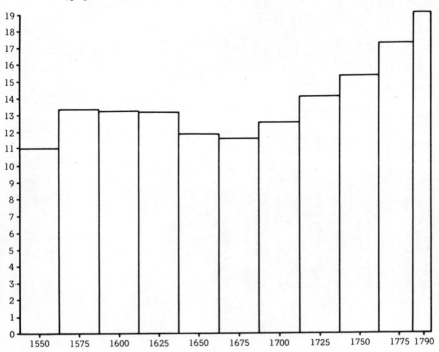

TABLE 1.2: Size of the principal Italian cities, 1550–1790

	10–20,000	20–30,000	30–40,000	40–50,000	50–60,000	60–70,000	over 70,000
1550 (30 cities)	Bari Bergamo Modena Modica/ Pozzallo Nicosia Pavia Reggio C. Siena Trapani	Catania Lucca Parma Piacenza Turin Vicenza	Cremona Mantua Messina Padua	Brescia Ferrara Rome	Bologna Florence Verona	Genoa Milan	Naples (227,000) Palermo (80,000) Venice (158,000)
1600 (32 cities)	Alessandria Ancona Bari Modena Modica/ Pozzallo Nicosia Pavia Reggio C. Siena Trapani	Bergamo Catania Lucca Turin	Cremona Ferrara Mantua Padua Parma Piacenza Vicenza	Brescia	Messina Verona	Bologna Florence	Genoa (71,000) Milan (130,000) Naples (289,000) Palermo (105,000) Rome (102,000) Venice (139,000)
1650 (35 cities)	Alessandria Ancona Bari Cagliari Leghorn Marsala Modena Modica/ Pozzallo Nicosia Pavia Reggio C. Siena Trapani	Bergamo Brescia Catania Cremona Ferrara Lucca Mantua Parma Piacenza Vicenza	?Messina Padua ?Turin Verona		Bologna	Florence	Genoa (90,000) Milan (109,000) Naples (265,000) Palermo (100,000) Rome (121,000) Venice (120,000)

TABLE 1.2: Size of the principal Italian cities, 1550–1790—continued

	10–20,000	20–30,000	30–40,000	40–50,000	50–60,000	60–70,000	over 70,000
1700 (36 cities)	Alessandria Ancona Bari Cagliari Leghorn Marsala Modica/ Pozzallo Nice Nicosia Reggio C. Siena Trapani	Catania Cremona Ferrara Lucca Mantua ?Messina ?Modena Pavia	Bergamo Brescia Padua Parma Piacenza Verona ?Vicenza	Turin		Bologna	Florence (72,000) Genoa (80,000) Milan (120,000) Naples (232,000) Palermo (100,000) Rome (142,000) Venice (138,000)
1750 (36 cities)	Alessandria Ancona Cagliari Marsala Modena Nice Nicosia Reggio C. Siena Trapani ?Bari	Bergamo Catania Cremona Ferrara Lucca Mantua Messina Modica/Pozzallo Pavia Vicenza	Brescia Leghorn Parma Piacenza	Padua Verona	Turin	Bologna	Florence (74,000) Genoa (87,000) Milan (124,000) Naples (315,000) Palermo (107,000) Rome (158,000) Venice (149,000)

1790					
Bari	?Alessandria	Bergamo	Catania	Verona	Bologna (71,000)
?Cagliari	Ancona	Brescia	Leghorn		Florence (81,000)
Modica/	Cremona	Parma	Padua		Genoa (91,000)
Pozzallo	Ferrara	?Piacenza			Milan (131,000)
Nicosia	Lucca				Naples (436,000)
Reggio C.	Mantua				Palermo (130,000)
Siena	Marsala				Rome (163,000)
	?Messina				Turin (82,000)
(36 cities)	Modena				Venice (138,000)
	?Nice				
	Pavia				
	Trapani				
	Vicenza				

52 and 50 per cent were under 20. At Pesaro, a century later, younger people were slightly less numerous, but they still constituted almost half the total population. Only about 15 per cent of the population was over 50 years of age. These censuses also reveal 'generations' in the population (see Table 1.3). Thus at Carpi, the 1–5 age 'cohorts', born in 1586–91, were unusually small (no doubt due to the harsh economic climate of these years) as were those aged 30–35, 40–45 and 50–55 (those born in 1556–61, 1546–51, and 1536–41, all periods of war, plague or famine).[2]

TABLE 1.3: The distribution of population by age groups: Carpi (1591) and Pesaro (1689)

Ages	Carpi (Emilia) 1591 Men	Women	Pesaro (Marche) 1689 Town	Country
81 and over	0.3	0.1	0.5	0.7
71–80	0.6	0.4	2.4	3.7
61–70	1.8	1.4	5.9	5.9
56–60	3.1	3.5	3.9	3.8
51–55	2.8	2.4	6.7	5.4
46–50	5.1	5.7	5.8	5.5
41–45	4.1	4.1	8.2	6.6
36–40	7.1	8.7	6.0	5.0
31–35	5.9	5.9	7.1	6.6
26–30	8.1	9.1	8.4	7.7
21–25	8.2	8.6	10.4	8.2
16–20	9.8	11.0	9.1	9.5
11–15	14.4	12.5	8.7	9.7
6–10	15.5	13.8	8.2	10.4
0–5	13.0	12.8	8.7	11.3

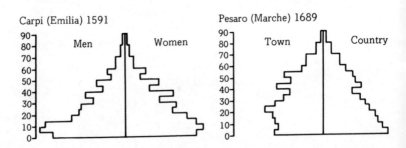

Carpi (Emilia) 1591   Men   Women

Pesaro (Marche) 1689   Town   Country

The fluctuations in the levels of Italy's population can be studied in more detail through surviving parish registers. As yet, however, this has only been done for certain towns. Moreover, because of incomplete burial statistics, we have only baptismal data to use.

These reflect, to some extent, the overall changes in the level of population, and in Figure 1.2 we can see the steady growth of the towns of southern Italy – Palermo, Bari and Naples – contrasting with the more sluggish performance of the towns of the north and centre.[3]

FIGURE 1.2: Annual averages of births in selected Italian towns (in thousands)

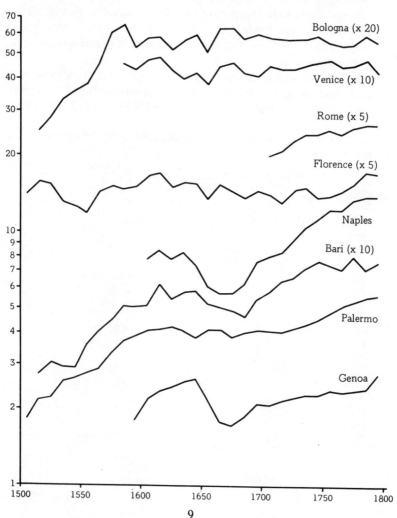

1.2 Agriculture

There are very few records of agricultural production, which was concerned chiefly with cereals and to a lesser degree with vines and olives. The surviving figures are limited to the last decade of the eighteenth century and relate to a few zones only of the peninsula; moreover they are based for the most part on the declarations of the producers themselves or on the reports of food commissioners. Those relating to wheat are the fullest, but even for this crop they are uneven. Some yield ratios have been interpolated to give an idea of productivity (see Table 1.4), but almost always they stem from a single estate (the 'yield ratio' is the number of grains harvested for each grain sown).

On the whole it is the diversity of the results that stands out: very high yield ratios in Sicily in the early eighteenth century (8 or 9 to 1); very low in Monferrat and Modena from 1660 to 1790 (2 or 3 to 1 and

TABLE 1.4: *Italian wheat yield ratios, 1510–1799 (grains harvested per grain sown)*

	Monferrat	Vercelli	Modena	Romagna	Sienna	Puglia	Sicily
1510–19				7.9			
1520–9				6.9			
1530–9				6.4			
1540–9				6.5			
1550–9				5.9			
1560–9			2.4	5.6			
1570–9				5.7	4.1		
1580–9				5.9			
1590–9			3.3	4.8			
1600–9				5.9			
1610–19				6.2			
1620–9				5.4			
1630–9				5.5			
1640–9				5.5	5.0		
1650–9			2.7	5.4			
1660–9	3.0			6.4			
1670–9	2.3			5.9	5.1		
1680–9	2.7			6.4		8.0	7.1–9.0
1690–9	1.8			6.1	5.4	6.3	
1700–09	2.9			5.7		6.3	
1710–19	2.2	3.6		6.1			9.8
1720–9	3.0			6.2		6.2	
1730–9	2.3			5.7		5.7	
1740–9		3.9		5.6		6.8	8.2–8.8
1750–9	0.9		2.6	6.0		5.9	
1760–9				5.7	6.4	6.3	6.0–8.0
1770–9			3.2	5.5			5.3
1780–9	3.6	4.6		5.9			5.6
1790–9				6.2			

less). In most of the peninsula during the eighteenth century the yield appears to have been between 4 and 5 to 1, rather more on good soil, rather less on poor land. Apart from the sharp decline in Sicilian productivity after 1750, it is possible to discern few salient trends during the period. There was clearly an improvement in the yield of *quintals* per hectare between the late sixteenth and the late eighteenth century on the mainland (see Table 1.5), but there was probably a drop in the seventeenth century.[4] (See German data on p. 198.)

TABLE 1.5: Italian wheat production, 1580–1799 (in metric quintals of grain harvested per hectare)

	Vercelli	Lombardy	Agro Romano	Sicily
1580–9		⎫		
1590–9		⎬ 4.5		
1600–9		5.5–5.7		
1660–1709				10.7–16.2
1710–19	6.1			⎫ 14.7–17.6
1720–9		⎫	8.0	⎬
1730–9		⎬ 5.0–12.0	8.0	
1740–9	⎫		10.1	
1750–9	⎬ 6.7		9.8	⎫ 12.3–15.8
1760–9		4.0–12.0	10.8	⎬
1770–9		8.5–10.5	8.7	
1780–9	7.3	6.5–8.5	8.7	
1790–9			8.3	

Information on the productivity of animal husbandry is even harder to obtain, although some isolated figures from Lombardy reveal an average daily milk yield of between seven and nine litres a day (with a maximum of twelve to thirteen litres) in the late sixteenth century, and an average of nine to twelve litres (with a maximum of fifteen to eighteen) in the mid-eighteenth century. In both periods, yields were significantly higher than in areas with less well developed farming, including the less favoured regions of Italy.

Data like these necessarily come from farm account books which record input and output faithfully. The same sources also noted income and expenditure on each estate and, therefore, profit and loss as well; but such material has been studied only for a very few farms. Foremost among these are the records of the Montaldeo estate in Piedmont, for which a long series of incomes has been calculated and expressed as a percentage of the land's value. Although the data of the years 1572–1632 seem too high (probably because the estate's value has not been increased in proportion to monetary devaluation), they point to a rise in the last decades of the seventeenth century, followed by a long decline (see Figure 1.3). Notwithstanding its limits, this series illustrates the usefulness of farm accounts in deepening our understanding of European economic development in the pre-industrial period.[5]

FIGURE 1.3: Agricultural profits at Montaldeo, Piedmont, 1570–1755 (estate's income as percentage of the land's value)

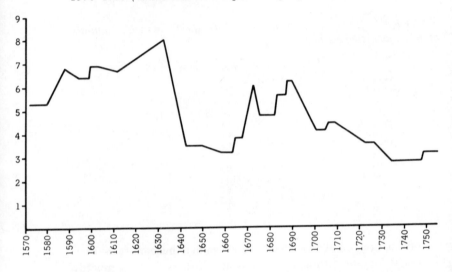

1.3 Industry

Textile production was the major industry in the peninsula throughout early modern times and, happily, we possess quite good statistics concerning the output of many major centres. The four series of woollen cloth figures given in Figure 1.4 all tell the same story: strong growth during the sixteenth century – and at Venice until 1620 – then prolonged and catastrophic decline to a minimal production in the eighteenth century. There were several reasons for this collapse. One was the competition of English and Dutch 'new draperies', which were lighter, cheaper and more colourful than the traditional 'broadcloths'. Another was the growth of cloth production in the smaller towns and villages of Italy, less regimented by the guilds and therefore operating on lower wages and undercutting the prices of woollens manufactured in Venice and

12

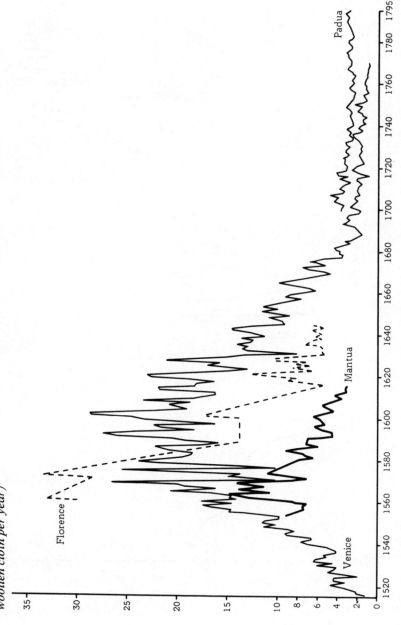

FIGURE 1.4: Woollen cloth production (Venice, Mantua, Florence and Padua) 1520–1795 (thousand pieces of woollen cloth per year)

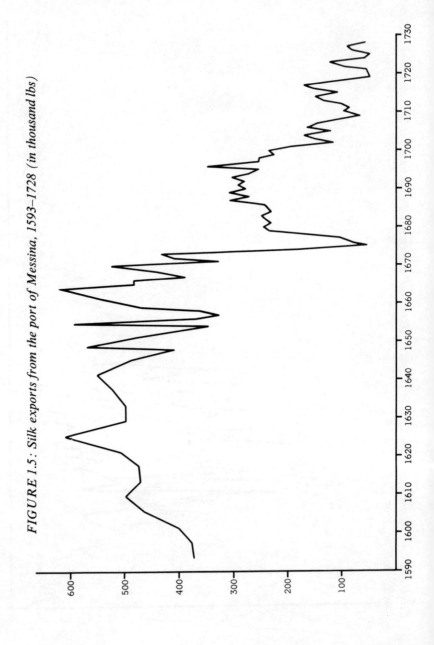

FIGURE 1.5: Silk exports from the port of Messina, 1593–1728 (in thousand lbs)

other cities. Finally, there was the string of misfortunes that afflicted Italy: plague in 1575–6, famine in the 1590s, plague again in 1630–1, war from 1635 to 1659 – all these disasters undoubtedly reduced consumption in one way or another and thus contributed to the decline in textile production.[6]

Another important aspect of the Italian textile industry was silk cultivation and manufacture. In Florence, around 1600, about three times as many people were employed in producing silk goods as in producing woollens (although the value of woollen exports was larger). Sicily had an even larger silk industry and it exported massive quantities of both raw and manufactured silk through Messina and Palermo (see Figure 1.5). Once again, however, there was a period of stagnation which lasted from the mid-seventeenth to the mid-eighteenth century.[7]

1.4 Trade and transport

Although there are sundry figures about trade in individual commodities such as silk, the subject of Figure 1.5, these do not reflect the collective trade balance of the peninsula. Ironically, the only overall view that we have is the fruit of the labour of the French Treasury, which noted the balance of trade between their country and Italy for almost the entire eighteenth century. Two salient features stand out in Table 1.6: first, the enormous growth in the value of the trade carried on, from around 20 million *livres* in the second decade to 80–100 million in the penultimate decade of the eighteenth century; and second, the contrast between the Kingdoms of Savoy and the Two Sicilies on the one hand, which regularly had a favourable balance with France, and the rest of Italy on the other, which after 1738 was regularly in deficit. Most of the fluctuations (e.g. the drop in Savoy's overall trade 1743–7) were largely the result of war.[8]

Figure 1.6 assembles some figures concerning the composition of merchant fleets flying the flag of Italian states in 1786–7, taken from an inquiry by French consuls abroad.[9] While it is clear from these figures that the chief ports of the peninsula in the early modern era were Livorno, Naples, Venice and Genoa, it is not easy to establish their order of importance owing to limitations in the records. At Naples, for example, movements of ships at the port are known only for 1760 (when there were 1009 larger ships, with a total tonnage of

TABLE 1.6: Trade between Italy and France, 1716–89 (yearly averages in million livres tournois)

	State of Savoy		Republic of Venice		Republic of Genoa		Kingdom of Naples and Sicily		Other Italian states		Total	
	Export	Import	Export	Import	Export	Import	Export	Import	Export	Import	Export	Import
1716–19	6.5	7.7							3.4	3.9	9.9	11.5
1720–4	8.2	10.2							5.9	4.3	14.1	14.5
1725–9	7.3	5.2							4.6	3.3	12.0	8.5
1730–4	6.6	3.8							5.5	4.6	12.1	8.5
1735–9	5.0	2.4							8.0	8.6	13.0	10.9
1740–4	3.0	2.6							13.7	25.8	16.7	28.3
1745–9	2.0	2.3							15.9	24.6	17.9	26.8
1750–4	7.4	3.5							19.3	32.3	26.7	35.8
1755–9	10.5	7.7							17.2	19.5	27.7	27.2
1760–4	11.5	7.6		0.2	5.7	2.8	8.9	1.8	5.4	15.5	31.5	27.8
1765–9	8.4	8.4	0.9	1.3	5.1	6.8	11.9	4.3	8.6	26.4	35.0	47.1
1770–4	5.3	7.7	1.8	1.7	3.9	5.0	11.0	5.7	9.3	25.7	31.3	45.7
1775–9	11.2	6.6	0.1	0.1	3.0	2.5	7.7	2.8	17.4	23.0	39.4	35.0
1780	26.0	6.8	0.1	—	2.5	1.4	5.9	0.7	15.9	19.0	50.5	27.8
1787–8	23.6	19.2	0.4	1.3	9.9	6.2	15.2	5.6	5.5	14.9	54.6	47.2
1789							26.9	7.1				

109,000 metric tons, as well as 555 smaller crafts). This isolated figure puts Naples at the top of the list by a long way – but how typical was the year to which it refers? At Genoa we have more data. Around 2000 ships used the port in the 1640s; by the 1780s this figure increased to 4000 ships per annum and more, which probably made it the busiest port of the peninsula by the time France took it over in 1797.[10]

FIGURE 1.6: Mercantile fleets of the Italian states, 1786–7

Naples	40·1%	943 ships	Naples	48·6%	120,800 tons
Genoa	27·4%	643 ships	Genoa	16·6%	41,200 tons
Venice	17·8%	418 ships	Venice	23·8%	59,100 tons
Papal States	7·8%	42 ships	Papal States	5·3%	13,200 tons
Sicily	4·3%	181 ships	Sicily	3·5%	8,700 tons
Savoy	1·8%	104 ships	Savoy	1%	2,600 tons
Tuscany	0·8%	18 ships	Tuscany	1·2%	2,900 tons

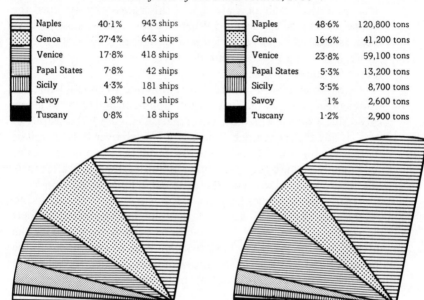

(A) DISTRIBUTION BY NUMBER OF SHIPS   (B) DISTRIBUTION BY TONNAGE

1.5 Currency and finance

The monetary system of Italy was binary: there were on the one hand gold and silver coins with considerable purchasing power (known as *monete grosse*), and there was on the other hand the 'small change' coins of base silver and copper (known as *monete piccole*). Because of the number of different coins in circulation at any one time (several hundreds were current simultaneously in many areas), it was necessary to have a common denominator and this was known as 'money of account': such were the *lira*, the *ducat* and the *oncia*. An actual coin would be worth so many *lire* or parts of a lira. These units of account almost never existed as specific coins, but they were divided up into minor units, materially represented by the *monete piccole*; thus the lira always had 20 *soldi* or 240 *denari* of account and although the lira rarely took the shape of a coin, the soldi and denari did. This relationship between real money and money of account meant that any change in the value of the *monete grosse* inevitably affected the *monete piccole*. Throughout the early modern period, in Italy and indeed all over Europe, the real value of the *monete grosse* increased as a result of scarcity and this necessarily devalued the copper coins used by the poor. Where the gold coin would once have been exchanged for 240 denari, it now exchanged for 300, 400 or even more. The rising price of gold and silver coins was thus in itself a powerful inflationary agent.

There are an almost infinite number of coins to choose from, but the changing value of the Spanish gold doubloon and of the Milanese silver ducat on the Milan exchange market (Figure 1.7) illustrate as well as any the rising price of *monete grosse* all over Italy. It will be noted that the price of gold coins rose faster than that of silver; this was mainly because gold was scarcer in Europe, especially after 1550. Then, as now, gold was a good investment in times of inflation.[11]

In early modern times Italy possessed many institutions similar to modern banks which accepted deposits and operated current accounts. However, few lent money to private clients. With the exception of the Monti di Pietà (which advanced small loans to the poor, secured by pledges) and the corn banks (which specialized in loans to farmers at seed-time), only private commercial bankers gave credit to individuals, often using sums deposited by other clients. By the late sixteenth century, we find institutions guaranteed by the state, termed 'public banks', which served as a depository for funds and performed the functions of a central clearing bank. But they too usually did not lend. The Banco di San Giorgio opened as a public bank in Genoa in 1584, the Rialto Bank in Venice in 1587, the Banco di San Ambrosio in Milan in 1593, with equivalents springing up in Naples, Rome and other major cities. However, the centre of Italian banking was undoubtedly Genoa. In the sixteenth century the city's financiers were denounced for their massive loans to the Spanish Crown. Between 1580 and 1620 their 'Fairs of Exchange' – the 'Fairs of Besançon' – handled transactions worth around fifty million *escudos* every year, most operations being of an international

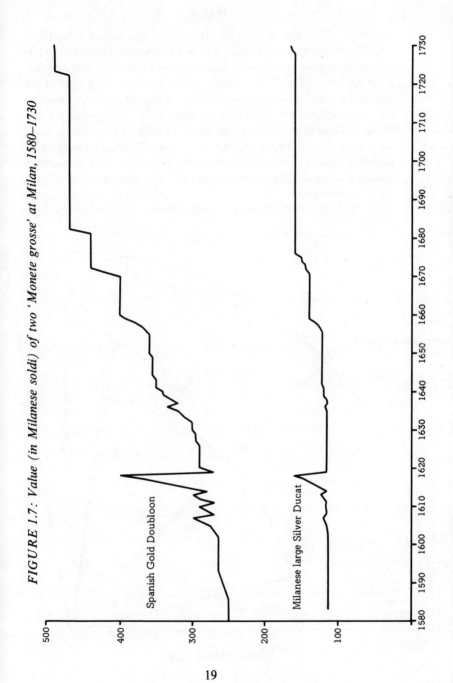

FIGURE 1.7: Value (in Milanese soldi) of two 'Monete grosse' at Milan, 1580–1730

Spanish Gold Doubloon

Milanese large Silver Ducat

19

character. After the 1620s, the activities of the Genoese bankers, severely crippled by the bankruptcy of the Spanish Treasury (1627), remained largely restricted to Italy, but the eighteenth century saw their operations flourishing once again in Europe on an even more influential scale. The Genoese nobility, of mercantile stock, needed no encouragement to take every opportunity of expanding their financial capitalism (Figure 1.8). By 1785 only 18 per cent of their total assets was tied up in real property; over 70 per cent lay in cash, loans and shares. This remarkable pattern of investment was unique among European aristocracies in the later eighteenth century.[12]

FIGURE 1.8: Distribution of wealth of the Genoese aristocracy, c. 1785

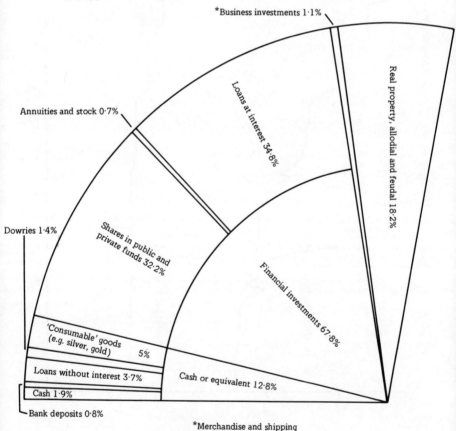

*Business investments 1·1%

Real property, allodial and feudal 18·2%

Loans at interest 34·8%

Annuities and stock 0·7%

Dowries 1·4%

Shares in public and private funds 32·2%

Financial investments 67·8%

'Consumable' goods (e.g. silver, gold)   5%

Loans without interest 3·7%

Cash or equivalent 12·8%

Cash 1·9%

Bank deposits 0·8%

*Merchandise and shipping

The geographical extent of Genoese financial capitalism in the eighteenth century is surprising. The Genoese always invested most heavily in their home government and after that in the government of Venice (another republic), the Papacy and France (Table 1.7). The three million or so lire on long-term loan to Spain represents, no doubt, the sorry legacy of Genoa's financial stake in Habsburg imperialism during the sixteenth and early seventeenth centuries, but the interest in the governments of northern and eastern Europe is noteworthy.

TABLE 1.7: Genoese investments in home and foreign bonds and in foreign loans in the eighteenth century (nominal capital in million Genoese lire)

	1 January 1725	1 January 1745	1 January 1765	1 January 1785
Government and private bonds (i.e. long-term borrowing)	270.8	287.8	300.9	246.8
Republic of Genoa	127.7	141.9	150.7	133.6
Republic of Venice	56.2	60.8	58.0	22.8
Papal State	45.0	44.0	35.6	30.9
States of Austrian Lombardy	14.8	10.6	7.7	6.9
Kingdom of France	7.3	10.0	29.1	38.4
States of the House of Habsburg	5.9	4.7	6.3	5.1
Grand Duchy of Tuscany	3.7	3.1	2.8	—
Kingdom of Spain	3.6	2.8	2.1	2.1
Kingdom of Naples	3.9	3.9	3.1	2.7
Kingdom of Sicily	2.1	2.1	1.5	1.3
Kingdom of Great Britain	0.6	3.4	2.8	2.4
State of the House of Savoy	—	0.5	1.2	0.6
Foreign loans (i.e. short-term borrowing)	4.7	18.4	31.3	95.7
Papal State	—	—	—	2.0
States of Austrian Lombardy	—	—	1.1	4.5
Duchy of Modena and Reggio	0.9	2.0	0.7	0.2
Duchy of Parma and Piacenza	0.6	0.5	0.5	0.3
State of the House of Savoy	—	1.6	—	0.6
Grand Duchy of Tuscany	—	0.5	—	—
Republic of Venice	—	0.6	—	—
States of the House of Habsburg	—	7.2	19.1	16.2
Duchy of Bavaria	—	—	—	3.5
Duchy of Saxony	—	—	—	5.2
Archbishopric of Trier	—	—	—	0.4
Kingdom of France	2.6	5.8	8.1	50.0
Kingdom of Denmark and Norway	—	—	0.9	5.4
Kingdom of Sweden	—	—	—	5.8
Kingdom of Poland	—	—	—	1.6
State of Malta	0.6	—	0.5	—
Kingdom of Portugal	—	—	—	0.1
Kingdom of Spain	—	—	0.3	0.1
Total	275.5	306.2	332.2	342.5

State borrowing and public finance is particularly difficult to describe in Italy, since public administration was divided into even smaller units than the very small political subdivisions might suggest. Many municipal and district bodies enjoyed a high degree of autonomy, assuming functions and collecting revenues appropriate to central government. The state administration itself was often made up of different departments, each with its own income and expenditure. In addition, the official accounts of many states do not include revenues managed directly by public creditors. This happened, for example, in the Republic of Genoa, where the Casa di San Giorgio handled the most lucrative revenues of the state, in the Kingdom of Naples, and in the Duchy of Milan. Finally, even where a centrally unified administration existed to control the whole management of public affairs, reports of its finances are scanty and almost always take the form of budget forecasts, not final balance sheets. However, it is reasonably safe to present figures of the consolidated public debt of certain Italian states in the eighteenth century. According to Table 1.8, one fact is immediately apparent: the low interest rates on funded debts (from 2 per cent to 4 per cent). Originally, several loans had been raised at higher rates, but very often those rates were later reduced by forced or voluntary conversions; in many cases capital and interest were paid in gold or silver, so that creditors could escape from the depreciation of money of account.[13]

TABLE 1.8: *Consolidated public debt in some Italian states in the eighteenth century*

State	Monetary unit in millions	1725		1745		1765		1785	
		Nominal capital	Annual interest	Nom. cap.	Ann. int.	Nom. cap.	Ann. int.	Nom. cap.	Ann. int.
Piedmont-Savoy	Piedmontese lire	6.5	0.3	30.8	1.2	49.2	1.8	52.6	1.9
Duchy of Milan	Milanese lire	110.5	3.3	112.8	2.9	104.3	2.6	114.8	2.9
Venetian Republic	Venetian ducat	73.5	1.8	77.1	1.9	75.9	1.8	43.2	1.4
Genoese Republic	Genoese bank lire	127.7	3.1	141.0	3.0	149.3	3.4	132.7	3.0
Tuscany	Florentine ducats	17.2	0.5	12.6	0.4	12.6	0.4	12.5	0.4
Papal States	Roman scudi	52.4	1.7	56.7	1.7	55.7	1.7	58.9	1.9
Kingdom of Naples	Neapolitan ducats	60.0							3.2

1.6 Prices and wages

The celebrated price rise of the sixteenth century started late in the Italian states and almost never attained the intensity of the inflation experienced in countries like Spain or England. The decennial averages of market prices at Florence (Table 1.9) show that some prices doubled in the course of a century, but only after a late start and with only one peak: the famine decade of the 1590s.[14]

TABLE 1.9: Market prices at Florence, 1520–1620 (in grammes of silver)

	Wheat (hl)	Olive oil (l)	Black grape (hl)	Beef (kg)	Tuscan cheese (kg)	Firewood (m)	Raw wool (kg)
1520–9	54.05	1.37	35.46	1.40	2.96	18.27	3.21
1530–9	54.77	2.10	36.11	1.82	3.06	18.43	2.95
1540–9	38.59	1.81	50.20	1.27	2.83	14.29	3.98
1550–9	66.59	2.08	45.70	1.53	2.97	18.26	3.07
1560–9	48.03	2.29	58.77	1.53	3.74	21.05	5.60
1570–9	61.47	2.33	—	2.14	4.33	25.55	6.20
1580–9	67.97	2.42	—	2.00	3.73	25.14	5.21
1590–9	114.94	2.97	—	2.19	4.65	26.03	6.20
1600–9	91.53	3.86	—	2.61	5.00	31.10	8.06
1610–19	76.37	2.75	79.58	2.75	4.83	31.87	6.62

There are two possible reasons for the moderate behaviour of Italian prices, the attractions of each depending on which theory of causation one adopts for explaining the 'price revolution'. The first reason, connected with the 'bullionist' interpretation, is that Italy did not receive her share of the American treasure until the 1550s, when Spain began to finance Habsburg imperialism through the bankers of Genoa. Vast quantities of silver were certainly injected into the Italian economy from Spain between 1570 and 1620. The second reason, which fits a 'demographic' or 'consumer-led' price rise model, is that the population of Italy did not grow as fast as the rest of Europe: wars and plagues probably kept down the rate of population increase and therefore the demand for food. The period of consumer pressure would thus coincide with the period of inflation. Figures 1.9 and 1.10 show the behaviour of wheat prices in four leading Italian markets throughout the period. Beyond the different curves, due to the various degree of monetary devaluation in each town, all series reveal two phases of strongly rising agricultural prices – 1560–1620 and post-1750; all reveal the long stagnation of the century

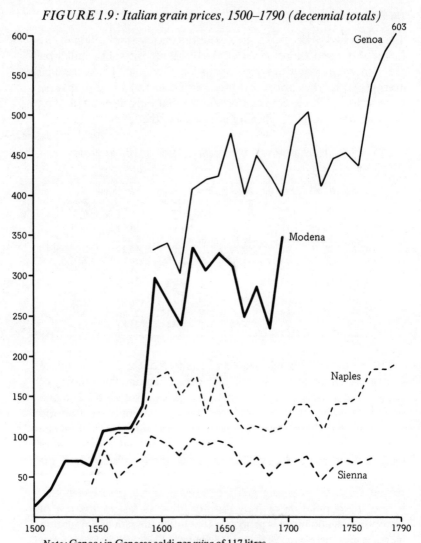

FIGURE 1.9: Italian grain prices, 1500–1790 (decennial totals)

Note: Genoa: in Genoese soldi per *mina* of 117 litres
Modena: in Modenese soldi per bushel of 63 litres
Naples: in Neapolitan *grana* per *tomolo* of 55 litres
Sienna: in Florentine soldi per bushel of 23 litres

1630–1730. We have focused upon the period 1640–60 in Figure 1.10 as a reminder of the violent fluctuations which periodically brought death by starvation to some and acute hardship to many. The three

24

bad harvests of 1648–50 were the worst of the century, in Italy as elsewhere in Europe, and in Naples the rise in the price of bread coincided with the rebellion of Masaniello.[15]

FIGURE 1.10: Italian grain prices, 1640–60 (annual average price; same units as Figure 1.9)

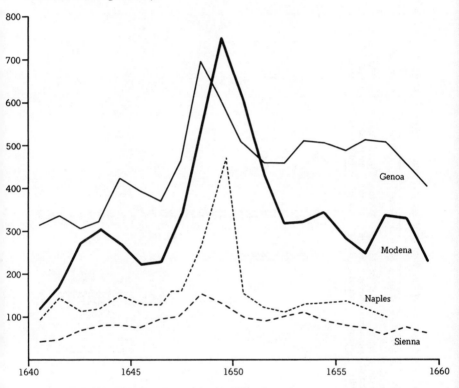

Researches into the level and variations of wages have been concerned chiefly with building construction work and to a lesser extent with agriculture and textiles. A few of the longest and most satisfactory series of daily wages for agricultural and building workers are given in Table 1.10. They are from edited sources except for the Genoese figures which are from researches still in progress. Whatever the method of computation used in each case, for the sake of consistency the figures here denote the wage rate mentioned most often in any year. Even if we consider the building labourers' wage

TABLE 1.10: Daily wages of building and agricultural workers in Italy, 1500–1799

Decade	Monferrat (Montaldeo) Agric. labourer (soldi)	Vercellese (Larizzate) Agric. labourer (soldi)	Milan Master mason (soldi)	Modena Master mason (soldi)	Genoa Master mason (soldi)	Florence Master mason (soldi)	Florence Agric. labourer (soldi)	Naples Master mason (grana)	Naples Agric. labourer (grana)
1500–9					8				
1510–19					9			?25	
1520–9					9				
1530–9				14	11–12	15–20	8	20	10
1540–9					13	21	10	20	14
1550–9				14	13				14
1560–9				14–15	14	21–28		?15	
1570–9	?10			18	15	35–40	10	?25	
1580–9				20	18–20	35	10		?19
1590–9	10			24	22	40	10	?20	
1600–9	10		35	27	24	40	10	30	?10
1610–19	?12		40	27	24	40–50		40	20–22
1620–9	12		40	27	26			38	
1630–9	?10		40	35	30				?25
1640–9			40	38	34			37½	
1650–9	12		40	43	34				
1660–9	12		40	43	36				
1670–9	12		40	43	40				
1680–9	12		40–35	45	40				
1690–9	12		35	50	36				
1700–9	12		35		36				
1710–19	12	13	32½		36–40				
1720–9	12	13	32½		36			35	20
1730–9	12	12	32½		40			35	20
1740–9	12	13	32½		38			35	?27¼
1750–9	12	13	32½		40				20
1760–9	12	13	32½		40				
1770–9		13	32½		40			40	20
1780–9	14	13	29		40				
1790–9		20	29		40				

which were fixed almost everywhere at 50–70 per cent of those of master masons, we can say that the nominal rates of wage reflected secular trends, but were not sensitive to short- and middle-term movements (with the exception of seasonal changes).[16] These figures, interesting as they are, take no account of inflation. The real test is to see how much food the common man's money wages could buy, although it must be remembered that wages were sometimes supplemented by payments in kind. For this purpose, we have taken five series of builders' monetary earnings and we have converted the nominal rates into the number of kilograms of bread that could be purchased with a day's wage. Although it must be remembered that for the seventeenth century the 'real wages' of Milanese workers have been calculated from the price of corn at Pavia, which could be somewhat lower than the price in Milan, the series from all the northern towns show increasing real wages for almost all the seventeenth century but a sharp decline after the 1760s. Apart from that, there is a surprising stability in the real wages paid during our period. In the five towns here considered, there does not appear to have been that catastrophic erosion of the standard of living that occurred in France during the later sixteenth and the mid-seventeenth centuries (see section 6.7 below).[17]

1.7 Wealth and social structure

In Italy, as in all countries, the population was made up of groups that possessed very different political, social, judicial and fiscal rights. The most privileged class was the nobility, whether of ancient feudal origin or of recent purchase, which represented about 1 per cent of the total population. There were, however, considerable local variations in this figure: 0.5 per cent in the Republic of Genoa in the seventeenth and eighteenth centuries, 1.3 per cent in the state of Venice 1766–70, perhaps 0.3 per cent in Tuscany and 1 per cent in Piedmont in 1760. In the city-states the percentage was far higher in the *dominante* town where the nobles tended to live: between 3 and 5 per cent of the populations of Venice, Milan, Genoa and Florence were noble. By contrast, in the states of feudal origin, or where there was no powerful city, the aristocracy was less concentrated and its distribution between town and country was more even: analysis of the social origins of newly married couples shows 1.4 per cent nobles in the first half of the sixteenth century at Naples and 2 per cent at Turin in the seventeenth and eighteenth centuries. This relatively even distribution is also found in the small rural towns of southern Italy: 2.4 per cent in Castellamare di Stabia in 1754 and 3 per cent in Bronte in

FIGURE 1.11: Real wages in Italy, 1500–1799 (expressed in kilograms of bread)

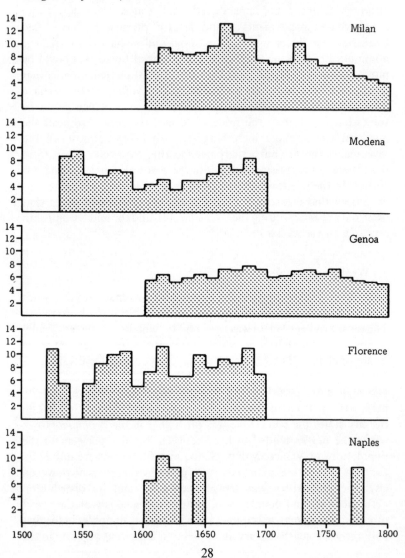

1756.[18] The clergy was another privileged class. In the eighteenth century its numbers ranged from 1 per cent in the Duchy of Mantua to 3.6 per cent in the Kingdom of Naples, with a 'national average' of about 1.8 per cent. Clergymen generally lived in the towns, where they might comprise as much as 5 or even 10 per cent of the population. In central Italy, which was closest to Rome, percentages of 12 and more are recorded.[19]

Information on the distribution of land and wealth between the various groups is sparse. Nevertheless, for the eighteenth century, at least, it is possible to make some general observations about the relative assets of the broader social divisions: 'the nobles', 'the clergy', 'citizens' and various institutions. The picture is far from clear or uniform. In Piedmont, for instance, the nobles held about 10 per cent of the allodial estates and an unknown part of the feudal lands in 1697–1711; in other countries they controlled over 50 per cent of real wealth (see Figures 1.12 and 1.13). A constant feature was the position of the secular clergy, who seem to have held about 3 per cent of the land in every area – even in the Papal States – although the landed wealth of the religious institutions varied considerably, being predictably high in the Papal States and predictably low in the Veneto.[20]

A complementary picture appears from an analysis of investments in the public debt of some of the same states. In Piedmont, the landed wealth of the noble and middle classes underwent a slight rise and their investments in government securities a slight diminution; an opposite evolution was experienced by religious and charitable institutions. The transfer of the wealth of these bodies from land into public debt was perhaps connected with the struggle against properties collected by the Church and with anti-clericalism in general.[21]

Below the level of landholders and bondholders, however, lay the poor, and about this sombre slice of humanity we still know tragically little. The earliest statistics on pauperism reflect only the exceptional situations arising from war, plague or famine. Thus in February 1580, during a plague, 57 per cent of the total population in Genoa was dependent on public charity. During the war of 1625, 17 per cent of the population of the same city was on poor relief; the same was true of 11 per cent of the people of Modena during the famine of 1620–1 and of 7 per cent of the inhabitants of Milan during the crisis of 1629 (war, plague *and* famine). These figures represent the upper limit. The lower limit was the hard core of people who were old or

FIGURE 1.12: *Distribution of real estate among the social classes of eighteenth-century Italy*

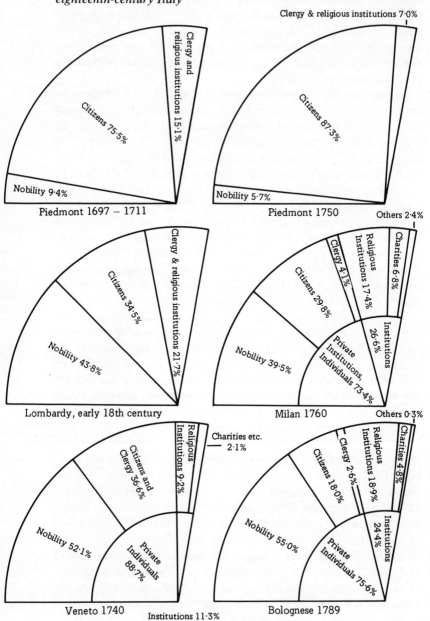

Piedmont 1697 – 1711

Piedmont 1750

Lombardy, early 18th century

Milan 1760

Veneto 1740

Bolognese 1789

FIGURE 1.12: Distribution of real estate among the social classes of eighteenth-century Italy—continued

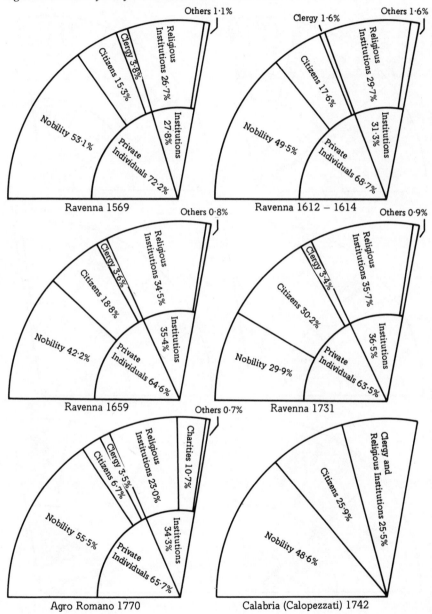

Others 1·1%
Clergy 3·8%
Citizens 15·3%
Religious Institutions 26·7%
Nobility 53·1%
Institutions 27·8%
Private Individuals 72·2%
Ravenna 1569

Clergy 1·6%
Others 1·6%
Citizens 17·6%
Religious Institutions 29·7%
Nobility 49·5%
Institutions 31·3%
Private Individuals 68·7%
Ravenna 1612 – 1614

Others 0·8%
Clergy 3·6%
Citizens 18·8%
Religious Institutions 34·5%
Nobility 42·2%
Institutions 35·4%
Private Individuals 64·6%
Ravenna 1659

Others 0·9%
Clergy 3·4%
Citizens 30·2%
Religious Institutions 35·7%
Nobility 29·9%
Institutions 36·5%
Private Individuals 63·5%
Ravenna 1731

Others 0·7%
Clergy 3·5%
Citizens 6·7%
Religious Institutions 23·0%
Charities 10·7%
Nobility 55·5%
Institutions 34·3%
Private Individuals 65·7%
Agro Romano 1770

Clergy and Religious Institutions 25·5%
Citizens 25·9%
Nobility 48·6%
Calabria (Calopezzati) 1742

FIGURE 1.13: Distribution of personal wealth among the social classes of eighteenth-century Italy

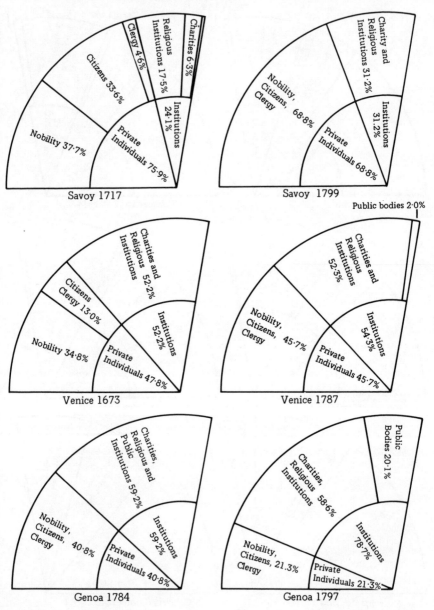

Savoy 1717

Savoy 1799

Venice 1673

Venice 1787

Genoa 1784

Genoa 1797

FIGURE 1.13: Distribution of personal wealth among the social classes of eighteenth-century Italy—continued

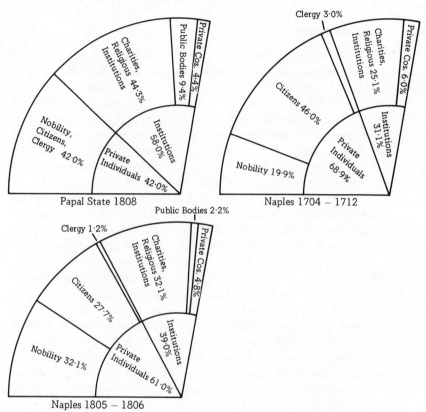

Papal State 1808

Naples 1704 – 1712

Naples 1805 – 1806

incurably ill and who therefore received permission to beg in public or to live in an almshouse: they made up 3.6 per cent of the population of Genoa in 1668–9, and 2.3 per cent of the inhabitants of Piedmont in 1734 (excluding those in hospitals). Of course, many more were reduced to begging without permission: in Venice between 1760 and 1787, for example, those licensed to beg made up between 3 and 5 per cent of the total population, but a further 13 to 15 per cent were unauthorized beggars. In Bologna in the same years 25 per cent of the population was described as 'unemployed' and therefore, probably, dependent on begging or public charity. Taking into account the lower-paid workers, the underemployed and the unemployed, 'the poor' must have normally made up between 40 and 50 per cent of the total population of Italy in the eighteenth century and beyond.[22]

1.8 Conclusions

When we examine the historical series contained in the preceding pages, we must always remember that they come from the separate endeavours of a large number of individual researchers. They were not inspired by a common purpose; they were not carried out according to a common plan. For this reason, it often happens that the same subject has been studied in depth for one region but remains almost unknown for another. Our knowledge is unequal, and the mosaic of evidence cannot permit a sure and detailed reconstruction of the economic history of all Italy for the early modern period.

At the same time, we do have enough data to make certain generalizations. There is no doubt here that in almost the whole of Italy the overall population trend was upward in 1550–1600, declining in 1600–75, then increasing again, at first very slowly but becoming more rapid as the eighteenth century advanced. One can distinguish two areas of different demographic performance: between 1550 and 1790 the largest population increases were registered in a crescent of territories stretching from the Kingdom of Naples and Sicily through Sardinia and Genoa to Piedmont and Lombardy; growth was far more sluggish in the Venetian territories, in the small states of Emilia, in Tuscany and in the Papal States. In both of these broad demographic 'regions' the increase in population was much more variable in the towns than in the countryside. There were several reasons for this. In the first place, famines, plagues and wars ravaged with particular severity urban populations, which depended for their subsistence on the surplus food produced by rural areas. They were also more exposed to epidemics because of their higher density of people and they might become primary military targets subjected to blockades, sacks and destruction. These were all short-term factors restraining natural urban growth. In the longer term, the capacity of the towns to increase depended on their ability to offer economic opportunities which would attract a steady flow of immigrants from the countryside. When their economic activity slowed down, their ability to attract and absorb immigrants diminished and the growth of their population therefore stopped.

There were several other influences on urban growth in Italy.

Conclusions

Towns might expand because they became a government capital, or because of the growth of central administration in the state, as at Turin, Naples and especially Rome, the spiritual centre of the Counter-Reformation as well as capital of the Papal States. In contrast, the political decline of small states (like Modena, Parma or Lucca) or the absorption of one state by another (like Mantua, Ferrara or Sienna) naturally caused the economic and demographic decline of their 'capital cities'. The development of certain other towns was linked to special economic activities. Thus the amazing and sustained expansion of Leghorn (Livorno) was a consequence of its status as a 'free port' (no transit dues); the rise of Genoa in the early seventeenth and in the eighteenth centuries was aided by its important financial operations and its fine port; the decline of Messina resulted from the collapse of Sicilian silk exports. The more famous 'decline of Venice' was the fruit of more complex developments, including the loss of overseas possessions to the Turks, the growing problem of building enough sound ships and the poor social mobility between Venice and its dominion. Urban demography in our period thus had its successes and its failures, but the overall picture was not positive: between 1550 and 1790 the population of the thirty-six 'biggest towns' rose from 1.3 million people to 2 million, but in relative terms the town-dwellers continued to make up only 11 or 12 per cent of the total Italian population. The urban economies were unable, in the long run, to increase their share of the economic product and of economic rewards. On the other hand, the series of prices and wages show that, if one excludes the consequences of monetary depreciation, the inhabitants of the Italian towns enjoyed a standard of living that held fairly stable throughout the period. This stability must be attributed to the towns' guild organizations, to the charitable institutions and to the development of local government which created more jobs in the public sector.

A very different situation existed in rural areas, where almost 90 per cent of the population lived throughout early modern times. From 1550 until 1790 an extra 7 million inhabitants were added to the 9.2 million already living on the land. Their 'arrival' was concentrated to a large extent in the eighteenth century and it increased the existing tensions within the rural world. Various solutions were attempted. In the plain of Lombardy and around Vercelli, for instance, efforts were directed to increasing agricultural productivity by improving farming techniques. In other areas there

35

was a switch from traditional crops to more profitable ones: vines and mulberries (for the silkworms) in the hills of Piedmont, mulberries and maize in some Venetian territories, hemp in the Romagna, mulberries again in Calabria, olives in Liguria. Not all of these new developments prospered, however; several were crippled by the tariff barriers erected by neighbouring states or by the high costs of transport. Another only partially successful answer to the growing demand for more land and more food was the reclamation of marshes and estuaries and the exploitation of previously uncultivated territory. But land reclamation, even when it succeeded, provided few new farms, while the exploitation of new land produced more food, but yield ratios remained very low. These improvements, such as they were, did nothing to relieve the social instability of the rural community or to reduce the growing opposition to feudal exactions. Plans by some governments to organize a redistribution of landed property came to nothing. Everything suggests that, for most Italians living in villages and small towns, the general standard of living deteriorated, especially during the eighteenth century.

2 Spain

2.1 Population

The highly centralized government of Habsburg Spain, and its even more highly centralized Bourbon successor, have left a regular series of official censuses dating from the early sixteenth century. Unfortunately the series are not entirely comparable, since the earlier enumerations dealt with only one province of Spain at a time and counted households (*vecinos*), not individuals, but they were still impressive bureaucratic undertakings. In order to facilitate comparisons, in Table 2.1[1] 'household' numbers have been multiplied by 4.5 to give a rough idea of the total population. It should be remembered that Castile covered 77 per cent of the Spanish territory, the crown of Aragon covered 20 per cent, and Navarre and the Basque lands (Vizcaya, Alava and Guipuzcoa) the remaining 3 per cent. Of course, not all places grew and declined at the same time and to the same degree. It seems certain, for instance, that the population of Old Castile began to decline after 1570; that of New Castile and Andalusia not until 1600, even 1620; that of the crown of Aragon perhaps hardly at all if one excepts the expulsion of the Moriscos in

TABLE 2.1: Spanish population, 1500–1800 (thousands)

	All Spain	Crown of Castile	Crown of Aragon			Basque provinces	Nav-arre
			Aragon	Catalonia	Valencia		
1541	6,300	5,300					
1553				294			139
1572					310		
1587–92	7,680	5,920					189
1603–9			319	400	450	206	
1646–50	5,250	4,500	102	250	380		
1712–17	7,000	5,500	406	390		225	
1756–68	9,300	6,460				280	
1787	10,410	7,180	614	815	792	305	529
1797	10,540	7,360	657	878	825	285	505

Note: Totals for 1787 and 1797 include the population of the Balearic and Canary islands (*c.* 350,000) and the clergy (140,000 in 1787, 66,000 in 1797 – cf. p. 58 below).

1609–14. It is also certain that the decline of some towns was associated with the ascendancy of others: thus Toledo lost to Madrid and Seville lost to Cadiz.[2]

There is some dispute about the reliability of all these figures, but there can be no doubt about the overall trend: rapid growth in the sixteenth century (22 per cent increase), followed by equally rapid decline in the seventeenth and recovery in the eighteenth century. The population of Spain in the 1590s was not matched again until the 1730s and even then growth was limited to a slow rate by late marriages and a relatively high incidence of celibacy: 72 per cent of females and 80 per cent of males between the ages of 16 and 25 were unmarried according to the census of 1787, and 11 per cent of the total adult population was unmarried. According to the census of 1768 the last figure was even higher: 13 per cent.[3]

We can glean some idea of the movement of the population between the isolated census dates from the registers of births, marriages and deaths, kept, in theory at least, in every parish. A number of data have been published for the Habsburg period and so far they all tell the same story: strong demographic growth until the 1570s, levelling off after about 1580 and then falling after 1620. Two sample urban communities can be studied. First Toledo, the largest city in New Castile, had a population of around 26,500 in 1530 rising to 50,000 by 1560; this level was maintained until 1600 but then fell to 20,500 in 1631 (see Figure 2.1[4]). The same pattern precisely may be observed in the city of Valencia, some 200 miles away on Spain's Mediterranean coast. (Figure 2.2[5]).

FIGURE 2.1: *Baptisms in Toledo, 1530–1650*

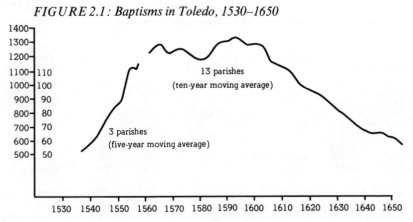

38

FIGURE 2.2: Baptisms, marriages and burials in Valencia, 1550–1650 (three parishes; nine-year moving averages)

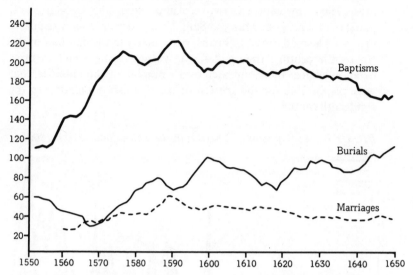

The baptism and burial 'scissors' at Valencia is particularly well marked owing to the inroads made into the local population by famine and plague between 1647 and 1652. In some years deaths exceeded births: the graph in Figure 2.3 of baptisms and burials in

FIGURE 2.3: Baptisms and burials in Simancas, 1555–1600

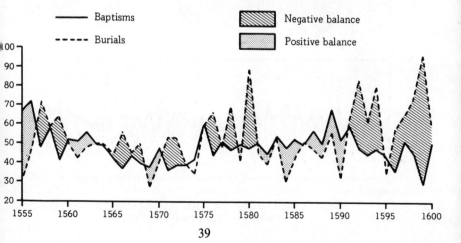

the rural parish of Simancas (home of the great archives, just west of Valladolid) in the later sixteenth century reveals an excess of deaths in most years; by contrast, two centuries later, the Catalan rural parishes of Arenys de Mar and Sant Andreu de Llevaneres regularly produced a small excess of births, particularly in the first half of the eighteenth century (figure 2.4). It was recurring small positive balances such as these, repeated over a number of communities, that were responsible for the growth of the Spanish population in the eighteenth century.[6]

FIGURE 2.4: Baptisms and burials in rural Catalonia, 1700–1800

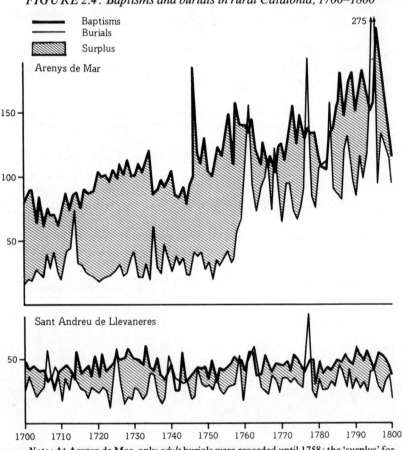

Note: At Arenys de Mar, only *adult* burials were recorded until 1758; the 'surplus' for 1700–58 is therefore artificially high. All burials included from 1759 onwards.

40

Compared with France, demographic studies in Spain are still in their infancy. It is noticeable that the Figures 2.1–2.4 were prepared by two Frenchmen, an Englishman and an American. But studies by Spaniards are now being published. An outstanding recent work concerns Talavera de la Reina, a town downstream of Toledo on the Tagus, for which very full parish registers have survived from the 1520s. It has proved possible to calculate fertility rates, conception patterns and illegitimacy rates as well as the standard fluctuations of births, marriages and deaths. The data on illegitimate births are particularly interesting, since they closely parallel the developments reported for other countries – including Protestant countries such as England – at the same time. Thus we find an illegitimacy rate in Talavera of around 6 per cent during the period 1570–1600 (in concrete terms, this meant 175 bastards in the 1570s, among 2789 live births), falling steadily throughout the seventeenth century until it reached 2 per cent in the last decade (or 36 bastards in the 1690s, among 1762 live births). The level of illegitimacy declined even further in the earlier eighteenth century (falling below 1 per cent from 1705 to 1734) but then rose slightly until 1764 and rapidly thereafter. The rate in the 1790s was just over 7 per cent (164 bastards among 2,242 live births).[7]

2.2 Agriculture

We have few figures concerning the production of agricultural or manufactured goods for early modern Spain. We do know, however, that as late as 1797 no less than 75 per cent of the total Spanish workforce was involved in agriculture, the vast majority of them occupied in arable farming. We also know that cereal yields, although in the region of 1 to 6 in the sixteenth century, had fallen by the eighteenth to 1 to 3 or 1 to 4. For actual yields, the rent-rolls of landowners and the tithe receipts of the clergy give some idea of the prevailing trends. All available figures suggest a severe fall in production, starting in the 1620s and lasting with the exception of only a few good years until the 1660s. Figures 2.5 and 2.6 show the harvest yields as measured by the tithes of the local clergy. The rhythm of production at Toledo in New Castile and in Andalusia, two hundred miles to the south, was remarkably similar. If the significant collapse of agricultural production in the first half of the seventeenth century was registered all over the heartland of the

FIGURE 2.5: Harvest yields in Andalusia: tithe yields at Puebla de Guzman and Bollullos, 1580–1800 (eleven-year moving averages; tithes paid in fanegas of wheat)

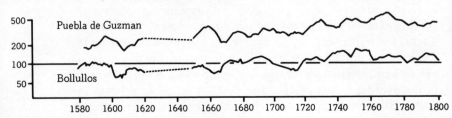

Spanish empire, we have an important new element to explain the decline of Spain as a great power.[8]

The real revival of Spanish agriculture came only after the 1760s when the prices for agrarian goods began to rise rapidly, encouraging new investment in the land and an increase in the area of land under cultivation. According to the 'Census of Agrarian and Manufactured Goods' of 1797, Spanish farmers produced 32 million fanegas of wheat, 16 million *fanegas* of barley, 11 million fanegas of rye and – an improvement on sixteenth-century diet – 4.3 million fanegas of maize and 16 million fanegas of vegetables (chickpeas, runner beans and French beans leading the way: the potato was still a minority crop). The fanega was roughly 1.5 bushels.[9] There was also considerable production of wine, olive oil (6 million *arrobas* per year), and certain

FIGURE 2.6: Harvest yields in New Castile: tithe yields at Ventas (Montes de Toledo), 1615–1688 (in fanegas of wheat and rye)

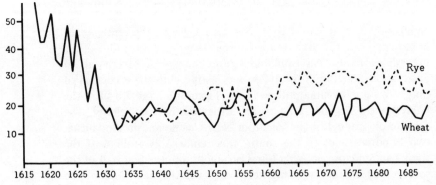

industrial crops. Gradually, therefore, Spain ceased to be dependent on the importation of food from abroad (which was a constant feature of her economy from the 1590s to the 1770s).

Perhaps the best-known aspect of the Spanish rural economy in early modern times was the migrant sheep flocks controlled by the Mesta – the sheep-owners' guild. These were sheep specifically kept for their wool, much of which was exported to northern Europe or to Italy, as opposed to the sheep retained by most towns and villages which were kept to provide mutton. There were perhaps 1.5 million of these 'local' sheep in Castile during the sixteenth century, compared with transhumant flocks totalling between 2 and 3 million and producing around 550,000 arrobas of wool (approximately 6000 tons). The number declined after 1600 until by the 1640s the size of the Mesta's flocks was down to only 500,000 sheep, but there was a considerable recovery later in the seventeenth century – perhaps to almost 2 million – and in the eighteenth century there was a further growth in the livestock population until by 1797 Spain had 16.7 million sheep, 2.5 million goats, 1.2 million pigs, 1.6 million oxen and 230,000 horses. The 'enlightened despotism' of the Spanish Bourbons, coupled with a situation of rising agrarian profits, did much to restore agricultural prosperity.[10]

2.3 Industry

Habsburg Spain had only one truly industrial city: Segovia, where over three-quarters of the total population (perhaps 25,000 people by 1580) were involved in manufacture, especially the manufacture of textiles.[11] The peak cloth production (Figure 2.7) of 13,000 pieces annually, lasting perhaps for two decades (1570–90), was surpassed only by the output of the far larger city of Córdoba (60,000 people in 1571) with 15,000 cloths. As yet there are no trustworthy figures or estimates available for the total textile production of Spain. However, as might be expected, production seems to have risen everywhere in the sixteenth and eighteenth centuries and fallen in the seventeenth. It would appear also that, except for the introduction of new industries like cotton-spinning, the industrial production of Spain did not regain its sixteenth-century levels until after 1800. Such recovery as there was took place mainly in the peripheral areas – particularly Catalonia – and not in the Castilian heartland.

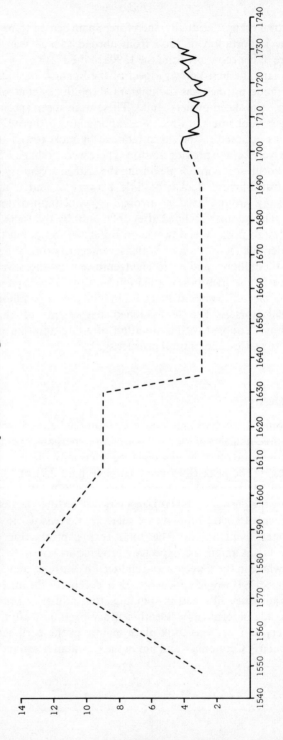

FIGURE 2.7: Cloth production in Segovia, 1540–1740 (in thousand pieces)

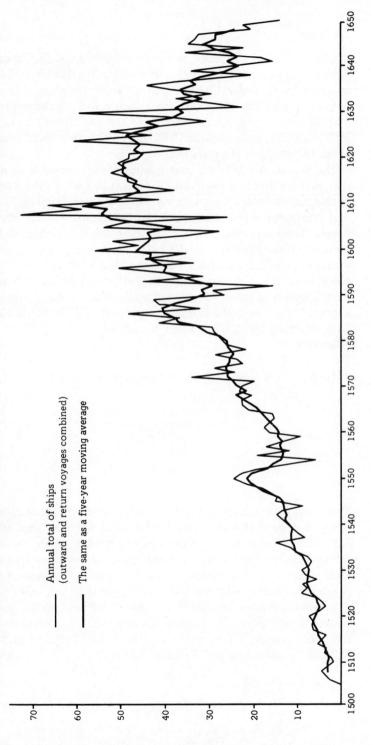

FIGURE 2.8: Trade between Seville and America, 1500–1650, by volume of shipping (in thousand tons of 2.83 cubic metres)

Annual total of ships
(outward and return voyages combined)

The same as a five-year moving average

2.4 Trade

The 'golden trade' of Spain – or more properly of Castile – in early modern times was the commerce with America. This has been studied in depth by H. and P.Chaunu, and although their methods and sources have been the subject of some criticism, there can be no doubt that the overall trends which they discerned are correct (see figure 2.8[12]): strong growth from the 1500s to the 1590s, then stability until about 1625, followed by rapid decline.

The figures after 1650 are incomplete, but they enable us to state that, in the course of the seventeenth century as a whole, the volume of shipping which traded between Spain and America fell by 75 per cent (see Table 2.2[13]). This, however, represents only the official figures. There was much contraband trade, some by Spaniards but mostly by other nationals: by the end of the seventeenth century, 95 per cent of the American trade was in the hands of foreigners. Of the 53 million *livres tournois* of goods that arrived at Cadiz every year from America in the 1690s, 25 per cent was accounted for by the French, 22 per cent by the Genoese, 30 per cent by the Netherlanders, 18 per cent by the English and Germans and only 5 per cent by Spaniards.

Table 2.2: Trade between Spain and America, 1600–1710

	OUTGOING		INCOMING	
	Ships	Tonnage	Ships	Tonnage
	(annual averages)		(annual averages)	
1600–4	55	19,800	56	21,600
1640–50	25	8,500	29	9,850
1670–80	17	4,650	19	5,600
1701–10	8	2,640	7	2,310

There were other important areas of commerce, the export of wool to northern Europe, for example; 17,000 sacks were exported from Santander alone in 1570 and even more probably passed through Bilbao. Although there was a disastrous recession caused by the Dutch Revolt in 1572, Spanish wool was regularly quoted on the Amsterdam market after the 1580s. From the 1630s until the 1670s annual wool exports fluctuated between 36,000 and 60,000 sacks. Also of some importance was the trade between Spain and the rest of the Mediterranean lands, especially France and Italy, which was handled by Barcelona and Valencia. Unfortunately, it has proved

FIGURE 2.9: *The balance of trade between France and Spain, 1716–82 (index numbers)*

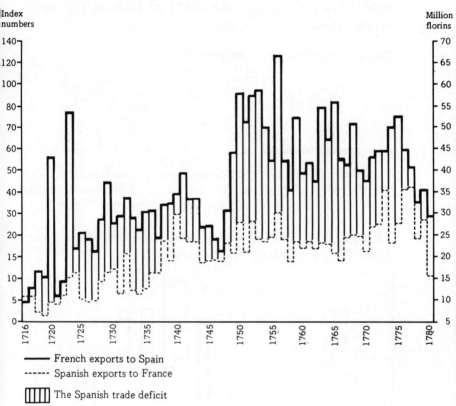

French exports to Spain
Spanish exports to France
The Spanish trade deficit

difficult to quantify, but for most of the eighteenth century we possess figures prepared by the French Treasury concerning the balance of trade between Spain and both Mediterranean and Atlantic France (see Figure 2.9[14]). In every single year of the series Spain was in deficit and the size of the deficit increased in the third quarter of the century while Spain was helping to fight France's foreign wars.

Spain's trade with other European countries was also in almost permanent deficit. When we have balance of trade figures for the whole of Spain, right at the end of the eighteenth century, they indicate the massive scale of the trade deficit (see table overleaf)[15].

It seems likely that Spain had had an unfavourable balance of trade since at least 1550, and that the deficit was paid for throughout by the re-export of silver imported from Mexico and Peru. Only the massive input of American treasure enabled the Spanish economy to continue to function as it did.

Spain's balance of trade (in million reales)

	Imports	Exports	Deficit
1789	717	289	428
1792	714	396	318

2.5 Currency and finance

The most important fact about Spain's history in early modern times was the inflow of American treasure, above all of silver from the mines of Zacatecas in Mexico and Potosí in Peru (see Figure 2.10).

FIGURE 2.10: Total imports of American treasure into Spain, 1500–1660 (five-year totals in million pesos)

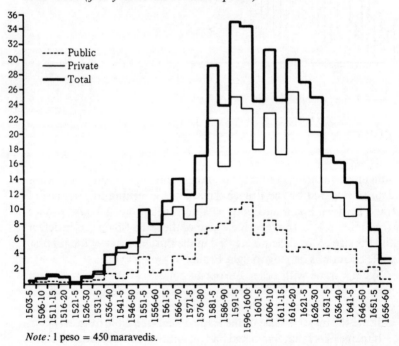

Note: 1 peso = 450 maravedis.

The famous table published by E.J.Hamilton in 1934 sets out the broad chronology of the arrival of the 17,000 tons of American silver, which was landed officially at Seville between 1500 and 1650.[16]

Alas, there has been no such series published for the inflow of bullion from the New World after 1650, although we know it to have been substantial.[17] It is true that very little of this largesse remained within Spain, but it stayed in circulation for a sufficient length of time to encourage a number of bankers, both Spanish and foreign, to set up shop and prosper; such enterprises, however, inevitably had their confidence shattered by the ruthless financial policies of the Spanish Crown. Habsburg imperialism eventually placed an insupportable burden on the resources of Castile. Because the country was so effectively tamed and so efficiently governed after the *comuneros* rising of 1520–1, it proved possible to levy far higher taxes from the Castilians than in any other European state. By the 1590s some farmers were obliged to pay half their incomes in taxes, tithes and seigneurial dues. The level of taxation doubled between 1556 and 1584, rising faster even than the level of prices. The yield of the *alcabala* sales-tax increased by 57 per cent more than prices in the course of the sixteenth century, as is shown in Figure 2.11.[18]

Even this rise in taxation was not sufficient to meet the needs of Habsburg imperialism. In some years the Crown of Castile spent double its income and the deficit had to be made good by borrowing (see Table 2.3[19]). At first the loans were short-term arrangements (known as *asientos*) made with bankers, but at measured intervals all outstanding obligations were forcibly converted by the Crown into long-term annuities (known as *juros*). The process by which the conversion was effected was known as a 'Decree of Bankruptcy' and there were at least eight in the course of the Habsburg epoch: 1557,

TABLE 2.3: State income and debt in Castile, 1515–1667 (in million ducats)

	Revenue	Debt	Interest on debt
1515	1.5	12	0.8
1557	5.3	21	1.6
1560	5.3	35	2.0
1575	6.0	50	3.8
1598	9.7	85	4.6
1623	15.0	112	5.6
1667	36.0	130	9.1

FIGURE 2.11: The rising burden of taxation in Habsburg Spain, 1504–96 (index numbers)

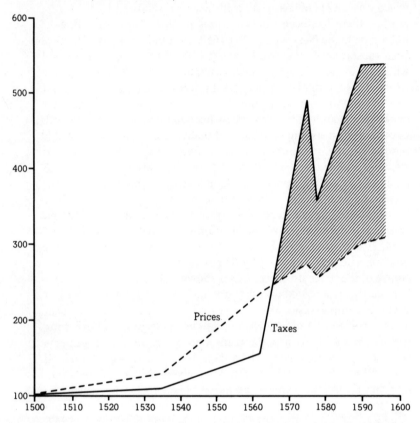

1560, 1575, 1596, 1607, 1627, 1647 and 1653. Each operation increased the total of Castile's national debt and the amount of current income required to service it.

It is well known that the taxes were raised and the debts contracted in order to finance Habsburg imperialism. There was the defence of the Atlantic against French, English and Dutch pirates; there was the defence of the Mediterranean against the Turks; and above all there was the war against the Dutch 'rebels' in the Netherlands. Figure 2.12 shows the money actually received by the Brussels government from Castile between 1561 and 1650; the cost to Spain was, of course, increased by the handling, interest and money-changing charges of the bankers (amounting perhaps to 10 per cent of each total) but this graph gives the basic rhythms of Spanish spending with its two peaks – 1586–1605 and 1621–40 – of maximum imperial effort.[20]

FIGURE 2.12: Money received from Castile by the military treasury of the Spanish Netherlands, 1561–1650 (in million florins)

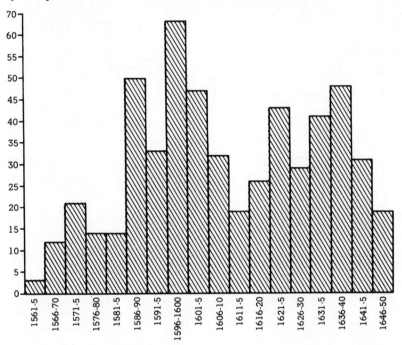

The Bourbon kings honoured some of the debts created by their predecessors – one-third of the total income of Philip v in 1702–3 (3.15 million ducats) went to the *juristas* – and they borrowed heavily themselves (see Figure 2.13). But they also managed to make the financial structure of the state more efficient and therefore enabled the Crown to attain some measure of financial solvency, although taxation levels continued to rise.[21]

2.6 Prices and wages

Thanks to the researches of E.J.Hamilton and P. Vilar we have a number of composite series of the prevailing prices and wages

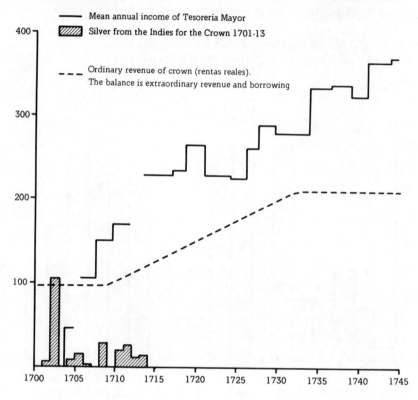

FIGURE 2.13: Government income under Philip V, 1700–45 (in million reales of vellon)

throughout Spain for the whole of the early modern period. On the whole the figures of Vilar are to be preferred since he based them on actual day-to-day market prices rather than (like Hamilton) on the records of institutions able to buy in bulk; however, the major trends are easy to see in all the tables.

There is some disagreement concerning the appropriate scale by which to measure prices. Hamilton used an arithmetical scale, giving all price increases the same weighting; others favour a semi-logarithmic scale which emphasizes the percentage increase. Thus an increase of 2p on an article costing 2p would appear the same on Hamilton's graph as an increase of 2p on an article costing £2; on a semi-logarithmic graph, however, the first would appear as an

FIGURE 2.14 : Two views of the 'price revolution' in Spain, 1500–1650 (index numbers)

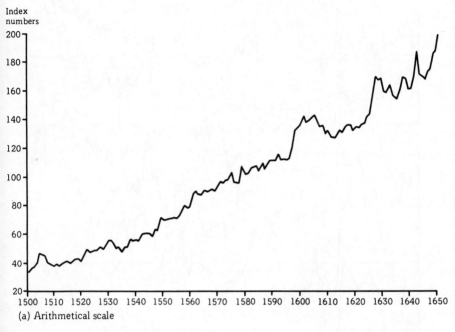

(a) Arithmetical scale

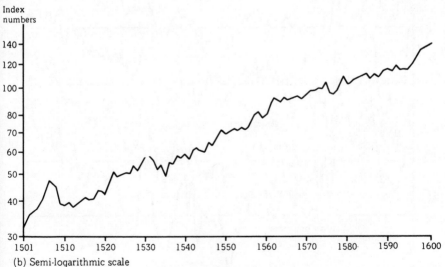

(b) Semi-logarithmic scale

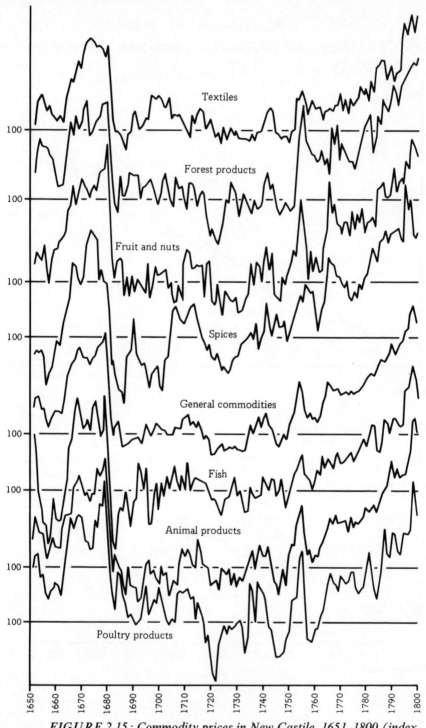

FIGURE 2.15: Commodity prices in New Castile, 1651–1800 (index numbers, 100 = 1726–50)

FIGURE 2.16: Grain prices in Spain, 1651–1800 (index numbers, 100 = 1726–50)

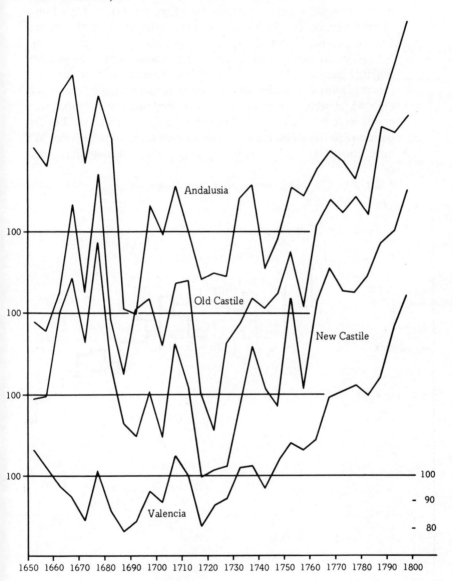

increase of 100 per cent, the second as an increase of 1 per cent. Both methods are technically correct, but they give a very different picture of the sixteenth-century price rise (see Figure 2.14): in Hamilton's original version the main increase comes after 1560; in the revised version it comes before.[22]

It is worth noting that in Spain prices and wages stayed close together between 1500 and 1650. The Spanish worker kept his earnings more or less abreast of inflation throughout the period, and high wages were said to be one reason why Spanish manufactured goods were more expensive than their foreign competitors. For the period 1650–1800 Hamilton provides a wide range of price series. We have chosen the table recording grain prices throughout Spain

FIGURE 2.7: Index numbers of real wages in Spain, 1651–1800 (100 = 1726–50)

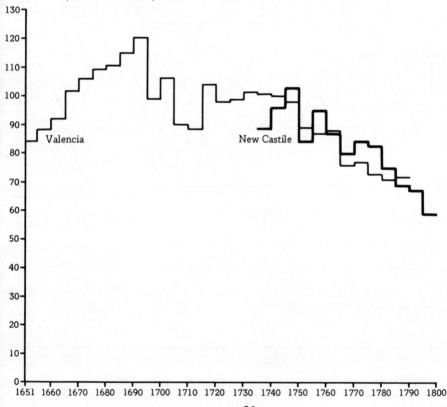

(Figure 2.16) and the table of group prices for New Castile (Figure 2.15) to illustrate the strong inflation of the late seventeenth century (caused in the main by debasement of the currency) and the late eighteenth century (caused in large part by population pressure). Food prices increased more rapidly than the rest. There is also a graph of wages (Figure 2.17), showing that – on this occasion – wages did not manage to keep pace with prices; on the contrary, real wages fell sharply after 1765.[23]

Finally, Figure 2.18 illustrates the significance of the grain price series: every rise in cereal prices was parallelled by a fall in baptisms and vice versa. The correlation would have been even more significant if conceptions (i.e. baptism minus nine months) rather than baptisms had been plotted against prices, but the 'scissors' effect is still very striking. High food prices, whatever the cause, were undoubtedly an effective restraint on human procreation.[24]

FIGURE 2.18: Grain prices and population in Gerona, 1670–1700

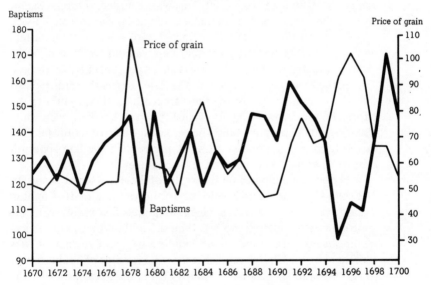

2.7 Wealth and social structure

The great census ordered by Philip II in 1590–1 as a preliminary to new tax increases provides a good guide to the social structure of the whole of Castile at the end of the first century of Habsburg rule. The enumerators reported the following:

hidalgo (tax-exempt noble) households		133,476
pechero (tax-paying) households		1,148,674
	no. of individuals	6,410,750
secular clergy	33,087	
regular clergy (male)	20,697	
regular clergy (female)	20,369	

The total clergy in Castile therefore amounted to 74,153 – 1.13 per cent of the total population. The total for the whole of Spain would have been 91,085. Almost certainly this marked a decline in power of the Spanish Church: in the fifteenth century there had been many more clergy per head of the population; there may even have been more clergy. In the course of the seventeenth and early eighteenth centuries there was a vast increase, until in 1737 the total Spanish clergy was estimated at 250,000. This was regarded as too large and by 1768 the number had fallen under combined pressure from Papacy and Crown to 176,057 (of whom 25,000 were subordinate ministers and only 15,639 were parish priests). This was still 1.9 per cent of the entire population and by 1787 it was still 1.8 per cent (191,000 clergy). The 650,000 or so *hidalgos* of the late sixteenth century also diminished in numbers during the eighteenth century, thanks to the efforts of the Crown and its Treasury: in 1787 there were only 480,000, in 1797 only 403,000. The percentage of aristocratic families in the total population fell from 11 per cent in the late sixteenth century to around 4 per cent in the late eighteenth.[25]

We know something about the wealth of these two social classes. In 1630 the Castilian Church enjoyed a total revenue of 10.4 million ducats every year – a figure which compared favourably with the state's income (although no less than 6.3 million ducats of clerical income were either paid to or handled by the Crown!). It was estimated by the Church itself that the total revenue of Spain – a sort of 'gross national product' – was 113 million ducats, and so the Church, with 1 per cent of the country's population, controlled perhaps 9 per cent of the country's wealth. By the eighteenth century this proportion had increased to 12 per cent. The *cadastro* compiled in the 1750s under the direction of the Marquis of La Enseñada reported a total clerical wealth of 2471 million *reales* or about 225

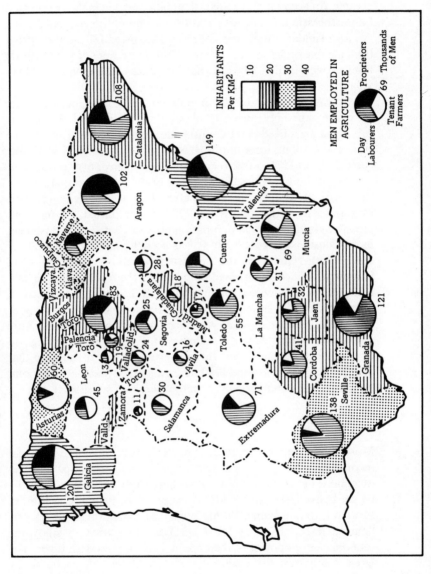

FIGURE 2.19: Population density and agricultural classes in Spain, 1797, by province

million ducats. It was hardly surprising that the Church became the reformers' prime target.[26] The social power of the nobility was even greater. An account of the Spanish nobility written in the 1520s listed 82 aristocratic families with a total income of 1.5 million ducats. Another similar enumeration of 1597–1600 listed 180 families with a total income of 5.7 million. By the 1790s there were 654 aristocratic families who owned between them 15 cities, 2286 towns and 4938 villages.[27]

The vast majority of the population, of course, were neither clergymen nor noblemen and about three-quarters of this under-privileged mass lived in the countryside, working in the fields. Of the rural population, according to the detailed census of New Castile carried out in 1571–5 (the *relaciones topográficas*), over 65 per cent were day-labourers (*jornaleros*), many of them living perpetually on the verge of destitution. The picture had scarcely changed two centuries later: the census of 1797 still reported 67 per cent *jornaleros* in the agrarian population of New Castile and 80 per cent in Andalusia (see figure 2.19). It was however, mostly under 50 per cent in other areas of the peninsula. In those areas the small landowner, the *labrador*, predominated. In the towns, too, the day-labourers were numerous, often grouped in the same 'poor' parishes, many of them driven in harsh years to dependence on alms or poor relief. Alas, we have as yet no reliable figures on poverty for the entire peninsula comparable to the estimates of Gregory King for England or Vauban for France, but there is every reason to suppose that conditions in Spain around 1700 were even worse and that 50 per cent or more of the population lived on the margin of subsistence.[28]

2.8 Conclusions

Most of the contributors to this volume lament the unevenness and incompleteness of the sources available to them. Spain is no exception: her economic history has been sadly neglected, especially by her native historians. With the exception of Felipe Ruiz Martín, Ramón Carande, Jaime Vicens Vives and a handful of others, few Spanish historians since the Civil War have tried to study the economic development of their country in early modern times. The 'great works' on the subject have been almost all produced by foreigners: by Americans like Julius Klein (on the Mesta) and Earl J. Hamilton (on prices and wages), or by Frenchmen like Pierre Vilar (on Catalonia) or Pierre Chaunu (on the trade between Seville and America). The situation is now beginning to change. A glance at the contents of any recent issue of the prestigious journal *Moneda y Crédito* demonstrates that Spanish historians are now deeply involved in economic history, and the reason is easy to see: by early modern standards, the Spanish economy was relatively well integrated and therefore research on one area can be extended relatively easily to others. The kingdom of Castile was particularly unified, at least in the sixteenth century. The cloths of Segovia were exported to England and the Netherlands, linking the industrialists of Segovia with the merchants of Burgos and the ship-owners of Bilbao; the produce of the Indies which arrived at Seville was distributed through the whole of Spain, linking Andalusia with the lands to the north. Seville seemed destined to become the metronome of the entire Spanish economy and, as the Indies trade expanded to its peak in the 1590s, it seemed poised to dictate the economic rhythms of the whole of western Europe. But this promise was never fulfilled. The economy of Spain was dislocated in the half-century following 1570. First the second revolt of the Alpujarras (1568–71) crippled the silk-production of Granada, because the Moors who cultivated the silk and wove the cloths were expelled. Then the trade with the Netherlands foundered in 1572 with the Dutch Revolt: little Segovia cloth could find its way north for several decades. Next, in the 1620s, piracy, smuggling and the saturation of the American market with home-made goods disrupted the trade between Seville and the colonies in the New World. Finally, after 1630, war, famine and plague caused the collapse of the Italian economy, entailing the decline of the trade of Barcelona and Valencia with Italy. These misfortunes were made worse by climatic disasters, over-taxation, the export of bullion to finance foreign wars, and prolonged and drastic debasement of the coinage. There was no real recovery until the advent of the Bourbon dynasty in 1700, and even then many areas were devastated by the war of succession which lasted until 1715.

In 1716, the Spanish Bourbons introduced a 'new order' (the 'Nueva Planta') which abolished most internal customs barriers (for instance those between Castile and Aragon) and made other changes intended to promote economic recovery. Later there were measures to create and protect new industries, to establish new factories and to encourage economic activities such as banking, mining and shipbuilding. They only appear to have succeeded in the areas on the periphery of the peninsula: in Andalusia, in the Basque provinces, above all in Catalonia. Most of central Spain remained economically backward, a sort of 'colony' producing raw materials and primary goods, a prey to the exploitation of the more developed areas like Catalonia, or to foreign powers like France and England. Even in the 1580s, some merchants had noticed that other Europeans were beginning to treat Spain 'as if we were the Indies'; it became more true as time passed. Rather like Portugal, the economy of Spain never 'took off', and the root cause of the failures was the same: the overseas colonies. The produce of the colonies flooded Spain, and attracted manufactured goods from the rest of Europe; between them, these two flows of commodities gradually damped down domestic enterprise and industrial activity. So, despite the advantages of a world empire, a strong government and natural resources, Spain's economic productivity, and with it the standard of living of most of her people, declined in relation to the rest of Europe throughout our period.

3　Portugal

By 1500 the Portuguese had discovered Brazil, the Indian Ocean and the goldfields of West Africa. Important quantities of gold and spice flowed into Lisbon and the city enjoyed a period of great prosperity. But not for long: already by the 1540s gold remittances were falling and the cost of defending the long route to the Indies exceeded the profits accruing from the spice trade. The future looked bleak, and in 1560 the Portuguese government declared itself bankrupt. About 1570, however, the colonists in Brazil began to produce cane sugar on a large scale and Portugal became the recipient of another windfall commodity, which began to arrive in Lisbon in ever-increasing quantities. Despite the temporary occupation of an important area of north-eastern Brazil by the Dutch (1630–54), Brazil and its sugar remained the mainstay and motive force of the economy of the Portuguese empire until the 1670s. Then, just as the sugar of the French and British Antilles began to challenge the Portuguese monopoly, explorers in the South American hinterland discovered gold. From the 1690s onwards, 'Portingale gold' came to Europe in massive quantities, reaching a peak between 1750 and 1760. The Portuguese overseas empire, which began its prosperity with gold from Africa, ended its days of glory with gold from Brazil.

It is easy to discern the major trends and the principal activities of the Portuguese economy between 1500 and 1800. The problem is to quantify them. In 1755 the famous earthquake of Lisbon destroyed a large part of the government archives as well as the legendary treasure of King John v. The papers and documents that survived, in Lisbon and elsewhere, have been neglected: few archives have been properly classified or catalogued; few studies and monographs have been based on statistical archive material. So, despite the obvious importance of Portugal in the European economy throughout early modern times, we know precious little about it.

3.1 Population

The demographic evolution of Portugal between 1500 and 1800 is a prime example of our present ignorance. There has been no serious study of parish registers, and even rough estimates of the total population are hard to come by. On the whole it appears that the kingdom was inhabited by more or less the same number of people throughout the period: about 1 million in 1500, perhaps 1.1 million in 1580, 1.2 million in 1640 and still only 1.5 million in the mid-eighteenth century. The reason for this stability lay in the dry, mountainous terrain, which could not feed a large population, and in the perpetual emigration towards the colonies and trading posts overseas in America, Africa and the Far East. The only counter-balance to this sustained loss of manpower was the import of slaves: a few from Brazil, far more from Guinea and Angola. Between 1450 and 1500, some 150,000 slaves were brought to Lisbon and sold – an average of 3000 a year. By the 1530s, Lisbon was handling about 10,000 slaves every year, many of them for use in agriculture and domestic service throughout Portugal. Thus Lisbon's population of more or less 100,000 included 9950 slaves in 1551 and 10,470 slaves in 1639. The number of slaves in Portugal did not really fall off until the later seventeenth century.

3.2 Agriculture

The economy of Portugal itself was backward in the extreme. It produced few commodities, and it produced fewer still in surplus. Its agriculture was based upon growing grain, oil and wine, those three staples of the Mediterranean economy in early modern times, and the only major distinction between the subsistence economy of Portugal and that of, for example, Provence or Catalonia was that, thanks to the trade with her colonies, Portugal's harbours were well developed and could therefore receive and redistribute vast imports of cereals (often sent by her own overseas possessions) in years of local famine. Fishing, too, provided a substantial quantity of food.

Unfortunately, we have no figures concerning actual agricultural production. One calculation suggests that the maximum cereal-producing area in Portugal in the seventeenth and eighteenth centuries was 550,000 hectares, each producing perhaps 8 hectolitres

– some 4,400,000 hectolitres in all. It was not enough, and Lisbon alone had to import some 660,000 hectolitres every year in the 1620s, much of it from the Azores.[1] We have scarcely more information concerning the production of other agricultural goods. Olive oil and dairy produce were on sale, but we do not know on what scale. Very little meat appears to have been eaten. There is rather more information concerning wine, of which Portugal itself furnished a surplus. Between 120,000 and 150,000 'pipes' of wine (each of 34.5 hectolitres) were produced annually in the sixteenth century. It was all *'petit vin'* – the 'port' we know and drink today originated only in the eighteenth century – but even so it was exported in some volume to northern Europe. The best wines were those made from 'malvoisy' grapes grown in Madeira and the Azores, and Madeira alone exported over 2000 pipes per year to Africa, America (North and South) and Europe. We have some more direct evidence of the production of Madeira wine between 1596 and 1640. The port of Funchal on the island levied a tax of $33\frac{1}{3}$ per cent of the value of all wine produced in the area, and this tax yield rose from 595,000 in 1596 to 833,333 in 1636 and 1,700,000 reales in 1655.[2]

3.3 Industry

Portugal had only one real industry during this period: the production of salt. Salt was the country's principal export and there were pans, both large and small, all along the Atlantic seaboard. Some of them dated back to the high Middle Ages. Thanks to the studies of Professor Virginia Rau, we know a considerable amount about Portuguese salt production. For the period 1562–1657 we can follow the progress of her salt exports to the Baltic (see Figures 3.1 and 3.2).[3] There is a remarkable stability about the quantity of salt exported to the Baltic over these ninety-five years. Despite some savage annual fluctuations, until the 1650s the annual average exported never fell below 22,000 lasts and never rose above 33,000. The number of ships passing through the Sound from Portugal did change, however. From an average of around 150 a year, there was a sharp fall in the 1620s to between 10 and 25, with only a modest recovery thereafter. In large measure the decline was caused by the reopening of the war between the Dutch and the King of Spain (who was also, between 1580 and 1640, King of Portugal). The Dutch

FIGURE 3.1: Portuguese salt shipped through the Danish Sound 1570–1660 (in thousand lasts)

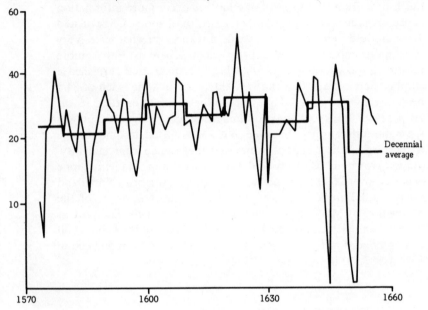

managed to corner an increasing share of the salt exported from western Europe to the Baltic: throughout the sixteenth and seventeenth centuries between 50 and 75 per cent of it was carried by Dutch ships, but their salt came from France, Spain and even Venezuela as well as from Portugal. Our series resumes in 1680, giving an indication of the total production of Portuguese salt as well as of quantities exported. The pattern is now somewhat different: the wars of Louis XIV of France and Charles XII of Sweden played havoc with Portuguese trade to the Baltic until 1720. Then followed a period of very slow recovery. It is noticeable from Figure 3.3 that the curve of salt produced closely matches the number of ships passing through the Danish Sound.[4]

3.4 Trade and Transport

The overseas trade of the Portuguese empire revolved around five commodities: grain, salt, spice, sugar and tobacco. The first two have been dealt with above; the other three were commodities which

Portugal did not produce herself, but imported from her overseas possessions and re-exported to the rest of Europe.

First, chronologically, came spices. We have fragmentary data on the quantities of spice that arrived in Lisbon from the Indies by the Cape of Good Hope during the sixteenth century (Figure 3.4). They reveal a steady decline in the trade.[5]

Portugal never acquired more than a fragment of the spice trade. Recent calculations suggest that the total production of Asiatic spices in the sixteenth century may have reached 1,500,000 tons, of which no more than 150,000 tons – 10 per cent – was sent back to Europe via the Cape of Good Hope.[6] Sugar was a different story. In 1500 it was still a spice, a costly condiment, and at first cultivation of the rare

FIGURE 3.2: Number of ships coming from Portugal passing through the Danish Sound, 1570–1660

FIGURE 3.3: Portuguese salt production and export, 1680–1766

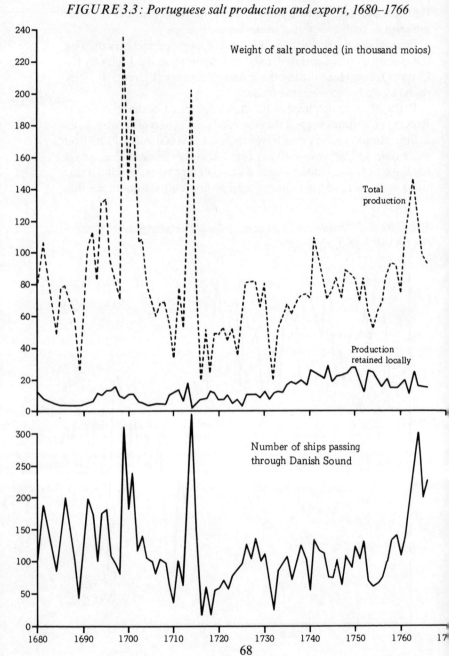

FIGURE 3.4: Arrival of spices at Lisbon during the sixteenth century (in thousand quintals)

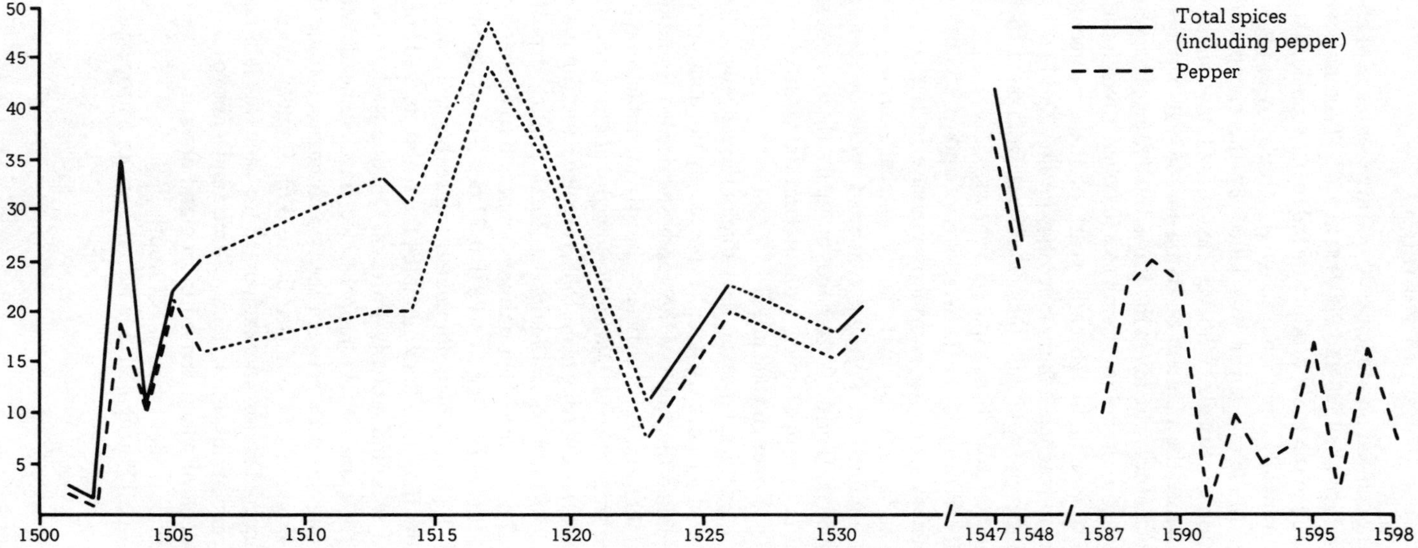

Total spices
(including pepper)

Pepper

sugarcane centred on Madeira: 70,000 arrobas (each of about 25 lbs) were produced in 1508 and 200,000 in 1570. This, however, was the apogee and in the 1580s production fell to between 30,000 and 40,000 arrobas annually and then died away completely in the seventeenth century. Madeira's sugar was killed by the cheap and plentiful production of Brazil. 'Whoever says Brazil says sugar and more sugar', wrote the planters of Bahía in 1662. It had been true for almost a century: already in the 1560s 180,000 arrobas were exported annually from the colony, rising to 350,000 arrobas in the 1580s and to over a million in the early years of the seventeenth century. Production reached 2 million arrobas a year (22,300 tons) by 1650. The number of sugar mills (*engenhos*) rose from 60 in 1570 to 346 in 1629 and 500 in 1670, as Figure 3.5 shows.[7]

Finally, Portugal, like the west of Scotland (p. 153 below) derived great benefit from the enormous increase in the consumption of tobacco in Europe during the later eighteenth century. Although the amount retained in Portugal remained more or less constant at between 50,000 and 60,000 arrobas annually, the amount re-exported to the rest of Europe tripled, from around 90,000 arrobas annually in the 1750s to over 260,000 in 1778.[8]

Taken together, however, the value of the salt, sugar, tobacco, oil, wine and other primary goods exported by Portugal never seems to have equalled the value of the goods she needed to import. Cloths, food, timber and other articles – mostly manufactured – had to be obtained from abroad. One of the few global estimates of Portugal's balance of trade, dating from 1685, revealed a total annual import bill of 5,228,883 *cruzados*, against a total annual export value of 3,275,627 cruzados. The resultant deficit had to be met by exporting bullion. It is interesting to note that 77 per cent of the imports came through Lisbon, which dominated the seaborne trade of Portugal even more than London dominated the seaborne trade of England.[9] England was undoubtedly Portugal's major trading partner after about 1660 and, as it happens, we have some detailed figures concerning the trade between the two countries, a trade that always ran in England's favour (see figure 3.6). English cloth, grain and manufactured goods were exchanged for wine (the famous port wine trade began at this time), sugar, tobacco and – above all – 'Portingale gold', much of which arrived in England aboard the weekly packet boat service from Lisbon to Falmouth.[10]

Almost all Portugal's trade with the rest of Europe was carried on

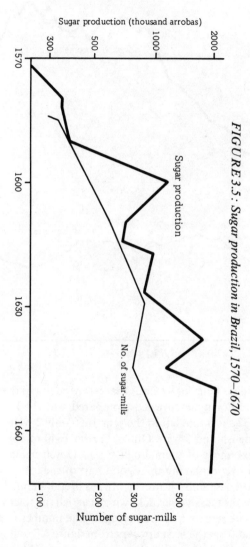

FIGURE 3.5: Sugar production in Brazil, 1570–1670

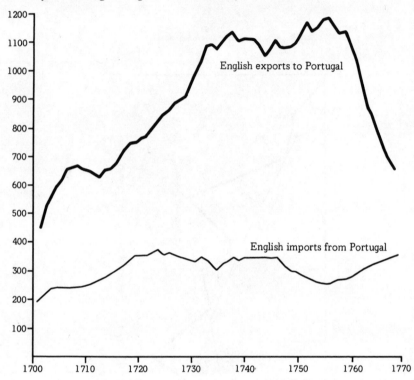

FIGURE 3.6: Trade between England and Portugal, 1700–70 (eleven-year moving averages, in thousand £s)

English exports to Portugal

English imports from Portugal

in foreign ships. Thus, of 42 ships that left Madeira in the year 1620, only 10 were Portuguese-owned (compared with 14 English and 8 Dutch); of 32 ships that left in the year 1650 only 2 were Portuguese (11 were English and 5 were Dutch). From 1640 to 1680, about 80 foreign ships (most of them English and Dutch again) docked at Lisbon every year, making up a good half of the total traffic of the port.[11] Portuguese ships, however, always preponderated in the East Indies trade: the massive carracks which carried the spices of the East to Lisbon were mostly built in Portugal. The number of these ships sailing to and from the East appears from figure 3.7 to have declined steadily from 1500 until 1800, but in fact the initial fall in numbers from 1500 until 1540 was more than compensated by the rising tonnage of each individual ship. The further fall after 1630 was a real one, however. The intensified privateering by the Dutch, and even more the successful competition of the English and Dutch East India Companies, made heavy inroads into the Portuguese trading empire in the east. When peace returned in the 1660s, and with it a new stability for the trade, only half as many ships sailed for the east every year as in the period before 1630.[12]

FIGURE 3.7: Number of Portuguese ships sailing to the East Indies 1500–1790 (decennial totals)

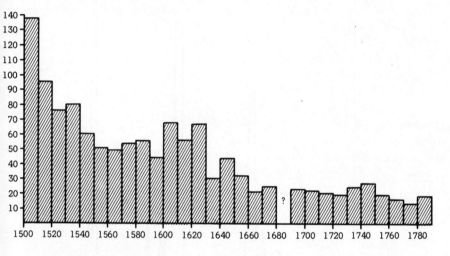

3.5 Currency

Paradoxically, we are better informed about the monetary situation of Portugal in early modern times than about almost any other facet of her economy. The records of the Lisbon mint – the Casa de Moeda – have survived in large quantities. Once a month after 1482, according to a Portuguese chronicler, a ship sailed from São Jorge da Mina, outport of the Ashanti goldfields, carrying gold to Lisbon, since the King of Portugal could not bear to wait longer than a month to see some more of his treasure. In all, about half a ton of African gold arrived annually in Portugal between 1482 and 1520. Later in the century there was gold from Monomatapa in Moçambique and silver from Spanish America (reaching a peak in 1623–8) (see figure 3.8).[13] Of course, not all of this treasure remained in Portugal. Much of it

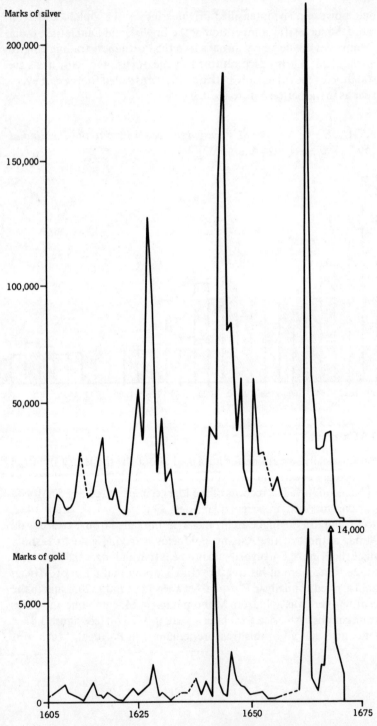

*FIGURE 3.8: Gold and silver delivered to the Lisbon Mint (*Casa de Moeda*), 1605–75*

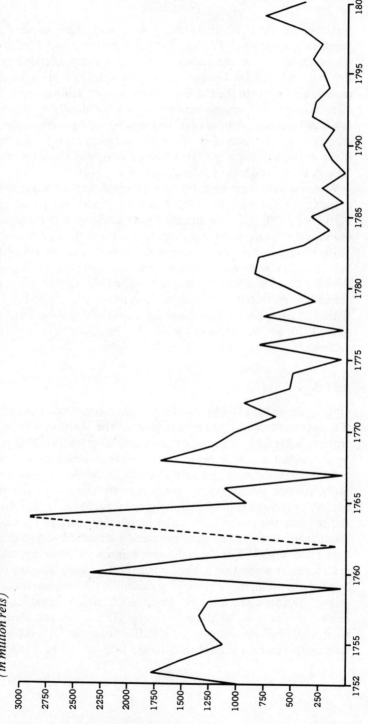

FIGURE 3.9: Total value of coinage (gold, silver and copper) struck at the Lisbon Mint (Casa de Moeda), 1752–1800 (in million reis)

was used to purchase the grain, timber and other goods from northern Europe which Portugal and her empire required. Much of it was shipped out to the Indies to purchase spices. According to Professor Magalhães Godinho, Portugal sent only about 50,000 cruzados annually to the Far East in the early sixteenth century, but after about 1580 the situation changed dramatically with up to 1,000,000 cruzados shipped east every year by the Portuguese, almost entirely in silver 'pieces of eight', while the Dutch exported far more silver to the east than the Portuguese throughout the seventeenth century in order to buy oriental luxuries for Europe.[14]

We know with some accuracy the total value of the coinage minted at the Casa de Moeda after 1752 (figure 3.9). There was a peak from 1750 until 1770, when the Brazilian gold made its greatest impact, enabling the Portuguese kings to manage without their Cortes. After 1770, however, there was a steady fall. Once again, much of the bullion inflow was immediately re-exported: this time to England. Between £1 million and £2 million reached the United Kingdom annually from 1700 to 1770, much of it carried, as noted above, by the Falmouth packet-boat. This supply of 'Portingale Gold' petered out after 1770 as the production of the Brazilian Minas Gerais declined.[15]

3.6 Prices

Once again we have fairly extensive data on this matter, above all for the seventeenth and eighteenth centuries. The problem is to select representative series. For the sixteenth and seventeenth centuries we have chosen the movement of wheat prices at Bragança in north-western Portugal, and at Ponta Delgada in the Azores (see figure 3.10). As one would expect, prices rose steadily in the sixteenth century, reaching a dramatic climax in the plague year 1598–9. In the Azores they fell away in the more favourable years of the earlier seventeenth century, but on the mainland a series of severe shortages kept prices high.[16] For the eighteenth century we possess excellent price series for several areas. For Lisbon, Porto, Evora, Bragança and Setúbal (for example) we possess the records of the corn market or the public weights-and-measures department, which listed current market prices with absolute accuracy. The series for Porto is particularly full, revealing the great stability of prices for much of the eighteenth century: a chicken cost 180–200 *reis* in the 1740s and

Figure 3.10: Prices in Portugal, 1570–1670: wheat

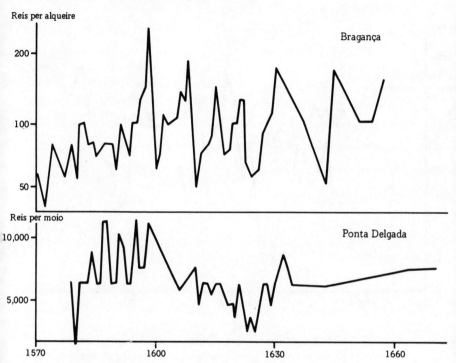

Note: 1 *alqueire* = 14 litres; 1 *moio* = 60 alqueires. 400 reis = 1 cruzado.

240–250 in the 1780s, a pound of butter cost 120 reis between 1740 and 1791, a sheep 600 reis between 1740 and 1782. Even grain prices, which fluctuated far more and showed a gradual upward trend, did not oscillate in the same brutal way as in the sixteenth and seventeenth centuries. After 1700 the price almost never doubled between one year and the next; in very bad years like the 1590s it had sometimes trebled or quadrupled.[17]

3.7 Conclusions

The Portuguese economy from the Age of Discovery to the Age of Enlightenment remained profoundly influenced by the sea. For example, in Figure 3.11, the price of rye at Bragança fluctuated far more than the price at Oporto because in a major seaport cereal

FIGURE 3.11: Prices in Portugal, 1740–1800: rye (in reis per alqueire)

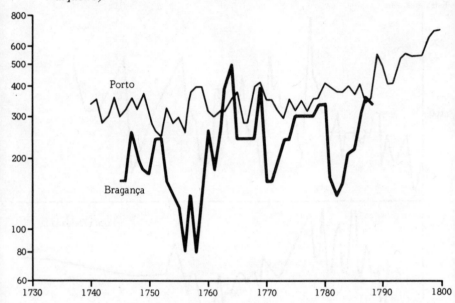

imports could reduce the impact of famines and even of temporary shortages. In an isolated region like Bragança, and in the case of the crop usually eaten by most of the poor, any shortage was immediately translated into rising prices. The ability to reduce food shortages by imports does not seem to have pre-dated the eighteenth century, however; figure 3.10 shows that between 1570 and 1670 wheat prices at Bragança and at Ponta Delgada in the Azores followed much the same rhythm.

The Portuguese economy was governed to a considerable extent by the great 'cycles' of the Atlantic economy: first by the 'gold cycle', which reached its peak around 1556, and the 'spice cycle', which never regained its initial high level of the years around 1500 but never entirely lost its importance until the general collapse of the 1640s. After 1500 there was also the considerable input of brazilwood – a 'spice' or 'drug' in the wider sense – which was imported in increasing quantities until the eighteenth century. But this economy of spices and gold collapsed in the mid-seventeenth century. It might have led to a substitute economy based on the manufacture of imported raw materials (which was the solution adopted by Venice after a similar collapse), but in fact the principal 'new industry' developed in Brazil: the growing and processing of sugar. The industry was demanding: it required large plantations and heavy capital investment; it gave rise to trade in slaves, to silver imports from Spanish Peru, to cattle raising on the *sertão* (the Brazilian interior), and to the development of new crops needed to sustain the growing workforce – maize, manioc, fruit, vegetables and later on tobacco, which came to be grown for export too. The entire Brazilian economy was based, more or less directly, on the sugar boom.

The outbreak of war between the Dutch Republic and the King of Spain – who since 1580 had also been King of Portugal – brought about a decline in the trade between Portugal and Brazil. Then in 1630 the Dutch managed to occupy Pernambuco, the part of Brazil where most of the province's sugar was grown and processed. There was at once an economic crisis in Portugal, which was suddenly deprived of her major source of wealth, and the government tried to develop the economy of other areas in the province (Bahía, Río). Although in 1640 Portugal broke with Spain, and although in 1654 the Dutch were driven out of Brazil, the situation of the prewar years did not return. Now the Dutch, and also the English and the French, were installed in the Antilles and producing sugar of their own which they sold at competitive prices on the international market. Chief Minister Ericeira, realizing the hopelessness of the position, tried to stimulate domestic industry to produce manufactured goods in Portugal from imported raw materials, but before his efforts could yield any fruits Brazil began to supply another treasure: gold.

Brazil gold began to flow to Portugal in the 1690s, and the amount increased (with some fits and starts) until the 1750s. As the quantity of gold began to decrease, other Brazilian products such as diamonds, tobacco, rice, maize, manioc, cattle and sugar (again) were imported to replace it. Under the direction of Pombal and his successors new industries were developed to deal with these imports and the Portuguese economy by the end of the eighteenth century had stabilized by using a permanent deficit in trade with Brazil to secure a permanent surplus in trade with the rest of Europe, especially England.

These observations about the conjuncture must not obscure the underlying structure. A small country of peasants and fisher folk, and a country of relatively few people, Portugal was able to play a major role in international commerce thanks to its sailors, its merchants and its colonial farmers. It played the role of middleman first in Asia and then in America until the moment (a different moment in each continent) when its role either became superfluous or was usurped by competitors from the north of Europe. The nineteenth century, when the final collapse occurred, was therefore a period of almost permanent economic crisis for Portugal: the colonies had sustained her for so long that nothing had been created to replace them. The initial solution to their loss was therefore to create a new colonial empire, in Africa, rather than to try industrialization. Now the second Portuguese empire has also collapsed, leaving only tourism and emigration to sustain the economy. The question now is whether the commercial and cultural ties that remain between Portugal and her former colonies will remain strong enough to keep her economy active, or whether there has to be a massive programme of industrialization. Or will there be yet another 'miracle' like gold or sugar?

4 The Low Countries

4.1 Population

General censuses of the population of the kind known today, held regularly under conditions of statistical accuracy, began in the Low Countries only in the early nineteenth century. For earlier periods information from several alternative sources is available, but it must always be used with extreme caution. We have to consider the intention of those who ordered the survey and the conditions under which the enumerators had to work. Practically all enumerations before 1800 differ from modern censuses in three important respects: first, instead of the count being made on a single day in all areas, there

TABLE 4.1: *The growth of population in the Low Countries, 1500–1800*

Province	*c.* 1500	*c.* 1530	*c.* 1620	*c.* 1690	*c.* 1750	*c.* 1795
Brabant	339,000	436,500	—	373,191*	447,282*	618,396*
Hainaut	102,000	154,000	—	—	—	—
Luxemburg & county of Chiny	57,000	72,000	—	—	—	—
Flanders	256,000	300,000	—	—	—	—
Holland	123,000	207,000	672,000	883,000	783,000	831,152
Veluwe	—	36,000	—	40,700†	54,150	65,801
Friesland	75,000	—	—	129,000	139,495	161,513
Groningen	—	—	—	—	—	114,655
Overijssel	53,000	—	—	71,000	122,434	135,600
Utrecht	—	—	[80,000]	—	[83,000]	92,904
Total Belgian provinces	—	—	—	—	—	2.273m.
Total Dutch provinces	0.95m.	*c.* 1.25m.	1.5m.	1.9m.	1.9m.	2.078m.

*Brabant in the eighteenth century was divided into two: Austrian Brabant and North or Dutch Brabant. The figures here refer only to the former; the population of the latter in 1795 was a further 211,063 people.
†Census of 1650.

were a number of separate surveys made over a period of time; second, they were not always based on identical criteria in all regions (some enumerators included young children while others omitted them, for example); third, instead of counting individuals, the earliest surveys counted 'hearths' or households. Therefore, in order to establish the approximate size of the population of the Low Countries in early modern times, as Table 4.1[1] attempts to do, it is necessary to allow for these idiosyncracies of the data and, where necessary, to multiply the number of 'hearths' by 4.5, the figure that recent research suggests was the average size of Netherlands households in early modern times.[2]

These total figures, fragmentary though they are, nevertheless indicate the strong demographic growth of the Dutch Republic in the sixteenth and earlier seventeenth centuries which turned to stagnation in the eighteenth. The records for modern Belgium are really too sparse to serve as a basis for generalization, but the population trends observed in individual towns over the early modern period reveal the prevailing pattern: growth until about 1560, after 1600 and again after 1750; decline in the later sixteenth century and stagnation in the first half of the eighteenth.[3]

TABLE 4.2: Population change in selected towns of the Low Countries, 1500–1800

North Netherlands	c. 1520	c. 1560	c. 1630	c. 1700	c. 1730	c. 1795
Amsterdam	13,500	30,900	120,000	190,000	186,200	217,024
Rotterdam	5,300	12,500	29,500	c. 51,000	49,400	57,510
Hague	5,500	9,300	16,600	c. 40,000	36,900	38,400
Leiden	11,461	22,600	44,000	c. 60,000	39,000	31,000
South Netherlands						
Antwerp	c. 50,000	89,996	c. 57,000	65,711	42,568	50,973
Brussels	26,100	—	—	—	57,854	65,977
Mons	c. 15,150	16,871	c. 13,800	13,800	17,250	c. 20,000
Namur	8,400	6,274	11,300	—	13,257	c. 15,000

In certain areas it has proved possible to estimate population size from parish registers of baptisms. The method was first used by the Chevalier des Pomelles in France during the 1780s: if one takes the annual average number of baptisms for a community over a ten-year period, and multiplies by 25.75, a reasonable indication of the total population is obtained. One has to be sure that almost all births are being registered but in the South Netherlands, a country of staunch Roman Catholics, the registers seem to be complete. Wherever we have census data for comparison, the correlation is surprisingly close. Let us demonstrate this from the figures for Antwerp:

Date	Population of Antwerp		Date
	According to census	According to baptisms	
1698	65,711	65,562	1695–1704
1755	42,568	43,656	1745–54
1784	50,973	50,351	1775–84

We may thus view population figures calculated by the des Pomelles method with some confidence (see also Table 6.1 below). For the South Netherlands we find, in the towns and rural areas surveyed (Table 4.3[4]), a heavy fall in population in the period 1570–1600, followed by about a century of growth. There was another setback at the end of the seventeenth century, due to Louis XIV's campaigns; and recovery from this was slow, at least in the towns.

The Netherlands, as is well known, were highly urbanized even in

TABLE 4.3: Parish register demography of parts of the South Netherlands, 1566–1795[4]

	Bruges	Ghent	District of Aalst	Evergem	Mechelen	
1566–75	—	—	95,000	[2,650–2,920]	—	1565–74
1576–85	—	—	32,500	—	—	1575–84
1586–95	—	—	35,500	[1,743–2,140]	10,972	1585–94
1596–1605	—	—	42,500	[1,970–2,480]	14,947	1595–1604
1606–15	—	31,073	55,000	1,865	15,273	1605–14
1616–25	27,278	37,380	67,500	2,400	18,073	1615–24
1626–35	30,223	40,797	78,500	3,000	20,901	1625–34
1636–45	32,230	43,829	83,000	3,300	21,371	1635–44
1646–55	34,255	46,059	90,000	3,473	19,460	1645–54
1656–65	34,993	49,310	97,500	3,939	20,501	1655–64
1666–75	36,813	50,680	94,000	4,105	21,895	1665–74
1676–85	37,580	51,030	84,000	3,605	24,136	1675–84
1686–95	37,243	51,887	86,000	3,855	22,700	1685–94
1696–1705	37,920	51,285	84,500	4,000	23,909	1695–1704
1706–15	36,799	49,781	93,000	3,681	22,965	1705–14
1716–25	35,367	44,120	103,000	4,049	21,947	1715–24
1726–35	31,757	42,732	113,500	4,209	20,694	1725–34
1736–45	28,532	44,226	127,000	4,507	19,284	1735–44
1746–55	27,932	45,400	134,000	4,668	20,968	1745–54
1756–65	28,266	43,661	147,000	4,939	16,944	1755–64
1766–75	28,878	45,465	157,000	5,139	16,789	1765–74
1776–85	29,971	49,023	164,000	5,702	16,989	1775–84
1786–95	31,837	51,104	171,000	6,557	18,833	1785–94

the sixteenth century. Already in 1500 there were at least twenty towns that could boast more than 10,000 inhabitants (England at the same time had but three). In Flanders and Holland over 40 per cent of the population lived in towns and several other provinces had a fairly high urban concentration, although, as Figure 4.1[5] shows, the percentage grew less the further one moved from the coast. There was nothing particularly remarkable about the structure of this population. As in the rest of Europe, females outnumbered males by about six to four in the adult population; children under ten years old made up about one-quarter of the total population (young people under twenty made up one-half); and about one-third of the total population was married.[6]

FIGURE 4.1: Urban population as a percentage of total population, c. 1500

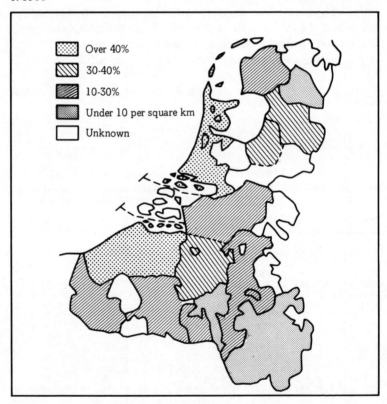

4.2 Agriculture and fishing

The Netherlands in early modern times were famed for their countryside as well as for their towns: the highest European yields in both arable and animal husbandry were obtained in the Low Countries. Rienck Hemmema, a Frisian farmer whose accounts have survived for 1570–3, obtained 1350 litres of milk per year from each of his dairy cows; on the Beemster *polder* in Holland in 1640, some animals produced 2000 litres annually. Yields like this were scarcely surpassed for two centuries, although the number of farmers specializing in the dairy sector increased. By the 1760s Friesland and Holland, still the centres of dairy produce, were turning out (respectively) 5.5 million and 18 million pounds of cheese every year.

TABLE 4.4: Yield ratios, 1570–1800 (weight of cereal harvested per weight sown)

		1570	1600–10	1775–1800
WHEAT	Brabant and Flanders	—	10.9	10.3–17.6
	Friesland	10.3	8.4	20–28
BARLEY	Friesland	7.5–9	5.8–7	27–33
	Flanders	—	—	16–22.8

1812: All Netherlands – Wheat 8, Rye 8.5, Barley 12.5, Oats 12.5

Yield ratios for cereal crops were no less impressive. Table 4.4 shows that Rienck Hemmema obtained a return on his wheat in the 1570s which was considerably higher than the national average in the early nineteenth century, after the 'agricultural revolution'.[7]

TABLE 4.5: Growth of agricultural area and use of land in the province of Overijssel, 1601–1812 (index numbers)

	Arable	Pasture	Total agricultural area
1601–2	100	100	100
1750	106.4	104.2	105.1
1812	135.6	223.3	186.1

Between the 1570s and the 1770s, the number of arable farmers producing for the market and the area in cultivation both increased dramatically. In Holland and Friesland in particular, with their rich soils and high profits, lakes, fens and estuaries, were reclaimed remorselessly in order to increase farmland. The same was true even in a poor province like Overijssel, where peat-bogs and heaths were brought under cultivation in the later eighteenth century in order to increase production (see Table 4.5[8]). It is significant that pasture increase was so much more rapid than arable: in 1601–2, 42 per cent of the cultivated land in Overijssel was arable, and this proportion was virtually unaltered in 1750 (43 per cent), but by 1812, 70 per cent of the land was pasture and only 30 per cent arable. This stability of agriculture between 1600 and 1750 was typical of most of western

FIGURE 4.2: The catch of the Dutch herring fleet, 1630–1800 (ten yearly averages, in lasts)

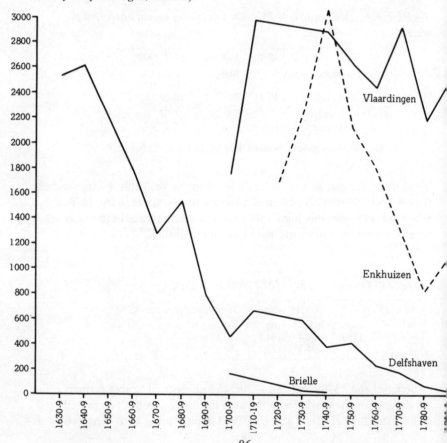

Europe: few areas changed the pattern of cultivation that was already established. Holland, Friesland and Flanders with their new crops and their new methods were the exception, not the rule.

As if burgeoning towns and prosperous fields were not enough, Holland was also the centre of a well-developed fishing industry. There was whaling off Greenland and cod-fishing off Iceland, but the main catch from the fifteenth century onwards was the herring.[9] Millions of herring were caught every year by Dutch ships, most of them controlled by a 'fisheries board' known as the 'Grote visserij'. As Figure 4.2 shows, the ports engaged in the herring-fishing changed in the course of time, but the total catch seems to have remained constant at about 5000 lasts until 1700, rising to a peak thereafter with catches of over 6000 lasts per year in the mid-eighteenth century. (Each last weighed about two tons and contained about 144,000 herring; we are thus speaking of catches of between 720 and 864 million herrings!).

4.3 Industry

There are three ways in which we can assess the level of industrial production in the early modern period, and all of them are defective. The first method is by means of the yield of the taxes, mostly excise or customs duties, levied on each item manufactured or on each item exported. Figures 4.3–4.5, all connected with cloth production, are compiled from fiscal records. Figure 4.3 shows the performance of the clothworks at Hondschoote in Flanders, the largest in Europe in the mid-sixteenth century, according to two different taxation records: the top set of figures are calculated from a tax on the number of serge and worsted cloths ('new draperies') exported; the lower set is the yield of an excise tax on all cloth produced. Both follow an identical trend, starting with a rapid rise until the civil wars of the later sixteenth century. (Hondschoote was sacked six times between 1578 and 1582; a town of 18,000 people in 1564, its population numbered just 385 in 1584.) The strong recovery in the first three-quarters of the seventeenth century is apparent – giving the lie to the 'century of misfortunes' legend. Only after 1670 and the wars against Louis xiv did the economy of the South Netherlands, including Hondschoote, collapse.[10]

The same pattern was repeated in the linen output of the area around Ghent (figure 4.4): there was a rapid growth from 1620 until

FIGURE 4.3: Production of serge cloth at Hondschoote, 1500–1700

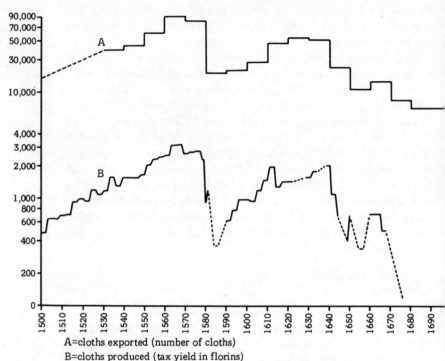

A=cloths exported (number of cloths)
B=cloths produced (tax yield in florins)

1670 – many of the cloths manufactured being exported to Spain – followed by decline until 1715. Then came further growth at an accelerating pace.[11]

The pattern of production at the largest clothworks in the North Netherlands, at Leiden, was remarkably similar after 1600 (see figure 4.5). In the earlier sixteenth century there had been a prosperous cloth-weaving industry (25,000 pieces per year from 1500 to 1530), but under pressure of competition from the south and (in the 1570s) of war, output shrank away to virtually nothing: only 510 pieces per year were produced in the 1580s. At precisely this nadir of the industry's fortunes, however, the manufacture of the 'new draperies', lighter cloths made with worsted yarn spun from combed long-staple wool, began to boom – a development not unconnected with the collapse of Hondschoote and the emigration of skilled Flemish weavers to the north. Well over 10,000 emigrants, most of them

88

FIGURE 4.4: Linen production at Ghent, 1620–1783

Note: 1620–1700 = yield of the farm of the excise on linen sold
1700–83 = actual yield of the excise on linen sold

FIGURE 4.5: Textile production at Leiden, 1570–1799 (number of cloths and total textile 'pieces')

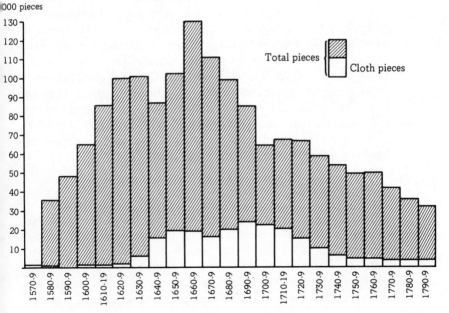

89

southern, arrived between 1580 and 1630.[12] There was rapid and steady growth from the 1580s until the 1670s. Thereafter, although there was a recovery in the output of old style broad cloths (spun from woollen yarn of carded short-staple wool), the total production of the Leiden clothing industry began to fall and the decline continued throughout the eighteenth century. It is likely that the very taxes that led to the compilation of this data helped, by their weight, to stifle the industry.[13]

The second source of evidence on industrial output is the accounts of individual enterprises, but surprisingly few concerns were worried about monitoring profit and loss for their own sake. Generally speaking, detailed accounts were kept only when it was someone else who was interested – shareholders, creditors and so on – and it was necessary to *prove* the profitability of the business. We have several records of this type relating to mining and metallurgy, where a percentage of the yield had to be surrendered to the landowner. Thus we know that the coal mines of Mariemont in Hainaut made 5300 florins profit annually between 1759 and 1769 and the mines of Houdeng, also in Hainaut, made 5000 florins in 1775 and 40,000 in 1790; but this, alas, tells us nothing about the development or the production of the Hainaut coal industry as a whole.[14]

A similar objection can be levelled against our third source of evidence: the vast corpus of statistics collected by the Austrian government of the South Netherlands in the eighteenth century. Here however the reproach lies not with the sources, which are relatively complete, but with the historians who have failed to use them! So far we have only the figures relating to individual enterprises. Thus we know that in the Charleroi area there were three steam-engines working in the coal mines around 1750, 6 in 1763, 10 in 1770 and 9 in 1785; but we know neither how typical this was, nor how important Charleroi's share was in the total production of coal.[15]

4.4 Trade and transport

Until the eighteenth century we have to rely partly on qualitative sources for our knowledge of the overall trading situation of the Low Countries. In 1567 an Italian merchant resident in Antwerp, Ludovico Guicciardini, published a remarkably detailed book entitled *A description of all the Low Countries*. It contained information on trade and production which has been used, together with additional material, to compile Table 4.6, showing both the geographical distribution and the composition of the Netherlands trade in the 1560s. The preponderance of manufactured cloths is notable; but more remarkable is the overall trade deficit caused largely by the enormous import of foodstuffs which made up 44 per cent of all imports.[16]

TABLE 4.6: The balance of trade of the Low Countries, c. 1560 (in guilders)

IMPORTS	
Italy (silk, alum, wine)	c. 4,500,000
Spain & Portugal (wool, cochineal, spices, sugar, oil, wine, salt, alum)	c. 4,684,000
England (wool, cloth)	c. 4,155,000
Baltic (cereals)	c. 4,500,000
France (wine, woad, salt)	c. 2,700,000
Germany (fustians, Rhine-wine, copper)	c. 2,000,000
TOTAL	c. 20–22,000,000

Raw materials		Industrial products		Foodstuffs	
woad	400,000	fustians	240,000	Rhine-wine	720,000
Span. wool	1,250,000	copper	80,000	Fr. wine	1,150,000
Engl. wool	500,000	Engl. cloth	3,240,000	Medit. wine	500,000
cochineal	225,000	Ital. silk	2,000,000	cereals	3,000,000
alum	240,000			spices	2,000,000
copper	80,000			oil	100,000
Ital. silk	2,000,000			sugar	250,000
				salt	425,000
TOTAL	4,695,000 (25.9%)	TOTAL	5,560,000 (30%)	TOTAL	8,145,000 (44%)

EXPORTS	
Italy (linen, cloth, other textile products, tapestries)	—
Spain & Portugal (linen, serges, cloth, other textile products, tapestries)	—
England (linen, other textile products, tapestries, silk)	—
Baltic (linen, cloth, other textile products, tapestries, silk)	—
France (linen, cloth, other textile products, tapestries, silk)	c. 3,000,000
Germany (linen, cloth, other textile products, tapestries)	—
TOTAL	c. 16,060,000

Industrial products		Foodstuffs and raw materials	
linen	2,500,000		
serges	2,500,000		
cloth	1,400,000		
other textile products	600,000		
tapestries	700,000		
silk	500,000		
re-exportation of imported textile products	270,000		
re-exportation of imported English cloth	3,120,000		
TOTAL	11,560,000	TOTAL	4,500,000

Of the international trade, the majority by the middle of the sixteenth century went through the metropolis of Antwerp. The largest town in the Netherlands, it handled three-quarters of the total exports of the whole country. Only Lille, sending Flemish cloths to France, possessed even a remotely respectable role compared with the domination of Antwerp. The total volume of exports in Figure 4.6 covers almost two years: the annual average for 1543–5 (compiled from the yield of an export tax) would thus be about 10 million florins, considerably below the estimated total of the 1560s.[17]

An indirect source of evidence confirms this suggestion that the trade of Antwerp expanded rapidly between 1545 and 1565. The records of the tolls collected in Brabant from all boats and carts

FIGURE 4.6: The commercial preponderance of Antwerp: Netherlands' exports, 10 February 1543–24 September 1545 (in £s Flemish)

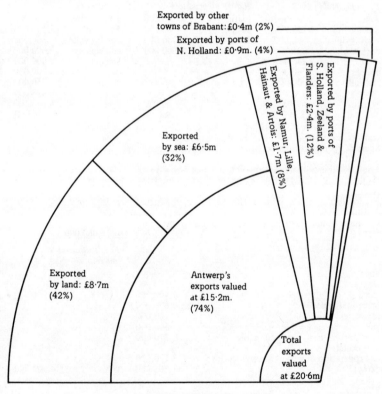

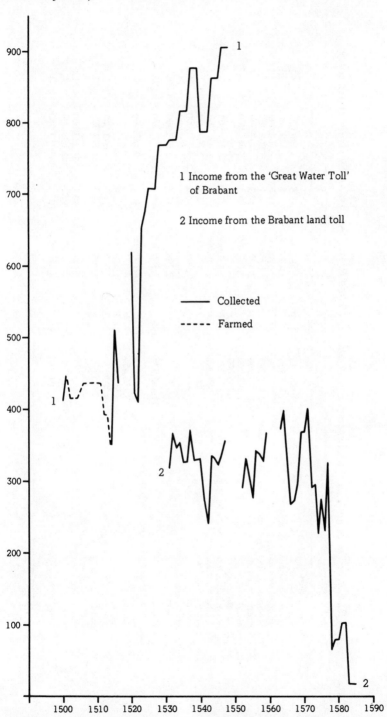

FIGURE 4.7: The income from the Brabant tolls, 1500–90 (in thousand florins)

1 Income from the 'Great Water Toll' of Brabant

2 Income from the Brabant land toll

—— Collected

- - - Farmed

TABLE 4.7: *The balance of trade between France and the United Provinces, 1635–1789 (in livres tournois)*

	1635-45	%	1750	%	1789	%
DUTCH EXPORTS TO FRANCE						
spices	3,193,130	14.9	3,482,000	15.5	1,180,000	3.2
sugar, tea, cocoa, tobacco	1,885,150	8.75	1,446,000	6.4	2,129,000	5.7
drugs, dyes, colours	1,877,300	8.75	2,390,000	10.6	1,904,000	5.1
precious stones, wool, cotton, ivory, silk, hair	1,835,200	8.55	1,820,000	8.1	803,000	2
cloth, serges, etc.	6,889,960	32.1	2,327,000	10.3	2,793,000	7.4
metal	1,500,000	7	2,137,000	9.5	2,485,000	6.7
war-materials	1,235,000	5.8	—	—	—	—
linen, hemp, wood, masts, leather, skins, furs	2,375,470	11.05	1,636,000	7.3	1,331,000	3.6
fishing-products, oil, lime	454,300	2.1	2,180,000	9.7	1,050,000	2.5
dairy-products	200,010	0.95	770,000	3.4	2,760,000	7.5
cereals	—	—	1,960,000	8.6	14,052,000	38.2
vegetables, brandy	—	—	—	—	3,490,000	9.5
others	—	—	c.2,238,000	c.10.6	2,872,000	8.5
Total	21,445,520	100	22,386,000	100	33,907,000	100
FRENCH EXPORTS TO THE UNITED PROVINCES						
wine, brandy	6,192,632	39.5	4,702,000	19.1	3,155,000	7.3
cereals	3,450,450	21.9	—	—	—	—
linen	1,583,432	10.1	1,450,000	5.9	—	—
salt, fruits & oil of Provence	3,203,927	20.35	922,000	3.7	1,073,000	2.4
textiles, paper, glass	915,525	5.8	1,794,000	7.3	1,014,000	2.4
fruit, honey, woad, etc.	355,500	2.3	—	—	—	—
colonial products	—	—	12,447,000	50.7	35,313,000	81.8
others	—	—	3,205,000	13.3	c.2,602,000	6.1
Total	15,701,466	100	24,520,000	100	43,157,000	100

taking merchandise to Antwerp have survived in considerable quantities for the sixteenth century (see figure 4.7). They reveal a tremendous surge of activity by river and canal between 1520 and 1540, and another somewhat smaller surge in land transport (and very probably in waterborne trade as well) between 1555 and 1565.[18]

It is not possible to assess the overall trade of the Netherlands after the revolt of the 1570s, partly because the warring governments were too preoccupied to collect the necessary statistics. We have, however, a number of estimates of the trade between France and the Dutch Republic (Table 4.7): for 1635 there is the estimate of the French merchant, Jean Eon; for 1750 and 1789 we have estimates compiled by the French government. It is interesting to compare the favourable balance of trade enjoyed by the Dutch in the mid-seventeenth century with the growing deficit of the balance in the later eighteenth century, a change that reflects some interesting alterations in the actual goods exchanged.[19]

A similar picture can be drawn up for the trade between the Southern Netherlands and Great Britain in the eighteenth century (Table 4.8). Here the balance always went against the Low Countries, and the size of the deficit increased steadily throughout the century.[20]

TABLE 4.8: The balance of trade between Great Britain and the Austrian Netherlands, 1715–89 (annual average, in £s sterling)

	Exports from the British Isles	Imports from the Belgian Provinces	Balance in Britain's favour
1715–40	246,300	101,135	+145,165
1740–48	232,963	95,353	+228,610
1748–74	517,877	92,717	+425,160
1774–83	1,298,401	571,744	+726,657
1783–89	1,109,483	251,173	+858,310

An idea of the total trade of the North Netherlands can be gained from fiscal records. From 1580 onwards all shipping had to pay 'convoy and licence money' to the Dutch Republic, and the trend of the receipts paid at Amsterdam or Rotterdam on the Maas shows the growth of the seventeenth century and the stagnation of the eighteenth. Even though port dues and taxes are notoriously incomplete (owing to evasion and smuggling), the trends of Dutch seaborne commerce are unmistakeable. The collection of the convoy and licence duties was entrusted to the Admiralties. Besides those of

FIGURE 4.8: Holland's seaborne commerce measured by the receipt of 'convoy and licence money', 1580–1799 (in Holland £s)

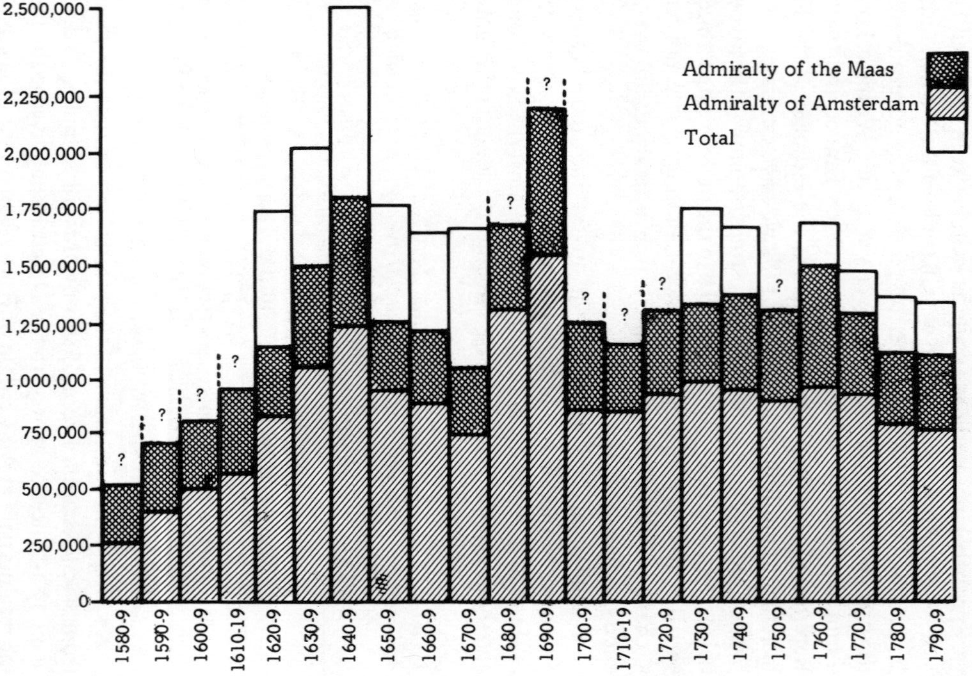

Admiralty of the Maas
Admiralty of Amsterdam
Total

Amsterdam and Rotterdam, the records of which have survived
entirely, there were three others: in the Northern Quarter of Holland
(at Hoorn, later at Enkhuizen), in Zeeland (at Middelburg), and in
Friesland (at Dokkum, later at Harlingen). They left incomplete
material which, whenever possible, has been added on top of the
Amsterdam and Rotterdam figures in Figure 4.8.[21]

A somewhat more reliable fiscal source which sheds light on Dutch
trade is the 'Sound Toll Register': the records of the dues paid at
Elsinore by every ship passing into and out of the Baltic. It is possible
to construct a table of the total trade of the Baltic with western
Europe over two centuries, and to assess the place of the Dutch in it
(Table 4.9). From 1562 until 1657 we find the Dutch carrying about
60 per cent of the trade, with a particularly high proportion of the
grain trade; from 1661 until 1783, however, there is both an absolute
and a relative decline. The total number of Dutch ships trading with
the Baltic fell, and their place in the total trade fell to 35 per cent,
almost half the figure for the preceding century.[22]

TABLE 4.9: Dutch traffic through the Sound, 1562–1783

Eastward		% of total traffic	Westward		% of total traffic
1562–1657	*c.*			*c.*	
number of passages	113,212	60	number of passages	113,212	60
salt (in lasts)	1,585,219	61	rye (in lasts)	2,807,011	77
herring (in lasts)	453,382	75	wheat (in lasts)	479,680	78
Rhine-wine (in amen)	380,005	79			
wine (in pijpen)	264,951	66			
cloth (in pieces)	1,234,667	35			
1661–1783					
number of passages	93,028	36	number of passages	92,088	35
salt (in lasts)	1,593,090	47	rye (in lasts)	2,335,182	70
herring (in lasts)	177,622	31	wheat (in lasts)	1,036,093	71
Rhine-wine (in amen)	123,932	67	wood (in pieces)	72,097,000	47
wine (in tuns)	337,326	35			
wine (in pijpen)	145,638	30			
wine (in oxhoofden)	169,089	30			
cloth (in rolls & pieces)	2,327,255	38			
colonial products (in pounds)	397,823,000	32			

Note: 1 'last' = 2918–2965 l (cereals); = 35.6 hl. (salt); = 12 tuns (herring) (1 tun = *c.*
850 herrings); 1 'aam' = 152.34 l. (wine); 1 'pijp' = 412.25 (wine); 1 tun = *c.* 150 l.
(wine); 1 'oxhoofd' = 228.51 l. (wine); 1 pound = 494 gr.

This overall decline after 1650 can be exaggerated: there was little
real fall in either the volume or the value of trade until after the final

struggle with Louis XIV ended in 1713, and rapid decline only set in after 1740.[23] At Danzig, the principal port for taking on Polish grain, over 300 Dutch ships docked every year even in the early eighteenth century, but by the 1760s the annual average was only 215 and by the 1780s it was only 91, accounting for 14 per cent of the total activity of the port (whereas at the beginning of the century Dutch shipping had made up 50 per cent of the total).[24] The same trend appears in the less complete records of other ports of northern Europe. The annual total of Dutch ships docking at Archangel in the 1580s was 6; by 1610–19 it had risen to 30. A century later the average was 57, but this fell steadily away to an average of 24 annually from 1720 until 1769.[25]

Several trading ventures have left us copious and detailed records of their commercial activities, including the famous East and the West India Companies. In the case of the former, the number of ships concerned was small, only 10 or 12 a year, but the value of the commodities carried was enormous. In the case of the West Indies trade, the records are less complete but the number of ships involved appears to have been considerable and profits large – although not as large as from the trade with the Far East. A description of this colonial commerce unfortunately lies outside the scope of this volume, but we cannot resist including a solitary example (Table 4.10) of the sort of things which the colonial trade involved.[26]

TABLE 4.10: The Dutch slave trade by the Middelburgh Commercie Compagnie, 1732–1802

Number of ships	29
Number of voyages	108
Crew (average per ship)	36
Number of bought slaves	31,095
Number of deceased slaves	3,751 (12%)
Profit and loss account (1732/4–1793/7, in £s*)	
debit	1,574,580
credit	1,625,802
loss (no. of times)	42
profit (no. of times)	59
result	+51,222 (3.2%)

*1 £ = 6 Holl. guilders.

4.5 Currency and finance

It is almost impossible to compile meaningful statistics concerning the currency of the Low Countries in early modern times because of the enormous number of foreign coins in circulation. Merchants' handbooks from Antwerp list over 1500 coins – gold, silver and copper – as being 'current' in the 1560s. Most of them were foreign. Almost certainly the majority of the money in circulation throughout the period covered by this volume was minted outside the Low Countries. The random figures in Table 4.11, taken from the declarations of coins received by customs collectors in three areas of the South Netherlands, reveal the preponderance of foreign coins even in the later eighteenth century.[27]

TABLE 4.11: Currency circulating in the Austrian Netherlands, 1761–71 (as percentage of total toll revenue)

	Brabant, Flanders, Hainaut		Luxemburg		Limburg, Gelderland	
	1761	1771	1761	1771	1761	1771
Gold:						
minted in the Netherlands	3.1	1.4	0.04	0.04	44.4	30.5
minted in France	3.5	0.3	62.9	11.7	13.5	0.3
minted elsewhere (mainly British)	2.3	0.8	—	—	1.5	0.3
TOTAL	8.9	2.5	62.94	11.74	59.4	31.1
Silver:						
minted in the Netherlands	14.8	85.7⎤	37.06*	88.26*	⎧ 3.8	30.0
minted in France and Spain	76.3	11.8⎦			⎩ 36.8	39.9
TOTAL	91.1	97.5	37.06	88.26	40.6	68.9

*Mainly French

If we bear this overall preponderance of foreign coins in mind, we can make better use of the fairly complete records of the production of the South Netherlands mints from 1598 to 1789. Their fluctuations, as one would expect, reflect above all the war-spending of the government, which necessitated an expanded volume of currency in circulation (see Table 4.12).

One of the most remarkable features of the sixteenth-century economy was the growth of credit and the concurrent fall in interest rates, which was clearly due to monetary abundance. Short-term loans, in particular, fell from 20 per cent in 1510 to 10 per cent in 1550, and although there was some rise in the years of war that followed, the overall trend was downwards. In the mid-seventeenth century loans were readily available in the Dutch Republic at under 10 per

TABLE 4.12: *Total mint output of the South Netherlands, 1598–1789 (in guilders*)*

	Gold	Silver	Copper	Total
1598–1600	2,181,117	304,449	—	2,485,566
1601–3	10,678,315	1,213,365	7,871	11,899,551
1604–6	6,561,248	1,610,628	14,718	8,186,595
1607–9	846,991	1,272,983	96,389	2,216,363
1610–12	308,933	3,037,617	120,198	3,466,748
1613–15	1,148,532	15,522,744	129,087	16,800,363
1616–18	1,157,650	8,366,682	141,615	9,665,947
1619–21	396,087	14,249,222	15,610	14,660,919
1622–4	235,567	18,441,016	5,522	18,682,105
1625–7	141,117	4,951,940	11,474	5,104,531
1628–9	153,010	2,643,732	4,109	2,800,851
1630–2	364,414	8,838,411	6,679	9,209,503
1633–5	476,996	16,554,079	—	17,031,075
1636–8	2,917,826	20,172,257	—	23,090,083
1639–41	2,950,150	8,102,988	—	11,053,138
1642–4	2,763,979	1,215,645	47,834	4,027,458
1645–7	3,505,544	5,852,834	14,811	9,373,189
1648–50	2,101,466	14,995,739	5,318	17,102,523
1651–3	1,359,800	10,221,276	20,086	11,601,162
1654–6	2,228,232	10,510,963	36,413	12,775,608
1657–9	2,193,480	6,604,871	6,542	8,804,893
1660–2	706,124	8,345,017	1,025	9,052,166
1663–5	376,205	5,361,763	—	5,737,968
1666–8	328,721	9,505,286	—	9,834,007
1669–71	95,351	4,823,445	—	4,918,796
1672–4	132,495	7,076,176	—	7,208,671
1675–7	109,050	2,067,000	91	2,176,141
1678–80	93,115	2,520,804	3,149	2,617,068
1681–3	66,393	1,650,889	1,403	1,718,685
1684–6	134,585	3,073,090	20,855	3,228,530
1687–9	116,805	1,463,920	17,839	1,598,564
1690–2*	248,251	793,062	114,038	1,155,351
1693–5	327,763	1,454,224	169,817	1,951,804
1696–8	206,714	719,245	83,289	1,009,248
1699–1701	152,847	450,396	42,572	645,815
1702–4	114,288	1,661,215	—	1,775,503
1705–7	33,202	526,909	—	560,111
1708–10	—	—	140,145	140,145
1711–13	65,607	603,540	151,000	820,147
1714–16	—	—	—	—
1717–19	19,565	—	1,003	20,568
1720–2	—	—	—	—
1723–5	—	50,000	—	50,000
1726–8	—	50,000	—	50,000
1729–31	—	—	—	—
1732–4	—	—	—	—
1735–7	—	—	—	—
1738–40	—	—	—	—
1741–3	—	—	—	—
1744–6	—	—	160,000	160,000
1747–9	5,000,000	2,000,000	100,000	7,100,000
1750–2	18,000,000	6,500,000	148,053	24,648,053
1753–5	7,500,000	3,500,000	—	11,000,000
1756–8	8,334,017	3,499,927	34,152	11,868,096

TABLE 4.12: —continued

	Gold	Silver	Copper	Total
1759–61	11,484,343	2,117,350	38,723	13,640,416
1762–4	7,152,431	11,084,209	—	18,236,640
1765–7	2,960,106	20,641,933	—	23,612,039
1768–70	490,048	7,476, 615	—	7,966,663
1771–3	541,592	2,413,221	—	2,954,813
1774–6	784,569	4,339,673	16,847	5,141,089
1777–9	2,962,580	1,736,360	154,457	4,853,397
1780–2	204,535	448,959	43,164	696,658
1783–5	298,000	7,797,709	—	8,095,709
1786–8	409,980	4,329,791	147	4,739,918
1789	28,572	76,498	—	105,070

*In current guilders after 1690 (7 current guilders = 6 guilders bank-money).

FIGURE 4.9: Short- and long-term interest rates in the Netherlands, 1510–70 (% interest per year)

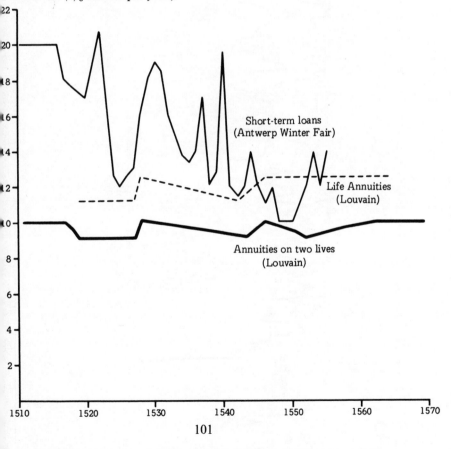

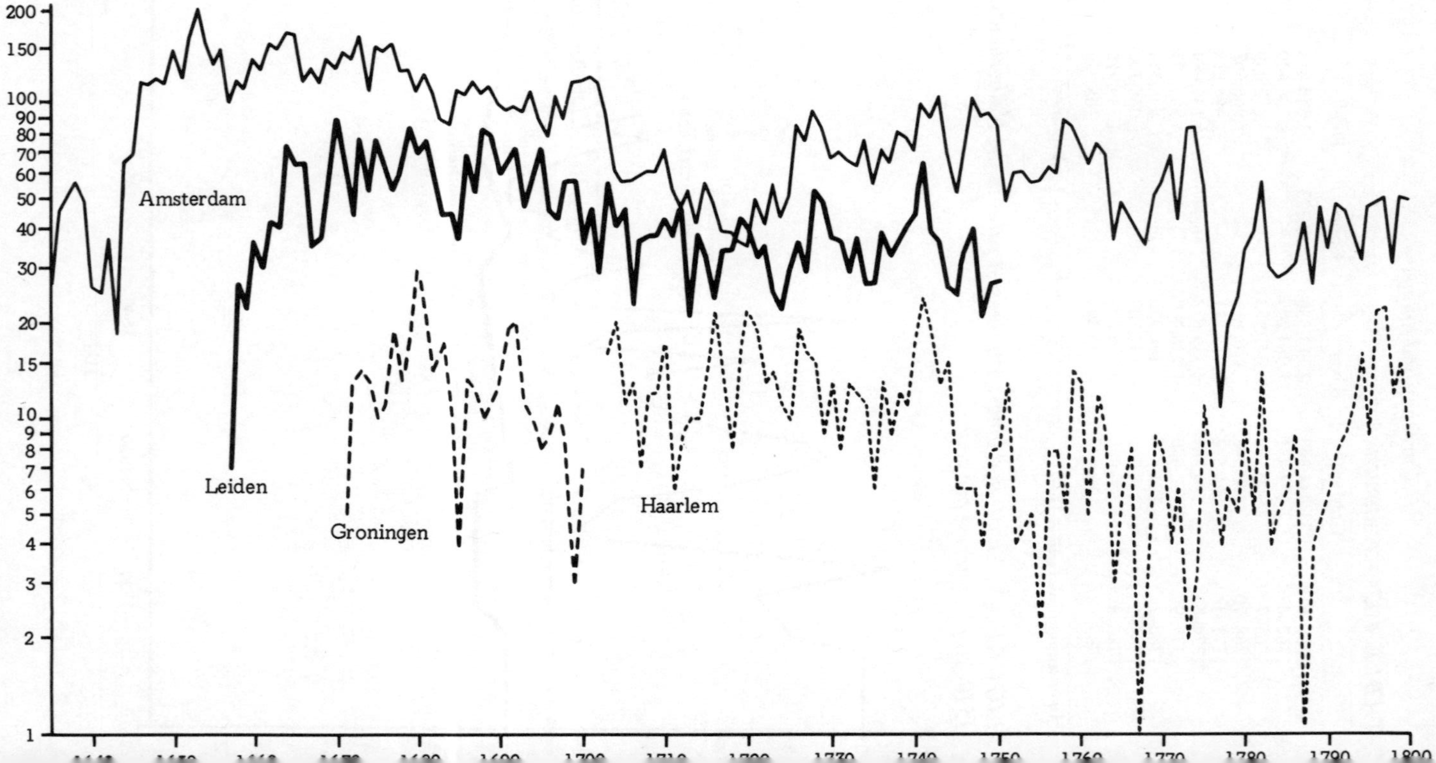

FIGURE 4.10: Number of annual bankruptcies in Amsterdam, Leiden, Haarlem and Groningen, 1635–1800

cent for short-term needs and at 4 per cent for long. Figure 4.9, compiled from merchants' letters and the municipal accounts of Louvain, charts the decisive drop in short-term interest rates in the first three-quarters of the sixteenth century.[28]

But despite cheaper money and better credit facilities, it still remained possible for commercial enterprises to become bankrupt. Figure 4.10 shows the number of bankruptcy cases recorded in four large towns of the North Netherlands during the seventeenth and eighteenth centuries. Rather surprisingly, the incidence of bankruptcy follows the prevailing economic climate: that is to say, there were more bankruptcies in the good decades in the later seventeenth century and less in the period of contraction and recession, 1700–20. Unfortunately, we do not know what proportion of the total businesses these bankrupt enterprises represented, but the series nevertheless has its interest.[29]

4.6 Prices

There are two major collections of published price series covering early modern times, one for the North Netherlands and one for the South.[30] Thanks to these and other publications, we possess remarkably full data on the price variations of a very large number of products throughout most of the three centuries covered by this volume. We have chosen rye prices at Antwerp, Amsterdam, Louvain and Utrecht (figure 4.11) and meat, milk and butter prices at Utrecht (figure 4.12) to illustrate the salient trends of agricultural goods. Perhaps the most striking factor is the pronounced variation between the different regions; for instance, between Antwerp the metropolis and Louvain the provincial town, and between the different products – the contrast between the rate of increase in cheese and butter prices at Utrecht is remarkable.

The same broad development of commodity prices appears to have been followed by rents: increase in the sixteenth and later eighteenth century, general stability or stagnation in between (see figure 4.13). The area around Nevele, some miles west of Ghent, shared in the prosperity of the sixteenth century, and even prospered in the middle decades of the seventeenth, but it passed through a serious depression between 1680 and 1740. The value of certain *polders* (reclaimed land) around Antwerp, for which we only have figures for 1500–1620, followed much the same pattern but with a different rhythm.[31]

FIGURE 4.11: Rye prices in the Netherlands, 1500–1800 (index numbers)

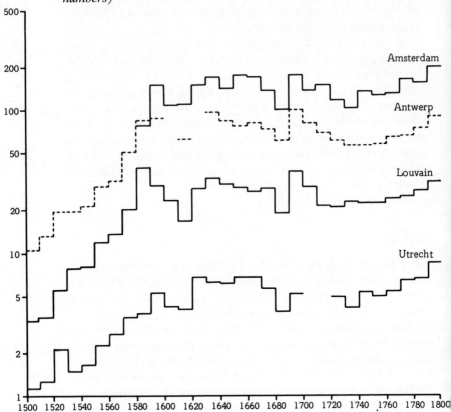

Note: Amsterdam: Prussian rye, in guilders per last; Antwerp: in stuivers per *viertel* (79.7 litres); Louvain: in stuivers per *halster* (29 litres); Utrecht: in guilders per *mud* (116.6 litres).

The behaviour of house rents in Antwerp and Ghent between 1500 and 1790 also reflects regional diversity. One of the readings plotted in figure 4.14 for each city gives the rent expressed in money (A1 and B1); the second reading (A2 and B2) gives the rents expressed in grain. The collapse of the Antwerp economy after its recapture by the Spanish army in 1585 is dramatically shown in the rapid fall in rents in terms both of money and of grain. Ghent, which experienced sluggish economic growth in the sixteenth century, only began to

FIGURE 4.12: Prices of animal produce at Utrecht, 1500–1800 (in guilders)

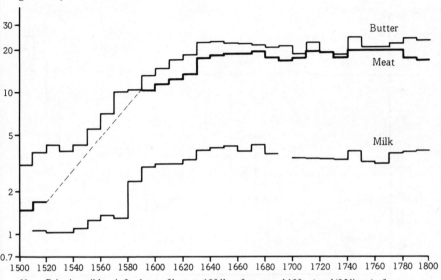

Note: Price in guilders is for ½ vat of butter, 100 lbs of meat and 100 *mingel* (85 litres) of milk.

recover after 1590; but, with the exception of the late seventeenth and mid-eighteenth centuries, the rise in rents continued until 1790, accelerating rapidly after 1750. Antwerp, ironically, stagnated throughout the eighteenth century. In Table 4.14, which is composed of index numbers, the base (100) for Antwerp is 1500; the base (100) for Ghent is 1570. The number of houses for which we have figures on rent differed somewhat from year to year, but the changes have been integrated to give a composite index number. As one would expect, rent levels faithfully followed the population trends recorded in tables 4.2 and 4.3.[32]

4.7 Wages

We have abundant sources for the rising wage-rates of the sixteenth century, but relatively little comparable data for the two centuries following. Between 1520 and 1590, all wages at least doubled and many trebled in a vain attempt to keep abreast of rising prices. After that there was a prolonged stability. Comparison of real wages,

FIGURE 4.13: Rents for farmland, 1500–1800 (index numbers, 1569 = 100)

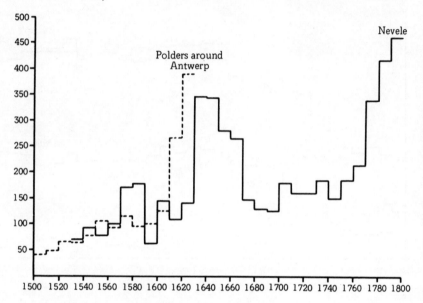

however, is complicated by the introduction of a piecework basis for calculating wages in place of daily rates. It is even more difficult to calculate the actual standard of living for the wage-earning population because we can never be sure how much was actually earned – we do not know for certain how many days or how many hours per day were worked. Nor have we much knowledge about the value or extent of payments in kind. There is indeed room for doubt concerning the value of wages as a measure of economic trends, and in Figure 4.15 we include only three series for the sixteenth century (two for master masons and one for unskilled building labourers) and three for the period 1590–1800. The first sets of data show remarkable consistency: wages rose at more or less the same rate in all three series. And yet the accelerated speed of inflation at Antwerp stands out: a master mason at Mechelen (Malines) earned 95 per cent of the wage of his Antwerp colleague in 1500, but only 77 per cent in 1600, and in the course of the seventeenth century all the advantages of higher wages were lost by the Antwerp workers. Although skilled craftsmen (such as typesetters in the printing industry) were well

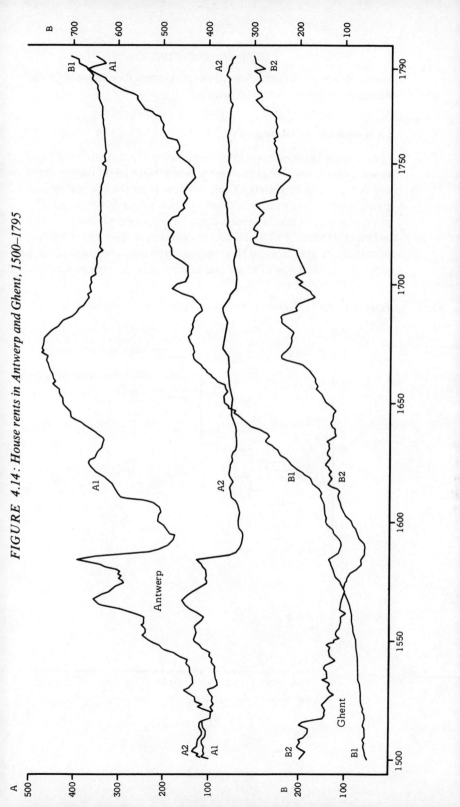

FIGURE 4.14: House rents in Antwerp and Ghent, 1500–1795

rewarded, a semi-skilled or unskilled worker was paid more in Ghent than in Antwerp from 1590 onwards.[33]

4.8 Wealth and social structure

The censuses of the eighteenth-century Netherlands, both North and South, provide the historian with abundant material on the structure and occupations of society. Table 4.13 analyses the occupations of the citizens of three southern towns and two northern provinces. The preponderance of textile manufacture emerges in most areas, urban and rural, a reflection of its massive importance in the economy of pre-industrial Europe. Beyond this, there is little similarity between the occupational patterns of town and countryside. A large proportion

FIGURE 4.15: Wages in the South Netherlands, 1500–1800

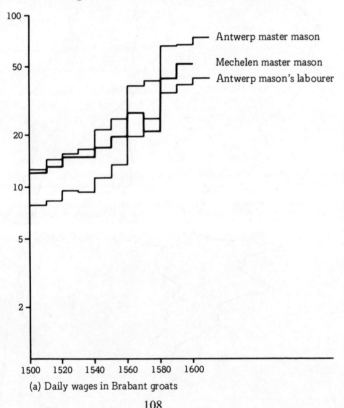

(a) Daily wages in Brabant groats

108

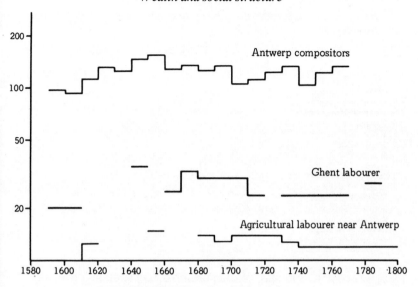

(b) Antwerp compositors: Weekly wages in Brabant stuivers; Ghent labourer: daily wages in Flemish groats; agricultural labourer: daily summer wages in Brabant stuivers

of the rural population, not surprisingly, worked on the land, although in some ways the number is smaller than one might expect: in Overijssel and Veluwe, two provinces justly celebrated for their agricultural produce, less than 50 per cent of the working population

TABLE 4.13: Occupational structure of selected communities in the eighteenth century (in percentages)

	Veluwe 1749	Brussels 1755	Antwerp 1755	Overijssel 1795	Mechelen 1796
public servants, clerks, etc.	3.7	5.20	3.91	2.8	3.20
professions	1.1	1.53	0.58	0.9	1.17
agriculture & gardening	46.1	0.94	1.10	47.0	5.31
food, beverages, tobacco	7.5	7.85	8.92	3.6	9.05
trade	5.7	6.51	8.13	5.4	5.57
clothing & textiles	10.2	25.95	31.40	17.9	37.83
leather	2.9	3.27	2.34	2.6	3.56
metallurgic industry	1.7	2.36	2.34	1.3	3.01
timber-, stone- & building trade	6.8	6.69	5.04	8.4	6.29
arts & printing	0.1	0.90	4.40	0.1	0.47
transport	3.4	2.31	2.23	6.2	3.23
house-servants & unskilled labour	4.6	32.14	27.87	2.7	20.70
others	6.2	4.35	1.74	1.1	0.61

TABLE 4.14: Approximate distribution of landed property (in percentages)

Area	Institutions (incl. Church)	Nobles	Peasants	Burgesses
Land of Schorisse (sixteenth century)	12	12	70.5	5.5
St Kornelis Horebeke 1572	6.1	8	82.5	3.3
St Kornelis Horebeke 1577	6.4	10.6	80.1	2.8
St Kornelis Horebeke 1664	5.7	9.9	80.8	3.5
St Kornelis Horebeke 1786	7.4	0.1	77.5	15
St Blasius Boekel 1571	24.4	6.5	62	7
St Blasius Boekel 1785	28.8	15	52.8	3.3
Salland (1601–2)	17.5	29.7	45	7.8
Twente (1601–2)	25.2	40.7	19.3	14.8
Austrian Brabant (eighteenth century)				
south-west	50	10	15–20	15–20
north-east	30	15–20	35	10–25
Principality of Liège (eighteenth century)	12.4	16	35.2	9.1

was involved in farming.[34] Within this broad occupational structure there were, of course, gross social inequalities. At Ghent, an analysis of 487 wills made between 1735 and 1740 revealed that the total value of the estates bequeathed was almost 8 million groats, of which 2.6 million, or one-third of the total, belonged to just 16 noblemen (only 3 per cent of the total testators). At the other end of the scale, 296 craftsmen, small tradesmen and farmworkers (61 per cent of the total testators) bequeathed only 900,000 groats between them, scarcely more than a tenth of the total.[35]

The same picture of aristocratic predominance does not emerge with such force from rural areas (see Table 4.14). There, the preponderance of the nobles was often dwarfed by that of institutions, above all the Church.[36] Inherent in this uneven

TABLE 4.15: The poor as a percentage of the total population, 1480–1765

	1480	1496	1526	1597–8	1675	1690	1716/23	1755/65
Brabant	27.3		20.5					
Antwerp	9.5							7.5
Brussels		21	20.5					7
Louvain	18.3		21.7	7.6		11		22
's Hertogenbosch			14.1					
Overijssel					21		19.7	c. 26
Salland								c. 17
Twente								c. 34

distribution of land was a high incidence of poverty (Table 4.15). Although not measured according to the same criteria in all areas, there was a terrifyingly high density of poor families in the towns of the Netherlands in the late fifteenth and early sixteenth centuries (23 per cent in Amsterdam and 63 per cent – *sic* – in Leiden in 1514). Although there was some decline from this peak, especially after 1700, it was still reckoned in 1801 that 10 per cent of the population of

FIGURE 4.16: The expenditure of a labouring family in Belgium, 1586–1961

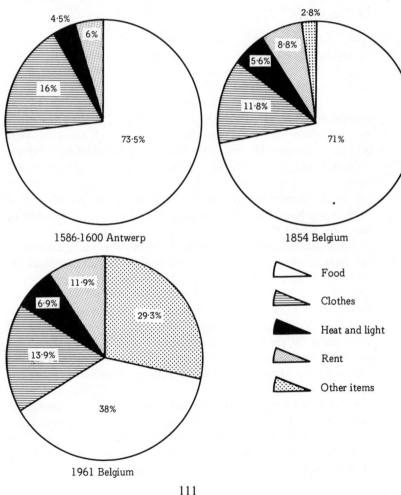

1586-1600 Antwerp

1854 Belgium

1961 Belgium

Food

Clothes

Heat and light

Rent

Other items

the 'Department of the Scheldt' (the present province of East Flanders) lived in abject poverty.[37]

Exactly what poverty meant for the people of early modern Europe is demonstrated by Figure 4.16: what a labouring man spent his money on. Right up to the middle of the nineteenth century, almost three-quarters of the income of the lower-paid went on food. Rent, clothing and heating took up the rest. The freedom to spend money on non-essentials – on household goods, on books, on luxury articles – is a very recent development in European society.[38]

4.9 Conclusions

From the middle ages onwards, the Low Countries have been distinguished by an unusually high degree of urbanization. Besides a considerable number of small and medium-sized towns, in early modern times they also contained two of the economic capitals of Europe: Antwerp in the sixteenth century, Amsterdam in the seventeenth and eighteenth centuries. As a result, the Low Countries were marked by an overall population density which was unequalled in other countries. By the 1790s there were 67 people per square kilometre (112 per square mile). This density was partly the result of a general growth in the population which began in the late fifteenth century, continued until around 1570 in 'Belgium' and until about 1670 in the North Netherlands, and started again in the southern provinces after 1750.

The prominence of the towns in economic life had a number of important consequences. For example, the merchants and industrialists were, comparatively, more important than in other countries; likewise, the urban bourgeoisie, for reasons of social prestige as well as for greater financial returns, invested heavily in land and agriculture. Netherlands farming was also distinguished, in most areas, by the virtual extinction of the manorial regime. The profitable outlets available for agricultural produce in the Low Countries and abroad favoured the peasant smallholders as well as the new bourgeois landlords.

But it would be wrong to overemphasize this picture of prosperity and wellbeing. Population nearly always grew faster than the demand for labour, so that wages seldom rose significantly above the vital minimum necessary for survival, and society was constantly burdened with a considerable number of poor.

Conclusions

Partly because of demographic pressure, small farms pre-dominated almost everywhere in the Low Countries. This fact, together with the still modest yields in agriculture (although they were the highest in Europe at the time), resulted in many areas of arable land being able to produce only enough food for the farmer and his family. The Low Countries were always dependent on imported cereals, while local farmers, when they produced for the market, specialized increasingly in industrial crops, livestock and fodder plants. Diets derived some benefit from the rapid growth of cod-fishing off Iceland and whaling in the Arctic, while the traditional herring fisheries continued to prosper until the depression of the eighteenth century when all fishing, like shipping and trade, experienced hard times. Throughout our period, the principal theatre of Dutch trade was the Baltic. In the later sixteenth century there was an increase in commercial exchange with southern Europe and the Levant, and in the seventeenth century the Dutch broke the Iberian monopoly of trade with America, Africa and Asia. Although this new commerce was largely handled by the North Netherlands, southern merchants were not entirely left out. Many Antwerp firms were able to trade with (for example) Italy and Brazil; many more in-dustrialists, artisans and merchants fled to the north after 1572 (and the creation of an independent, Protestant state in Holland and Zealand) and provided capital for new enterprises and expertise for technical improvements. Thanks partly to them, Dutch commerce and industry dominated Europe for much of the seventeenth century, although there was some stagnation and even decline after about 1700. From 1572 onwards, the river Scheldt was closed to sea-going vessels by Dutch warships, and this prevented direct participation in overseas trade by the South Netherlands. However the southern provinces did not share in this eighteenth-century depression. Their industries recovered from the devastation of war and, after 1750 in particular, protected by the mercantilist policies of its Austrian rulers, the 'Belgian' provinces resumed their economic expansion.

The concentration of a large measure of international trade first in Antwerp and then in Amsterdam made both cities in succession into important centres of European finance. The inflow of capital led to a fall in interest rates, which benefited economic life in general, and the operation of the money market was facilitated by technical improvements such as the system of 'discounting' bills of exchange or the organization of a public clearing bank in Amsterdam in 1609.

Abundance of capital largely remedied the economic ills caused by the shortage of currency: Dutch coins were rarely a prey to fluctuations and disorders. By contrast, the currency of the south Netherlands was frequently tampered with as the 'cockpit of Europe' was overrun time and again by foreign troops carrying with them inferior coins. In this, as in other economic matters, the North Netherlands did rather better than the south for most of our period. But in the eighteenth century, on the whole, the roles were reversed. The 'Belgian' provinces may not have enjoyed political independence, and they may not have possessed a world empire; but for those very reasons they did not have to pay the enormous costs of defending that liberty and that empire against the attacks of jealous and remorseless enemies. In the eighteenth century there was no profit allowed to those without power, and in 1795 both North and South Netherlands, both independent and dependent provinces, fell to the conquering French.

5 The British Isles

'British' history, Professor John Pocock has observed recently, has never really been written. There is no single work which deals simultaneously with the history of all the peoples inhabiting the British Isles. This section is no exception. The majority of the data presented here concern England, and southern England at that, and information on Ireland, on Wales and on Scotland after its union with England in 1707 has been included with series of data on England. Only Scotland before the union has been given separate coverage, partly because it alone possessed an economic system that was entirely independent of England, partly because it alone was also politically separate from England, and partly because its economic performance can be easily studied through the surviving printed and unprinted sources. The pre-union Scottish data appear in section 5.9 below (pp. 145–54).

5.1 Population

Unlike almost all the other countries of western Europe, the population of England and Wales more than doubled between 1500 and 1700 and almost quadrupled between 1500 and 1800 (Table 5.1). The population of Scotland and Ireland also increased rapidly during the eighteenth century (the first period for which we have proper records).[1]

The total population of the British Isles thus stood at about 5 million at the beginning of the sixteenth century and at about 16 million by the end of the eighteenth. Needless to say, the rate of growth was nowhere smooth and steady. In England and Wales, for which we have most information, the overall increase masked some periods of stagnation and even decline.[2]

The strong demographic increases of the sixteenth and eighteenth centuries shown in Table 5.2 were common to most of western

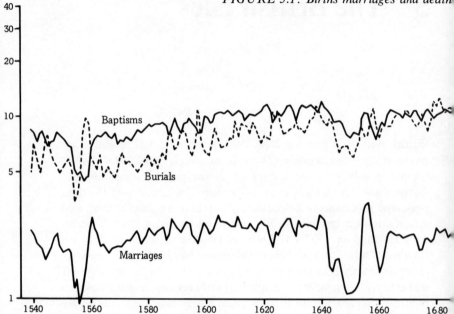

Europe, but in the case of England we know a great deal about the mechanics of the increases, and of the seventeenth century stagnation that separated them, thanks to the work of the Cambridge Group for the History of Population and Social Structure. Figure 5.1, prepared by Dr E.A.Wrigley of the Cambridge Group, shows the total number

TABLE 5.1: The population of the British Isles, 1522–1801 (in millions)

	England and Wales	Scotland	Ireland
1522–5	2.5	—	—
1545	3.0	—	—
1603	4.1	—	—
1670	5.8	—	—
1701	5.8	1.0	2.5
1731	5.9	—	3.0
1751	6.1	1.25	3.1
1761	6.6	—	—
1771	7.0	—	3.5
1781	7.5	—	4.0
1791	8.2	1.5	4.7
1801	9.2	1.6	5.2

nglish parishes, 1540–1840 (in thousands)

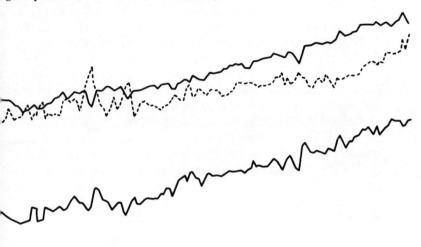

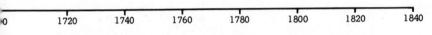

of births, marriages and deaths for 404 English parishes (about 4 per cent of the total in the country) between 1540 and 1840. The data are preliminary only, and will appear in a somewhat different form in the Group's forthcoming book, but the salient trends are clear. Thus

TABLE 5.2: England and Wales: percentage increase of population per decade, 1570–1801

% increase per decade	
1570–1600	+ 5.6
1600–30	+ 5.5
1630–70	+ 0.8
1670–1700	+ 1.5
1701–11	+ 2.7
1711–21	+ 0.3
1721–31	− 0.9
1731–41	− 0.3
1741–51	+ 3.6
1751–61	+ 7.0
1761–71	+ 7.3
1771–81	+ 6.8
1781–91	+ 9.5
1791–1801	+11.0

117

although the greatest 'aberration' in the period covered – the fall in births, marriages and deaths between 1642 and 1660 – was due to poor registration during the English Civil War, and not to any demographic catastrophe, the other peaks of mortality – during the 1550s, the 1590s, the 1620s, the 1670s, the 1720s and the early 1740s – were all the result of plague or famine, sometimes complicated by wars. The mortality crises of the early eighteenth century made a surprisingly sharp impact on the overall trend, but it is noteworthy that after 1743 the total of deaths never exceeded the total of births registered, while between 1760 and 1800 deaths remained almost constant while births and marriages increased prodigiously. Herein lies the key to the dramatic population growth that accompanied the first Industrial Revolution.[3]

TABLE 5.3: Average regional birth rate (B/r) and death rate (D/r) in England, 1701–1800 (per thousand)

Region	1701–50		1751–80		1781–1800	
	B/r	D/r	B/r	D/r	B/r	D/r
North-west	33.6	28.0	39.6	26.7	39.8	27.0
North	32.6	28.5	35.1	26.8	35.1	25.3
South	32.8	30.6	36.6	29.0	37.1	26.0
London area	38.0	48.8	38.5	43.3	37.9	35.1
England and Wales	33.8	32.8	37.2	30.4	37.5	27.7

The widening gap between births and deaths was not, however, a feature found in all areas (see Table 5.3). A regional analysis of the data reveals that London constantly had a death rate that exceeded its birth rate until the 1780s. In the south of England too, the number of births only just exceeded the number of deaths up to 1750. The surplus of births was provided, until 1750, largely by the north and north-west regions, and throughout the century they recorded the largest surplus.[4]

The persistent heavy excess of deaths over births in London was a problem that exercised many of the 'political arithmeticians' who, after 1660, occupied themselves in making demographic calculations and projections. The London 'Bills of Mortality', which recorded deaths and causes of deaths, were an ideal source and William Petty, for example, was able to argue from their evidence that, although the number of burials regularly exceeded the number of christenings, nevertheless the total number of burials consistently increased, indeed quadrupled, and that this was an accurate index of the growth of the metropolis:

... there dyed in London, [he wrote] At a Medium between the Years

1604 and 1605	5185
1621 and 1622	8527
1641 and 1642	11883
1661 and 1662	15148
1681 and 1682	22331

He also correctly concluded that the constant surplus of deaths over births would mean that: 'London would in time decrease quite away, were it not supplyed out of the Countrey where are about Five *Births* for Four *Burials*, the proportion of Breeders in the Countrey being greater than in the City.'

Encouraged by his successes in this area, Petty took his new statistical tools into the realm of theological dispute in order to confute a sceptic who thought to deny the Resurrection: 'by saying that the surface of the Earth [would not] furnish Footing for so vast a Number: whereas we did ... shew that half the Island of Ireland would afford them all, not only Footing to stand upon but Graves to lye down in. ...'[5]

5.2 Agriculture

The 'political arithmeticians' were equally concerned with the amount of farmland in England. At the end of the seventeenth century Charles Davenant and Gregory King came to the conclusions about the land of England and its products shown in Table 5.4.[6] We can perhaps discount some of the estimates of the animal population (rabbits with a stock of one million breeding at the rate of two million a year seems more of an inspired guess than an accurate computation!), but estimates of acreage and land utilization at least appear to be reliable. The inferiority of the area of arable land to pasture, in particular, has been confirmed by recent research[7]. The corn-growing regions were predominantly in the east of England, but even there they were broken up by fen, heath and forest.

The massive and rising output of beef cattle, many of them coming from Scotland, is indicated in Table 5.5[8] by the numbers auctioned at Smithfield in the eighteenth century. The number of sheep raised and sold for meat also grew steadily but less spectacularly.

TABLE 5.4: English Agriculture in 1688

	Acres	Value per acre			Rent
		£	s.	d.	
Arable land	9,000,000	0	5	6	2,480,000
Pasture and meadow	12,000,000	0	8	8	5,200,000
Woods and coppices	3,000,000	0	5	0	750,000
Forests, parks and commons	3,000,000	0	3	8	570,000
Heaths, moors, mountains, and barren land	10,000,000	0	1	0	500,000
Houses and homesteads, gardens and orchards, churches and churchards	1,000,000	The land The buildings			450,000 2,000,000
Rivers, lakes, meres, and ponds	500,000	0	2	0	50,000
Roads, ways, and waste land	500,000				
In all	39,000,000	about 6	2		12,000,000

	Yearly breed or increase	The whole stock	Value of each besides the skin			Value of the stock
			£	s.	d.	£
Beeves, sterks, and calves	800,000	4,500,000	2	0	0	9,000,000
Sheep and lambs	3,600,000	12,000,000	0	7	4	4,440,000
Swine and pigs	1,300,000	2,000,000	0	16	0	1,600,000
Deer and fawns	20,000	100,000	2	0	0	200,000
Goats and kids	10,000	50,000	0	10	0	25,000
Hares and leverets	12,000	24,000	0	1	6	1,800
Rabbits and conies	2,000,000	1,000,000	0	0	5	20,833
	7,742,000	19,674,000	0	0	0	15,287,633

TABLE 5.5: The passage of sheep and cattle through Smithfield market, 1731–1800

	Smithfield cattle (000s)	Smithfield sheep (000s)
1731–40	84	565
1736–45	82	542
1741–50	79	570
1746–55	72	633
1751–60	78	616
1756–65	84	609
1761–70	82	614
1766–75	86	607
1771–80	95	649
1776–85	99	686
1781–90	98	687
1786–95	104	711
1791–1800	114	756

It was, however, grain that was the basic agricultural product in early modern times, and here too there was great improvement by virtue of more scientific farming methods and (perhaps) a more benevolent climate. The changing yield ratios obtained on English

TABLE 5.6: Average number of grains harvested for each one sown in various areas of Europe, 1500–1820

	Great Britain, Belgium, Netherlands	France, Italy, Spain	Germany, Switzerland, Scandinavia	Russia, Poland, Bohemia
1500–49	5.9	6.7	4.0	2.4
1550–99	6.7	—	4.3	4.5
1600–49	6.2	—	4.2	4.2
1650–99	7.0	6.4	4.1	3.7
1700–49	—	5.9	4.3	3.7
1750–99	9.7	7.0	4.8	3.4
1800–20	11.3	5.9	5.4	4.4

and Low Countries farms tell a clear story especially when compared with the performance of other areas of Europe (Table 5.6[9]). The increasing yields were also aided by the rationalization of landowning known as 'enclosure', a process that could cause much local hardship. Between 1455 and 1637, 744,000 acres, or 2.1 per cent of the total area of England, were enclosed. In the eighteenth and nineteenth centuries over $6\frac{1}{2}$ million acres of common fields and commons, or nearly 20 per cent of the total, were enclosed by Act of Parliament, besides many other enclosures that had no legislative sanction. In some areas the percentage was as great as 25 or even 50 of the total. But whatever the causes, and however high the costs, social and economic, the results

TABLE 5.7: Estimates of corn output in England and Wales in the eighteenth century (000s and 000 quarters)

	Population (E. & W.)	Home consumption	+ Net exports − Net imports	Output
1700	5,826	13,109	184	13,293
1710	5,981	13,457	362	13,820
1720	6,001	13,502	491	13,993
1730	5,947	13,381	343	13,723
1740	5,926	13,334	522	13,855
1750	6,140	13,815	1,006	14,821
1760	6,569	14,780	485	15,265
1770	7,052	15,867	−250	15,617
1780	7,531	16,945	−238	16,706
1790	8,247	18,556	−672	17,884
1800	9,024	20,305	−1,313	18,991

were impressive: production of corn in England and Wales increased by 40 per cent in the eighteenth century (Table 5.7), although this was not sufficient to keep pace with the powerful population increase, and considerable quantities had to be imported both from the continent and, in the case of Scotland, from North America as well.[10]

5.3 Industry

It is impossible to present a complete picture of the British economy during early modern times. Nothing like a 'Gross National Product' can be calculated. However, it is possible to trace, for the eighteenth century at least, the use of certain key industrial commodities (see Table 5.9): raw materials like wood, cotton or flax; manufactured goods such as Scottish linen, Cornish tin and copper, and local beer.[11] This daunting table, which reflects the labours of many economic historians to explain in a quantitative fashion the course of British industrialization, demonstrates what might be categorized as an industry-led economic takeoff in eighteenth-century Britain. The scale of increased activity was unprecedented: cotton imports up from 1.14 to 42.92 million lbs, Cornish copper ore production up from 6,600 to 52,900 tons and so on. Perhaps the very diversity of the information makes it harder to grasp the overall reality. A conversion of the data to index numbers may prove illuminating (Table 5.8).

TABLE 5.8: Index numbers of British economic output in the eighteenth century (1700 = 100; numbers in brackets indicate number of sources used)

	Export industries (18)	Home industries (12)	Total industry and commerce (30)	Agriculture (43)	Rent and services (20)	Total real output
1700	100	100	100	100	100	100
1710	108	98	104	104	103	104
1720	125	108	118	105	103	109
1730	142	105	127	103	102	111
1740	148	105	131	104	102	113
1750	176	107	148	111	105	123
1760	222	114	179	115	113	137
1770	256	114	199	117	121	147
1780	246	123	197	126	129	151
1790	383	137	285	135	142	189
1800	544	152	387	143	157	231

TABLE 5.9: *Selected indicators of British industrial growth in the eighteenth century*

	Retained imports of raw cotton (m. lbs)	Silk Imports (000 lbs)	Flax (rough) imports (000 cwts)	Linen yarn (raw) imports (m. lbs)	Scottish linen stamped for sale (m. yards)	Bar-iron imports (000 tons)	London coal imports (000 London chaldrons)	Cornish copper ore production (000 tons)	Cornish tin production (tons)	Tin retained for home use (tons)	Strong-beer production (000 barrels)	Wood imports (£000)	Glass production (000 cwts)
1695–1704	1.14	525	34	2.1	—	16.4	327	—	1,323	232	3,446	114	—
1700–9	1.15	499	34	2.1	—	16.0	339	—	1,426	308	3,673	114	—
1705–14	1.00	482	34	2.1	—	16.3	355	—	1,476	174	3,387	112	—
1710–19	1.35	557	42	2.8	—	17.3	389	—	1,453	194	3,483	115	—
1715–24	1.68	629	44	3.1	—	19.0	433	—	1,396	326	3,744	135	—
1720–9	1.55	675	48	2.7	—	19.7	468	—	1,482	333	3,669	146	—
1725–34	1.44	685	66	2.7	3.87	21.5	475	6.6	1,632	345	3,588	143	—
1730–9	1.72	645	80	2.7	4.53	25.5	475	7.7	1,667	278	3,606	138	—
1735–44	1.79	563	74	2.8	4.81	24.2	484	7.4	1,691	290	3,512	136	—
1740–9	2.06	552	79	3.1	5.68	22.5	480	6.3	1,744	251	3,536	140	—
1745–54	2.83	607	98	3.6	7.50	26.6	492	9.1	2,159	474	3,679	153	60
1750–9	2.81	670	113	4.2	9.04	29.3	508	13.8	2,658	937	3,777	168	78
1755–64	2.57	777	119	4.9	10.82	33.0	527	16.7	2,669	1,023	3,818	176	94
1760–9	3.53	906	127	5.2	12.42	39.7	582	19.5	2,728	913	3,775	203	116
1765–74	4.03	946	129	6.5	12.58	44.9	634	25.2	2,851	990	3,744	239	131
1770–9	4.80	950	131	8.4	12.84	44.5	653	28.8	2,751	1,089	3,957	248	130
1775–84	7.36	1,083	125	9.1	14.68	43.0	666	29.7	2,657	808	4,220	249	121
1780–9	15.51	1,132	132	9.0	17.49	44.1	709	33.3	2,958	918	4,329	275	131
1785–94	24.45	1,177	—	—	19.38	—	771	37.1	3,327	945	4,690	—	155
1790–9	28.64	1,181	242	8.7	20.89	49.9	825	46.7	3,245	822	5,278	489	157
1795–1804	42.92	1,128	317	8.8	21.42	43.0	875	52.9	2,881	861	5,407	558	167

TABLE 5.10: Estimated growth of woollen manufacture in England and Wales in the eighteenth century

Circa	Wool consumed (including imports) million lbs	Value added in manufacture £s millions	Value of final product
1695	40	3.0	5.0
1741	57	3.6	5.1
1772	85	7.0	10.2
1799	98	8.3	13.8

Despite the apparent completeness of these data, some extremely important industries are not represented. For example there is no mention of the vital woollen industry, which clothed much of the population, down even to the woollen buttons on their coats (see Table 5.10).[12] There is also insufficient information in the main tables on the rise of the British coal industry, which tripled its production in the course of the eighteenth century (Table 5.11). Between 1550 and 1800, coal production in the British Isles increased around 52-fold, representing 'something like a revolution in the use of fuel'.[13]

TABLE 5.11: Estimated Annual Coal Output of the Principal Mining Districts (in tons)

Coalfield	1551–60	1681–90	1781–90
Durham and Northumberland	65,000	1,225,000	3,000,000
Scotland	40,000	470,000	1,600,000
Wales	20,000	200,000	800,000
Midlands	65,000	850,000	4,000,000
Cumberland	6,000	100,000	500,000
Kingswood Chase	6,000 ⎫		140,000
Somerset	4,000 ⎬	100,000	140,000
Forest of Dean	3,000	25,000	90,000
Devon and Ireland	1,000	7,000	25,000
Total	210,000	2,982,000	10,295,000
Approximate Increase		14 fold	3 fold

5.4 Trade

The concern over the 'balance of trade' of the British Isles is not a recent phenomenon. It springs from deeply rooted apprehensions about the supposed inadequacy of the national trading performance. The handful of estimates that have come down to us from the sixteenth and seventeenth centuries do not, it is true, always show an adverse balance; but such estimates were usually made in the first place because it was *expected* that they would reveal a deficit. Even the last figure in Table 5.12[14], with its healthy trade

TABLE 5.12: *The English Balance of Trade, 1530–1700 (in £s sterling)*

	Exports	Imports
1530s	721,117	686,352
1613	2,487,435	2,141,151
1622	2,320,436	2,619,315
1663/69	4,100,000	4,400,000
1669/1701	6,419,000	5,849,000

surplus, concealed a large deficit in England's trade with non-European countries. It was the re-export of colonial produce to Europe that made the profit, as Table 5.13[15] shows (see also p. 174

TABLE 5.13: *Analysis of English foreign trade by commodities and areas, average of 1699–1701 (000 £s)*

	Total	Europe including Turkey and North Africa	West Africa, America and the East
A. Imports			
Manufactures			
Textiles	1,597	1,123	474
Other	247	169	78
Foodstuffs, etc.	1,969	910	1,059
Raw materials	2,036	1,784	252
Total	5,849	4,086	1,863
B. Exports			
Manufactures			
Textiles	3,125	2,815	310
Other	458	182	276
Foodstuffs, etc.	488	431	57
Raw materials	362	344	18
Total	4,433	3,772	661
C. Re-exports			
Manufactures			
Textiles	672	456	216
Other	74	35	39
Foodstuffs, etc.	941	898	43
Raw materials	299	271	28
Total	1,986	1,660	326
D. Total of exports and re-exports	6,419	5,432	897

FIGURE 5.2: *British foreign trade in the eighteenth century (in £s million)*

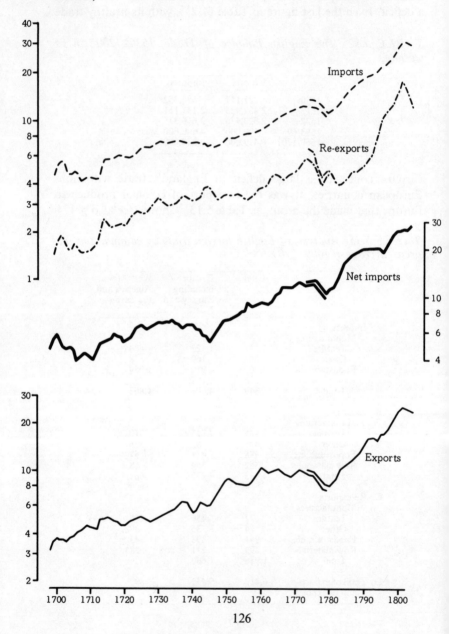

below for a similar observation about French commerce). This pattern survived throughout the eighteenth century with the volume of trade expanding despite the slumps caused by periodic wars (especially the American War, 1776–83, which shows up very clearly in Figure 5.2). Its various aspects are illustrated by the Tables 5.14 and 5.15, compiled from the ledgers of imports and exports at the Public Record Office, London.[16]

TABLE 5.14: The rate of growth of Britain's international trade, 1700–1800

Compound rates per cent per annum in volumes (decade averages) of domestic exports plus retained imports

England and Wales	%
1700–30	1.2
1710–40	1.0
1720–50	1.1
1730–60	1.5
1740–70	1.9
1750–80	1.1
Great Britain	
1760–90	1.8
1770–1800	2.3

The overwhelming predominance of woollen goods in the eighteenth-century figures of Table 5.15[17] was not exceptional. Woollen cloth had always been the principal English export, increasingly through London, which handled 60 per cent of the total in the early sixteenth century, 80 per cent by 1550 and perhaps even more by the seventeenth century. It is therefore of singular importance to chart the fluctuations in this trade (Figure 5.3); it serves as a valuable barometer of English commerce as a whole.[18]

TABLE 5.15: Exports of manufactures from England (000 £s)

	1699–1701	1722–4	1752–4	1772–4
Woollen goods:				
Continental Europe	2,745	2,592	3,279	2,630
Ireland and Channel Islands	26	19	47	219
America and Africa	185	303	374	1,148
India and Far East	89	72	230	189
Other manufactures:				
Continental Europe	456	367	647	987
Ireland and Channel Islands	60	40	168	280
America and Africa	290	376	1,197	2,533
India and Far East	22	15	408	501

FIGURE 5.3: *Export of English woollen cloth, 1500–1640 (in thousands of 'shortcloths')*

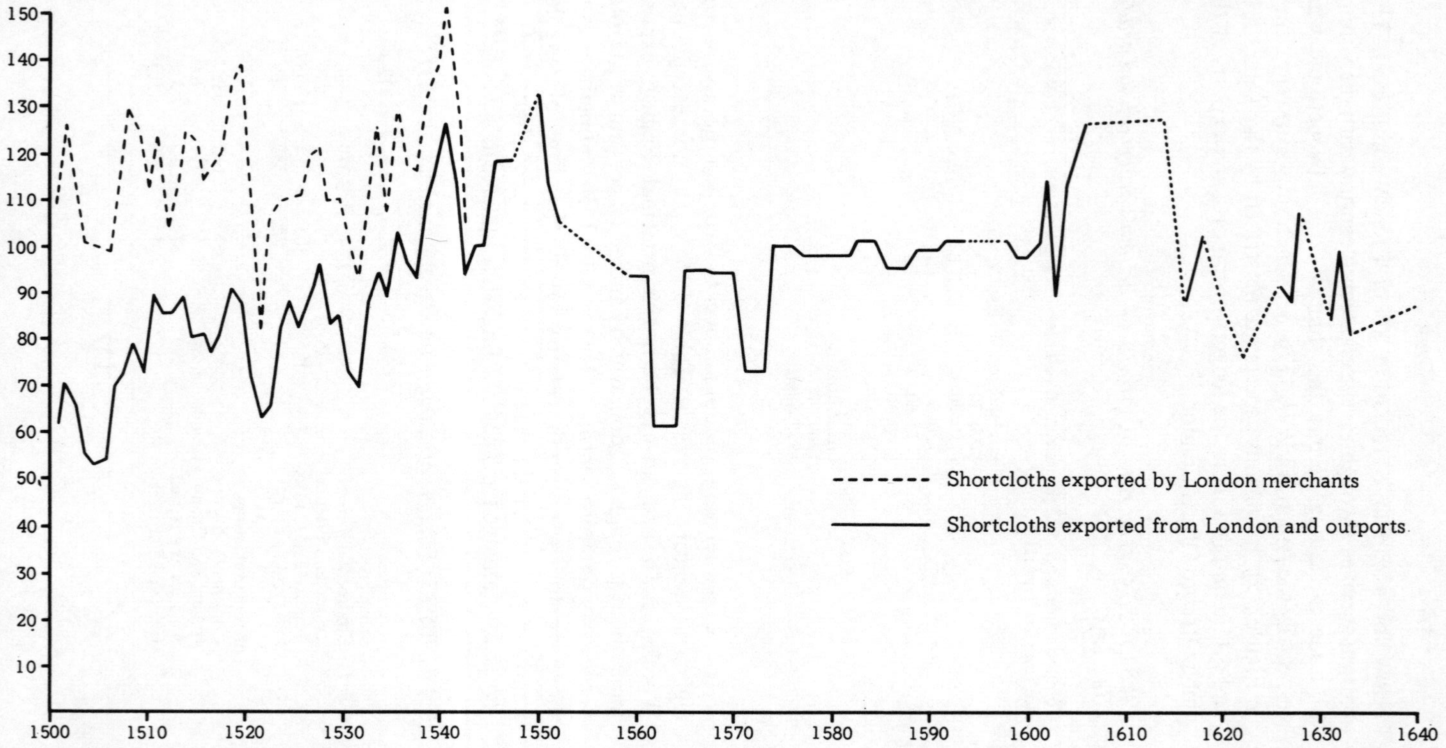

------- Shortcloths exported by London merchants

——— Shortcloths exported from London and outports

5.5 Transport

Given the notable growth in English trade during this period, and given that Britain is an island, a parallel growth in English shipping in early modern times comes as no surprise. But the increase was also stimulated by a variety of other factors, for instance the prosperity of the Newfoundland fishing fleet or the development of the Tyneside coal mines. As Tables 5.16[19] and 5.17[20] show, however, the bulk of the extra shipping was involved in foreign trade, above all

TABLE 5.16: The distribution of English shipping by tonnage, 1582–1773

	Total tonnage	Collier trade	Other coast trade	Newfoundland and Greenland fisheries	Other fisheries	Foreign trade
1582	68,433	7,618	10,607	6,000	11,316	32,892
1609–15	101,566	28,223	15,743	13,312	14,409	29,879
1660	161,619	70,899	25,051	20,330	3,159	42,180
1702	267,444	78,212	41,454	16,157	8,763	122,858
1773	581,000	125,346	89,631	38,585	23,646	303,792

TABLE 5.17: Tonnage of shipping required to serve overseas trade (000 tons), 1663–1773

	1663	1686	1771–3
Northern Europe	13	28	74
Nearby Europe and British Isles	39	41	92
Southern Europe and Mediterranean	30	39	27
America and West Indies	36	70	153
East India	8	12	29
Total	126	190	375

TABLE 5.18: Percentage of total English tonnage owned in various regions, 1582–1788

	1582	1702	1788
London	18.7	43.3	29.9
East Anglia	27.1	11.6	7.7
South-east	16.2	8.4	5.3
Total, all south-eastern England	62.0	63.3	42.9
South-west	20.9	17.6	13.9
North-east	15.0	13.1	28.1
North-west	2.1	6.0	15.1
Total, rest of England	38.0	36.7	57.1
Total tonnage (000)	67	323	1055

transatlantic trade. The overall expansion was accompanied, especially in the seventeenth century, by a growing concentration of shipping in London at the expense of the south-eastern and south-western ports, which lost most of their independent trade to the capital (Table 5.18).[21] The league-table of ports in 1700 looked something like Figure 5.4: London was far ahead of the field even by then.

FIGURE 5.4: Shipping owned in the principal English ports, c. 1700 (in tons)

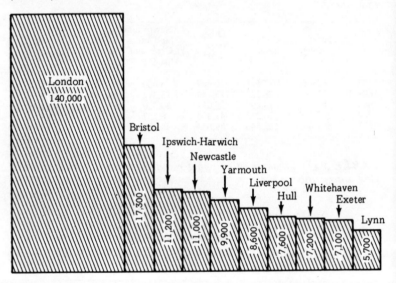

5.6 Currency and finance

It has been estimated from the figures of Mint output that the total monetary stock of England and Wales stood at about £1 million in the 1540s and increased to £2 million with the 'great devaluation' of 1551. By 1700 it seems likely that the monetary stock had risen to £12 million and perhaps to £15 million if one includes the various banknotes, bills of exchange and other credit devices, and that by 1800 the total stock of the United Kingdom must have exceeded £25 million. This increase was accompanied by a sizeable fall in the value of money and it did not go unnoticed by contemporaries. Sir John

Sinclair, a Scottish landlord and civil servant, was characteristically sensitive to the falling value of the pound in his pocket. In 1806 he penned the following 'Hints regarding the value of money at different periods and the Depreciation thereof'. He observed (correctly) that the pound sterling had lost over half its value in the course of the eighteenth century (see Table 5.19).[22]

TABLE 5.19: Observations of Sir John Sinclair on the falling value of the £ sterling, 1700–1800

In 1700	— — — —	0 8 5¼	
1710	— — — —	0 8 9½	
1720	— — — —	0 9 1¼	
1730	— — — —	0 9 8	
1740	— — — —	0 10 2½	Were equal to a
1750	— — — —	0 11 2	pound sterling in
1760	— — — —	0 12 2	1800
1770	— — — —	0 13 7¾	
1780	— — — —	0 15 2½	
1790	— — — —	0 17 7¾	
1800	— — — —	1 0 0	

This phenomenon was one that observers on the continent often overlooked, but what they almost always both noticed and admired was the efficient organization and control of British public finance. Between 1689 and 1715, over 100,000 men were almost permanently under arms for the Crown's wars against Louis xiv of France. Taxation swiftly reached its limits, and it became necessary to seek out new sources of income. Given the relative backwardness of the British economy and the serious problems that stood in the way of efficient tax collection, government tax revenue was plainly never

TABLE 5.20: The National Debt and debt charge (cumulative totals), 1697–1802 (£s)

	National Debt	Debt Charge
1697	14,522,925	1,232,519
1702	12,767,225	1,215,324
1714	36,175,460	3,063,135
1739	46,391,421	2,044,104
1748	75,448,809	3,149,661
1757	77,817,182	2,735,925
1763	132,120,664	5,008,918
1776	130,451,006	4,814,714
1781	187,756,281	7,343,949
1786	243,206,140	9,525,038
1793	244,720,976	9,534,738
1802	523,274,057	19,481,252

TABLE 5.21: War expenditure and public borrowing 1688–1815

Years (each inclusive) (1)	Total expenditure (2)	Total income (3)	Balance raised by loans (4)	Col. (4) as % of Col. (2) (5)
	£s	£s	£s	%
1688–97	49,320,145	32,766,754	16,553,391	33.6
1702–13	93,644,560	64,239,477	29,405,083	31.4
1739–48	95,628,159	65,903,964	29,724,195	31.1
1756–63	160,573,366	100,555,123	60,018,243	37.4
1776–83	236,462,689	141,902,620	94,560,069	39.9
1793–1815	1,657,854,518	1,217,556,439	440,298,079	26.6
Totals	2,293,483,437	1,622,924,377	670,559,060	33.3

going to expand sufficiently to cover more than a part of its expenditure. This was the dilemma in which public borrowing was developed on the basis of a parliamentary guarantee from 1689 onwards. Some loans were negotiated directly between government and investor (the annuities); some were channelled through the medium of the great companies and the Bank of England. Either way, private funds flowed into the government's coffers in ever-increasing quantities from 1689 onwards (see Tables 5.20[23] and 5.21[24]).

Much of the money borrowed by the British Government came from foreign investors. This practice was viewed with considerable suspicion by some contemporaries, a suspicion that could only be increased by the Government's extreme reluctance to publish any figures on the subject. Table 5.23, referring to 1762 (when Britain was at war), reveals that under £15 million was invested by foreigners out of a public debt of about £132 million. This, however, did not include such important 'funds' as those of the East India Company, those still known as the South Sea Annuities or the stock of the Million Bank, London Assurance and Royal Exchange – all well-known attractions to Dutch investors. What the real proportion was is not known. An

TABLE 5.22: The budget of the English Commonwealth, 1654–8 (£s)

	Revenues paid paid into the Exchequer	Assessments	Total revenues	Expenditure
1654	800,596	785,579	1,586,175	2,877,079
1655	871,873	697,732	1,579,605	2,327,512
1656	1,018,803	796,745	1,815,548	2,067,357
1657	953,438	380,976	1,334,414	2,878,174
1658	832,498	333,036	1,165,534	2,197,985

TABLE 5.23: Foreign investment in British government stock, 1762

'An abstract of certain accounts drawn up in 1762, shewing how much of the several Funds transferable at the Bank of England, stood in the Names of Foreigners, or their Agents; drawn up from the respective Dividend Books, at the Dates hereinafter mentioned.'

Date	FUNDS	Number of Foreign Creditors in each Fund	Sums in Foreigners Names £ s d	In their Agents Names £ s d	Total Sums belonging to Foreigners £ s d	Amount of Interest annually received by Foreigners £ s d
1762 July 5	**1. Perpetual Annuities**					
	1. Consolidated £3% Annuities	2,440	5,782,464 16 7	348,613 9 8	6,131,078 6 3	184,132 7 1
	2. £3% Annuities (1726)	78	167,492 10 —	—	167,492 10 —	5,024 15 8
	3. £3½% Annuities (1756)	137	194,185 — —	2,820 — —	197,005 — —	6,895 3 6
	4. £3½% Annuities (1758)	150	287,526 — —	39,300 — —	326,826 — —	11,438 18 2
	5. Consolidated 4% Annuities (1762)	725	1,637,464 — —	189,555 — —	1,827,019 — —	73,080 11 8
Oct. 10	6. Bank Stock (then at 5%)	2,025	4,578,630 4 6	49,228 — 10	4,627,858 5 2	231,392 18 5
	7. Reduced £3% Annuities	775	1,669,216 16 7	9,900 — —	1,679,176 16 7	50,373 10 —
		6,330	14,316,979 7 8	639,416 10 6	14,956,395 18 —	562,338 4 6
1762 July 5	**2. Temporary Annuities**					
	1. Long Annuities amounting to £128,250 per annum of interest, but properly speaking without any capital (1761)	103	3,563 19 6	5,141 14 10	8,705 14 4	8,705 14 4
	2. Long Annuities of £120,000 per annum, but without any correspondent capital (1762)	87	1,675 — —	3,895 10 —	5,569 10 —	5,569 10 —
		6,520	14,322,218 7 2	648,452 15 4	14,970,671 2 4	576,613 8 10

133

estimate (sometimes attributed to Lord North) that the Dutch owned some 43 per cent of British stock in 1777 is probably too high, but most commentators believed that the proportion was high enough to exercise a powerful influence on the market for the funds and therefore on public finances in general.[25]

The mainstay of the National Debt and other funds was taxation.* From Tudor times until 1688, the mainstay of royal taxation was the customs, although income from land, land sales and other sources was often considerable. Needless to say, it was never enough. The

TABLE 5.24: The principal taxes in force in England in 1702

I. DIRECT TAXES

The land tax; now annual.
On houses, 1696.
On trades: hackney coaches, 1694; hawkers, 1697.
Burials, births and marriages, 1695.
Bachelors, 1695.

II. TAXES ON ARTICLES OF CONSUMPTION

(*a*) Eatables:
   Salt, 1694. Spices, 1695.
(*b*) Drinks:
   The brewery; Malt, 1697.
   Wine. Tunnage and special duties.
   Spirits – (Distillery and imports).
   Tea, coffee and cocoa } The subsidies and the new duty, 1695.
(*c*) Tobacco: The subsidies and special tax.
(*d*) Articles not eatables, drinks, or tobacco:
   Timber (from Europe), 1690.
   Coals (sea-borne), 1695.
   Whale-fins, 1698.
   Imported and exported articles, generally, 2 subsidies of 5 per cent., viz., the old subsidy and the new subsidy of 1698, making 10 per cent.
   French goods, 50 per cent additional.
   East India and China goods, additional duties under the impost of 1690.

III. THE STAMP DUTIES, 1694

On various deeds and instruments.
On law proceedings.

---

*To all computations of taxation as it bore on the taxpaying class should be added the poor rates, which were already comparable in value to the land tax or customs, though the benefits of the tax were passed directly from the local authority to the poor and did not affect the government revenue. They are therefore set out under section 5.8 below on social structure rather than in the present section on taxation.

later Tudors and early Stuarts were normally debt-ridden. During the Interregnum, therefore, new taxes were imposed by Parliament – mainly the 'monthly assessment' – in an attempt to balance the nation's budget. They too failed, thanks largely to the cost of the army and navy maintained by the Cromwellian regime. As Table 5.22[26] shows, the Republic never managed to break even.

Charles II did little better, but notable improvements were made after 1688. The government now drew its income from an unprecedented range of taxes. Table 5.24[27] lists the principal taxes in force in 1702 (with the date at which the recent ones were first levied): as can be seen, almost all had been introduced during the reign of William III. Of these taxes, the most important was not the customs on 'eatables' and the rest, but the land tax. Early in Anne's reign it was standardized at four shillings in the pound with a yield of £2 million a year. However, the assessment and collection of the land tax fell more heavily on London and the home counties than the 'monthly assessment' that it replaced, while counties in the far north and west escaped more lightly. A 'political arithmetician' of the day, Charles Davenant, was so intrigued by the discrepancies in the burden of different taxes upon different areas of England that he drew up a table (Table 5.25) which showed that Charles I's notorious 'ship money' had established a fairer balance between the home counties and the rest of the country than any other tax.[28]

TABLE 5.25: The regional incidence of taxation in seventeenth-century England

Tax	Home counties (1)			Rest of England (2)			(1) as % of (2)
	£	s	d	£	s.	d.	
Ship Money	57,800	0	0	129,000	0	0	45.8
Assessment of (1643)	134,172	12	6	214,155	15	11	61.2
Produce for £2,000,000 on assessment of 1660.	626,000	0	0	1,234,400	0	0	50.7
Monthly assessment (1691)	529,615	2	0	946,118	2	0	56.0
Land tax (1694)	632,388	19	6½	1,038,184	19	1	60.9

The rising burden of taxation on the home counties was partly the result of the appearance in London of important and numerous concentrations of capital: rich merchants, joint-stock companies and banks. By 1695 there were at least 140 companies in England with a total capital of £4,250,083 (of which 50 per cent was tied up in three enterprises: the East India, African and Hudson's Bay Companies, all based on London). By about 1717 the Bank of England alone, with a capital of only £720,000 in 1695, was worth £5.5 million and the total share capital of companies in existence at the time exceeded £20 million. Many companies were specifically designed to attract capital to industry – 'The company for making Iron with Pit-coal', 'Convex-Lights Company', 'The Glass-Makers of London' – but this promising development was ended by the speculative South Sea Bubble. After that, industry financed itself, from profits, from partnerships based on kinship or religious affinities (Quakers, Jews), or from bank loans.[29]

TABLE 5.26: *Comparison of the highest and lowest prices of certain stocks and shares, 1692–7*

	East India Company	Royal African Company	Hudson's Bay Company
Highest price 1692–7	200 (1692)	52 (1692)	260 (1692)
Lowest price 1692–7	37 (1697)	13 (1697)	80 (1697)
	Bank of England	Royal Lustring Company £25 shs. issued at £5 Prem.	King's and Queen's Corporation for the Linen manufacture in England £10 shs.
Highest price 1692–7	48 Prem. (1696)	32 (1692)	45 (1693)
Lowest price 1692–7	48½ Disc. (1697)	18 (1697)	5 (1697)

The 'Bubble' itself was the result of the proliferation of joint-stock and marketable annuities, which created a vastly expanded market in government stocks and company shares. Since much of this debt was perpetual, the stocks passed from hand to hand by purchase and sale and their prices responded to sentiments and expectations as much political as economic. The outbreak or even the prospect of war invariably sent up the rate of interest on government stocks, lowering their price and the price of other shares. Thus the years from 1690 to 1697, for example, saw the fall in Bank stock from a premium of 48 to a discount of 48½ (Table 5.26[30]). Other prices moved in parallel fashion.

The year 1701 saw another crisis, this time caused by the Bank of

England's assistance to the New East India Company. The Old East India Company organized a run on the Bank, causing a general financial crisis in which several private bankers failed (Table 5.27). Trade, especially in London, was affected, and widespread though temporary unemployment followed.

TABLE 5.27: Comparison of the highest and lowest recorded prices of certain stocks during the crisis of 1701

	Old East India Co.	New East India Co.	Bank of England	Million Bank
Highest price 1700	142	154	$148\frac{1}{4}$	97
Lowest price 1701	$75\frac{1}{2}$	100	97	57
Depreciation	$66\frac{1}{2}$ (53%)	54 (35%)	$51\frac{1}{4}$ (34%)	40 (41%)

These pronounced fluctuations in prices had a number of side effects. They increased the problems of the genuine investor who might want to cash his holdings when prices were low; they offered capital gains for those who were able to come out at the top of the market (and then re-invest on favourable terms); and they encouraged the growth of professional speculators and of systems of speculation (margin or time-dealings, premiums, puts-and-calls) to exploit the mobile market. The extent to which such individuals and groupings could influence dealings in stocks was inimitably demonstrated by the successive rise, decline and collapse of major share prices in the course of 1720 during one of those fits of speculative insanity that periodically sweep the stock markets of the world. Between January and July, the index of South Sea Company stock rose from 120 to 950: between July and December it plunged down to reach its January level once more.[31]

Although the 'South Sea Bubble' was by no means the last stock market crisis of the eighteenth century – there were fluctuations of up to 50 and 60 per cent during the Seven-Year War (1756–63) – the scale was never the same. This was partly, perhaps mainly, because alternative investment opportunities materialized to absorb floating capital. There were company 'bonds', which were guaranteed in value and yielded a fixed dividend; there were the insurance companies, which sold fixed value annuities; and there were above all the banks. Starting with the goldsmiths' shops in the 1630s, fully fledged joint-stock banks appeared in London in the 1690s. There were 24 in

London by 1725, 32 by 1763 and 51 by 1776; in the provinces there were only perhaps a dozen in 1750, but 119 by 1784 and about 300 in the 1790s. In Edinburgh the Bank of Scotland was founded in 1695, and a number of other chartered and unchartered joint-stock banks soon followed. By 1750, however, the total assets of the Scottish banks still totalled only £600,000; the real boom only came later – by 1770 their total assets had leapt up to £3.7 million. Not all of the banks either in Scotland or in England were absolutely secure, but the majority remained solvent and served their clients well. The growth of British banking in the eighteenth century was of the greatest importance for the country's future agricultural and industrial development.[32]

5.7 Prices and wages

The behaviour of prices during our period falls into two almost symmetrical halves: a period of prolonged inflation from 1500 to 1640, followed by a century and a half of more stable prices. As might be expected, wages failed to keep abreast of the sevenfold increase in food prices: in terms of purchasing power, they fell by 50 per cent between 1500 and 1650 and they did not regain their 1500 level until the late nineteenth century (see Figure 5.5). The early seventeenth and the late eighteenth centuries were both particularly hard periods for wage-earners; both were periods of considerable political unrest and instability.[33]

If we look more closely at the 'price revolution' of the period 1500–1650, we find that food prices increased twice as fast as industrial prices, and the cost of grain for a man's daily bread increased faster than anything else. Thus between the 1500s and the 1640s, industrial products increased from 98 index points to 306, but grain products rose from 112 points to 786. Other arable crops rose from 98 points to 664.[34]

5.8 Wealth and social structure

Gregory King (1648–1712), herald, genealogist, engraver and statistician, compiled a series of 'Natural and Political Observations and Conclusions upon the State and Condition of England' which he completed in 1696 (see Table 5.28). It was received by the Board of Trade on 27 September 1697 but it was not printed until 1801, when

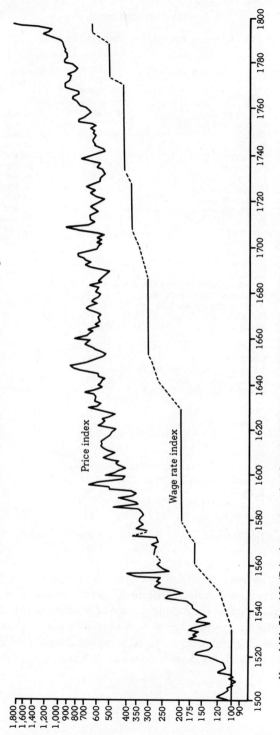

FIGURE 5.5: Prices and wages in southern England: a composite series 1500–1800

Price index

Wage rate index

1,800
1,600
1,400
1,200
1,000
900
800
700
600
500
400
350
300
250
200
175
150
120
100
90

1500   1520   1540   1560   1580   1600   1620   1640   1660   1680   1700   1720   1740   1760   1780   1800

Note: 1451–75 = 100. 'Prices' = a composite 'shopping basket' of goods. 'Wages' = building craftsmen's wages.

TABLE 5.28: The social structure of England in 1696

Number of families		People per household	Number of persons	Yearly income per family
160	Temporal Lords	40	6,400	2,800
26	Spiritual Lords	20	520	1,300
800	Baronets	16	12,800	800
600	Knights	13	7,800	650
3,000	Esquires	10	30,000	450
12,000	Gentlemen	8	96,000	280
5,000	Persons in Offices	8	40,000	240
5,000	Persons in Offices	6	30,000	120
2,000	Merchants and Traders by Sea	8	16,000	400
8,000	Merchants and Traders by Land	6	48,000	200
10,000	Persons in the Law	7	70,000	140
2,000	Clergymen	6	12,000	60
8,000	Clergymen	5	40,000	45
40,000	Freeholders	7	280,000	84
140,000	Freeholders	5	700,000	50
150,000	Farmers	5	750,000	44
16,000	Persons in Sciences and Liberal Arts	5	80,000	60
40,000	Shopkeepers and Tradesmen	4½	180,000	45
60,000	Artizans and Handicrafts	4	240,000	40
5,000	Naval Officers	4	20,000	80
4,000	Military Officers	4	16,000	60
511,586		5¼	2,675,520	67
50,000	Common Seamen	3	150,000	20
364,000	Labouring People and Out Servants	3½	1,275,000	15
400,000	Cottagers and Paupers	3¼	1,300,000	6 10
35,000	Common Soldiers	2	70,000	14
849,000		3¼	2,795,000	10 10
	Vagrants		30,000	
849,000		3¼	2,825,000	10 10

SO THE GENERAL ACCOUNT IS:

511,586 Families	Increasing the Wealth of the Kingdom	5¼	2,675,520	67
849,000 Families	Decreasing the Wealth of the Kingdom	3¼	2,825,000	10 10
1,360,586	Nett Totals	4¹⁄₂₀	5,500,520	32

George Chalmers appended it to the second edition of his *Estimate of the Comparative Strength of Great Britain*. It is the best surviving account of the economic state of Britain towards the end of the seventeenth century, based on King's own observations during his tours of England, while engaged in his genealogical research.[35]

Recent research has confirmed many of King's observations. His estimate of household size at $3\frac{1}{4}$ for the poor and $5\frac{1}{4}$ for the rich, or about 4 overall, is born out by the findings of modern demographers (see Figure 5.6).[36] The pattern of household size in the period covered underwent a clear change. In the early half of the period the greatest number of households (22 per cent) contained just four people; in the latter half the commonest size (20 per cent) was five. There had therefore been a significant increase in family size.

FIGURE 5.6: Household size in 100 English communities, 1650–1821

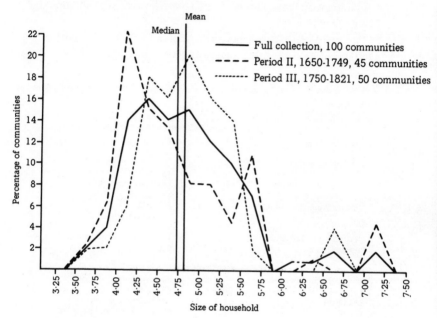

Demography tells us nothing about the wealth of the individuals under consideration, but Gregory King concluded from his observations that just over half the population of England and Wales was living below subsistence level and in this estimation he was probably right: to use his lapidary phrase, over 50 per cent of the people were 'decreasing the wealth of the kingdom'. (At about the same time Vauban estimated that five-eighths of the French population lived at or below subsistence level.) For such individuals there was only poor relief to fall back on.

From insignificant beginnings in the early sixteenth century –

£20,000 a year, a figure probably surpassed by expenditure on almshouses, pious donations and other forms of charity – the yield of the poor rate leapt to £700,000 by 1677, £900,000 by 1701 and £2.1 million by 1776–85. It was in effect a local tax levied on householders and assessed under the authority of the Poor Law of Elizabeth. This was a very small part of the 'gross national product', as King pointed out. He thought the sum levied – £600,000 in his day – represented about 1 per cent of the total income of the people of England and Wales (Table 5.29[37]). It was not a large amount, but it was a beginning from which larger – and some thought, alarmingly larger – things were to grow.

The extreme disparity between rich and poor in Gregory King's England formed a sombre background for the Industrial Revolution.

TABLE 5.29: The social accounts of England and Wales in 1688 (in £s million)

I. NATIONAL PRODUCT AND EXPENDITURE			
1. Indirect taxes		4. Consumption of goods and services	46.0
(a) Central government	2.1	5. Government expenditure on goods and services	2.4
(b) Local government	0.7	6. Domestic capital formation	1.7
2. National income at factor cost	48.0	7. Exports	5.1
		8. Less imports	−4.4
3. National product at market prices	50.8	9. Expenditure on national product	50.8

II. PERSONAL INCOME AND EXPENDITURE			
10. Consumption by persons		14. Incomes	
(a) Food	20.0	(a) Rents	13.0
(b) Drink	1.3	(b) Wages and salaries	17.7
(c) Rent	2.5	(c) Cottagers and paupers	2.6
(d) Clothing	10.4	(d) Profits, interest and other mixed incomes	14.7
(e) Domestic service	4.5		
(f) Other goods and services	7.3		
11. Direct taxes	0.2	15. Transfers to poor	0.6
12. Saving	2.4		
13. Total personal expenditure	48.6	16. Total personal incomes	48.6

5.9 A note on Scotland before the union

The quantitative sources for Scottish economic history before 1707 form a difficult and underworked field, where even the limits of the possible have often not been established. The basic problem is the relative scarcity of central government fiscal record. Scotland by 1500 was a unified but extremely decentralized polity, composed of a network of semi-autonomous local societies. The heads of these societies, the Scots magnates, regarded the Crown as an essential pivot around which national life revolved; but they expected the Crown to remain politically – and therefore fiscally – relatively inactive. The Stuart dynasty accepted this somewhat invidious role. The Scottish crown thereby escaped the fate of its English sister, which changed hands by violence six times between 1399 and 1485, but only at a price: it was not allowed to raise much money. Mary Queen of Scots, for example, raised only one new tax during her at first very successful personal rule, and that was one of £40,000 Scots for her son's baptism in 1566. The union of the crowns of England and Scotland in 1603 did not abolish this traditional Scottish polity, which survived, theoretically unchanged, until the parliamentary union of 1707. Lacking power, the government also lacked the incentive to collect and keep statistics on the economic state of the country. The economic historian therefore must look elsewhere for his material.[38]

Estimates of the size of the population of Scotland before the middle of the eighteenth century have to be based on fragmentary or indirect evidence and are generally regarded with extreme caution even by those who produce them. However, in 1755 Scotland suddenly became the third European country (after Sweden and Austria) to publish a comprehensive census. Its author was Alexander Webster, well-known as the minister of the Tolbooth Kirk in Edinburgh and as a *bon viveur*. He had government support and he was moderator of the General Assembly of the Church of Scotland in 1753, so he had no difficulty in securing co-operation from ministers of the Kirk by law established. Recent testing by historical demographers in Edinburgh University suggests that his results are extremely reliable (see Table 5.30[39]).

Pushing our estimates back beyond 1755 is difficult. Poll tax returns exist for 1694–5 and Hearth tax rolls for 1683–4, but recent researchers have experienced grave difficulty in finding even a single large closed parish suitable for family reconstitution. Baptismal records tend to be erratic. Marriage records are confused by the Scottish habit of being married by your favourite, rather than by your parish, clergyman, and are not tidily kept by pre-1750 kirk sessions.

In any case, formal marriage was neither popular nor necessary (given Scots law) in some parts of Scotland. Burial registers and bills of mortality are more complete, lending themselves to aggregation and identification of crises of subsistence. They strongly suggest nil population growth between 1695 and 1755, which would give a 1695 population of a million and a quarter or so. There is only one other population figure before the first state census of 1801 on which some reliance may be placed, and this is the figure for around 1795

TABLE 5.30: The population of Scotland, 1755 and 1795

Sheriffdom	Webster 1755	Sinclair 1795
Aberdeen	116,168	122,921
Angus	68,883	91,001
Argyll	66,286	76,101
Ayr	59,009	75,030
Banff	38,478	38,487
Berwick	23,987	30,875
Bute	7,125	11,072
Caithness	22,215	24,802
Clackmannan	9,003	8,749
Dumfries	39,788	52,329
Dunbarton	13,857	18,408
East Lothian	29,709	28,966
Fife	81,570	87,250
Inverness	59,563	73,979
Kincardine	23,057	26,799
Kinross	4,889	5,302
Kirkcudbright	21,205	26,959
Lanark (including Glasgow)	81,726	125,254
Midlothian (including Edinburgh)	90,412	122,655
Moray	30,604	26,080
Nairn	5,694	6,054
Orkney and Shetland	38,591	43,239
Peebles	8,908	8,107
Perth	120,116	133,274
Renfrew	26,645	62,858
Ross and Cromarty	48,084	55,430
Roxburgh	34,704	32,020
Selkirk	4,021	4,314
Stirling	37,014	46,662
Sutherland	20,774	22,961
West Lothian	16,829	17,570
Wigtown	16,466	20,983
All Scotland	1,265,380	1,526,492

produced by Sir John Sinclair (1754–1835), an eccentric improving laird who as secretary to the Board of Agriculture harried the parish ministers plus some few others into producing between 1791 and 1797 the material for twenty-one volumes of a *Statistical Account* of Scotland, unique in the Europe of his day and of immense permanent value to historians. From these volumes he later extracted population figures (also listed in Table 5.30).

The demographic increase between 1755 and 1795 – over 20 per cent or 0.5 per cent per annum overall – was felt in almost every county. Only Moray and the Northern Isles lost substantially. The main centres of growth, as one would expect, were around Edinburgh and Glasgow: the population of Midlothian increased by 36 per cent, Lanark by 53 per cent and Renfrew by 136 per cent.

The spectacular growth of the Lowland towns in the late eighteenth century, however, does not alter the fact that agricultural activities were the preoccupation of the vast majority of Scotsmen between 1500 and 1800. Quantifiable evidence on this subject is not abundant, but there is a certain amount of suggestive indirect evidence.[40] For instance, we have good statistics of Scottish Baltic trade from the later sixteenth century onwards owing to the existence of the Sound toll registers, and it was to the Baltic that Scotland looked to relieve grain shortages. In good years virtually no grain was imported. Table 5.31[41], of westward shipments of grain and flour carried in Scottish ships passing through the Sound, is therefore a sensitive barometer of the state of Scottish grain harvests.

TABLE 5.31: Westward grain and flour shipments in Scots ships from the Baltic, 1562–1709

(Annual average, in Bolls, to nearest thousand)			
1562–9	3,600	1630–9	5,400
1574–9	7,200	1640–9	4,400
1580–9	3,700	1661–9	200
1590–9	7,300	1670–9	1,300
1600–09	3,300	1680–9	2,000
1610–19	1,600	1690–9	300
1620–9	5,800	1700–9	100

Note: 1 Boll = 140 lbs.

The Sound toll registers cease to be very valuable for Scottish history after 1650 because of the partial replacement of Baltic grain by supplies from England and Ireland. There is, however, another quantitative source for the seventeenth and eighteenth centuries which is not only valuable in its own right, but is also a fairly sensitive indicator of dearth. This is what is known as 'fiars prices', which were struck every year, nominally at Candlemas, at the sheriff courts of the Scottish counties. These fixed a mean price for the crop harvested the previous year (and therefore still in the market: thus the fiar of 'Candlemas 1738' would have been fixed for the 1738 crop at the end of February 1739). Since the fiars related to grain actually harvested – mostly oatmeal and 'bere', a hardy four-row barley – and since they were used for calculations and accounts, we can be fairly sure of their substantial accuracy. A comparison of fiars from a number of different areas reveals several interesting features. First, it is clear that the Scottish grain market was regional, not national; only in the 1730s does a clear overall pattern become observable, with most regions deviating less than 10 per cent from the 'national average'. However, even in the seventeenth century a severe famine, like that experienced by Scotland in the 1690s, would create a high price peak

FIGURE 5.7: The price of East Lothian oats, 1643–1810, and Aberdeenshire meal, 1693–1756 (in shillings per Boll, seven-year averages)

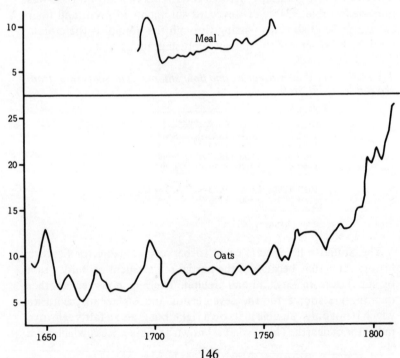

in all areas. A century later, however, high prices and dearth had been separated: grain prices rose to unprecedented heights (Figure 5.7), but the people did not starve.[42]

Overseas trade was important to the Scottish economy, precisely because that economy was underdeveloped compared with the economies of richer and more integrated neighbouring states like England and France. Capital accumulation and economic growth hinged mainly on the expansion of overseas commerce, and the special relationship between the Crown and the royal burghs hinged mainly on the monopoly of foreign trade which the former granted to the latter. Crown revenues from commerce were collected, when they were collected at all, in the form of export duties. The yield was small and the money was collected indirectly. In the reigns of James III (1460–88) and James IV (1488–1513) the annual value of the customs was about £3000. In 1582, during the reign of James VI (1567–1625), despite inflation, the customs were let at an annual tack of a little over £4000. This situation could not long continue, and in 1597, after his finances had virtually collapsed, James VI secured an act from the Scots Parliament which for the first time imposed a general import tariff, nominally at a flat rate of a shilling in the pound. It is from circles around King James that we probably derive the remarkable document reproduced in Table 5.32. It was a survey of the volume and value of all goods shipped from every port in Scotland between November 1611 and November 1614, divided by three to give an

TABLE 5.32: 'The wairris and commodaties that ar shippit and transpoirtted furthe of this kingdome yeirlie, be sea, ar:'

The commodaties that the land yeildis yeirlie, and is transpoirtted, extendis to	£375,085
Summa of the commodaties that ar maid and wrocht in the land, yeirlie and everie yeir ourheid, is	£169,097
Summa that the commodaties of the sea extendis to yeirlie, is	£153,354
Summa of the foirrane commodaties that ar transpoirtted agane, is	£39,047
Summa	£736,986

Conforme to the comptis maid and produceit.
Nota. – This is besydis and attour the greit quantetie of lynning claythe, lynning yairne, sheip, nolt, etc., that is transpoirtted be land dalie.

Note: All figures in £s Scots. There were £12 Scots to £1 English. The total value of Scotland's exports around 1614 was therefore £61,415 sterling. The total value of England's exports at the same time (see p.125 above) was £2,487,435 sterling.

annual average. The survey was divided into four parts: (1) the produce of the land (wheat, 'bere' and malt, oats, flour, bread, beef, 'aquavita', hides, skins, wool, feathers, Orkney butter, lead and coal), which was valued at £375,085; (2) goods manufactured in Scotland (salt, cloth, linen, hose, gloves, leather, cushions, bed-covers and shoes), which were valued at £169,097; (3) sea produce (salmon, herring, fish and fish oil), which were valued at £153,354; and (4) foreign goods re-exported, which were valued at £39,047. Three-quarters of the total value, £736,986, was thus made up of food exports – although it was noted that more cloth and livestock were sent out of the kingdom by land. Unfortunately, this document is unique – it is the only 'global' estimate of Scottish trade before 1700.[43]

This particular list of exports and re-exports gives us a picture of the Scottish economy which is confirmed by almost all other evidence. It was an economy that exported surplus primary products like skins, hides, wool, salmon and other fish, coal and in good years grain. Manufactured exports were of the simplest – salt (produced in coal-fired coastal pans) and coarse woollens. The Scottish lead-mining industry was subject to extreme fluctuations, so the very high value of its exports in 1614, which nearly matched the value of coal exported, was probably abnormal.[44] Normally coal was a very important export, especially to the Scots Staple in the Netherlands, which through most of this period was sited in the Walcheren town of Veere (which the Scots habitually referred to as Campvere). Of the 66 Scots ships recorded as paying dues at the staple port between 1 August 1626 and 1 October 1627, 40 carried only coal, 10 carried coal plus other staple goods, 14 staple goods without coal, and 2 had their cargoes unrecorded.[45] The great bulk of the ships carrying coal came from the southern ports of the coal-rich peninsula of Fife, and this is a pattern that persisted beyond the union of 1707, being admirably

TABLE 5.33: Destination of coal exports from Kirkcaldy customs area, 1754–86 (in percentages)

	Hamburg	Holland	N. Europe
1754–6	10	75	15
1764–6	38	30	32
1774–6	59	21	20
1784–6	43	9	48

documented in the records of the customs administration set up in Scotland as a very unpopular part of that union. In the Kirkcaldy customs records from 1743 to 1792, for example, of 3195 recorded voyages outwards, 2938 (92 per cent) showed coal as part of the cargo, and with the vast majority coal was the sole item exported (Table 5.33[46]). The same records show that the Netherlands did decline as a market for Scots coal as the eighteenth century progressed, being replaced to some extent by north Germany and Baltic lands.

TABLE 5.34: Average annual number of Scots ships recorded at the Sound, 1497–1657

	All ships (1)	Scots ships (2)	(2) as % of (1)
1497–1547	1,336	55	3.4
1557–8	2,251	40	1.8
1560–9	3,158	67	2.1
1574–9	4,300	135	3.1
1580–9	4,921	92	1.9
1590–9	5,623	133	2.3
1600–09	4,525	123	2.7
1610–19	4,779	102	2.1
1620–9	3,726	107	2.8
1630–9	3,383	127	3.7
1640–9	3,499	79	2.3
1650–7	3,015	20	0.7

Note: Assuming a round trip, individual ships appear twice in columns (1) and (2).

Prior to the imposition of a British customs service, we cannot hope to have detailed quantitative information on Scottish overseas trade save in abnormal sectors such as the Baltic trade, where the Sound toll registers provide detailed information, albeit of a kind whose validity, as far as cargo manifests are concerned, has been much debated. Detailed comparison of the Sound toll registers with Dundee shipping lists suggest that, at least until 1618 when inspection was intensified, evasion (or exemption) was common. Much more remains to be done in this field, but in the meantime it would appear perfectly safe to take the totals of Scottish ships passing through the Sound (between 1497 and 1657 these never exceeded an annual average of 68 and apart from the disastrous slump in Scots trade in the 1650s never fell below 20 – see Table 5.34) as an index of the fluctuations in and relative importance of the Scottish Baltic trade.[47]

Much detailed work remains to be done on the shipping of

individual burghs. Customs books are scarce, and apart from the Leith books between 1626 and 1628 and the Aberdeen ones for the 1580s and 1639, all of which give skippers, cargoes and destinations, they preserve merely lists of traders' names and isolated payments. Burghs did, however, keep other records, and among those recently published one may mention the abstract of ship entries at Dumbarton 1595–1648, and the Aberdeen shore-work accounts. The latter preserve a day-to-day record of cargoes entering and leaving the port between 1596 and 1670, massive in bulk and rich in statistical potential.[48]

TABLE 5.35: The tax rolls of the Royal Burghs, 1612–1705 (percentages paid by towns and regions)

	1612	1649	1670	1683	1692	1697	1705
Edinburgh	28.75	36.00	33.33	33.33	32.33	40.00	35.00
East Lothian	2.62	3.10	2.45	2.25	2.15	1.55	1.75
S.E. Fife	8.60	8.37	6.82	6.55	4.41	2.99	2.85
Upper Forth	5.10	5.15	5.60	5.40	4.37	4.05	4.10
Dundee	10.75	7.00	6.10	5.00	4.67	4.00	4.00
Perth	6.16	4.00	3.85	3.85	3.00	2.40	4.00
Cupar	1.50	1.10	1.00	1.00	0.90	0.75	0.75
St Andrews	2.67	3.33	2.33	1.20	0.60	0.40	0.35
Tay	24.83	18.68	16.43	15.20	12.32	9.78	12.13
Aberdeen	8.00	6.67	7.00	6.00	6.05	4.50	4.90
North East	12.27	11.77	12.71	11.86	11.02	8.30	9.83
Glasgow	4.00	6.50	12.00	15.00	15.00	15.00	20.00
Dumbarton	0.93	0.60	0.50	0.50	0.25	0.25	0.30
Renfrew	0.60	0.40	0.40	0.40	0.30	0.20	0.20
Rutherglen	0.20	0.20	0.15	0.15	0.10	0.10	0.20
Lanark	0.80	0.60	0.60	0.60	0.50	0.45	0.60
Upper Clyde	6.53	8.30	13.65	16.65	16.15	16.00	21.30
Ayr	2.17	1.40	1.73	1.73	1.07	1.07	1.06
Lower Clyde	3.57	2.70	2.93	3.03	1.92	1.97	2.05
Solway	4.24	3.73	3.62	3.27	2.92	2.81	2.81
Borders	2.52	2.42	2.47	2.47	2.25	2.55	2.16

When it comes to quantitative assessments of the wealth of Scottish society before 1700, the position is predictably difficult. The Highlands and Islands in particular were beyond all but the most minimal of central government supervision, while even the Lowlands were enviably free of those fiscal burdens calculated to leave comprehensive central record. However, we do know a good deal about the revenues of the clerical estate in the sixteenth century, owing to the 'assumption of thirds' of benefices by the crown from 1561, partly for its own uses and partly for the stipends of the ministers of the Reformed Kirk (the remaining two thirds went to the pre-Reformation holders of benefices). The accounts of the 'collectors of thirds' survive and from them one can reconstruct the wealth of the religious houses of Scotland, which were technically never dissolved as in England.[49] Another indirect measure of wealth of great interest can be derived from the records of the 'Convention of Royal Burghs'. Centralization of sovereignty in a parliament was quite alien to Scottish political thought. The General Assembly of the Kirk claimed to meet and rule *iure divino* (despite royal hostility to the idea). Taxation agreed by the Estates was apportioned between individual burghs by the Convention of Royal Burghs, which also managed the overseas Staple. It is the changing percentage of the tax burden ascribed to individual burghs that reflects their relative fortunes, and in Table 5.35 one can see among other things the gradual decline of the Fife burghs and the steady rise of Glasgow.[50]

For the period after 1707 it is possible to obtain full British government statistics of such phenomena as the great surge of tobacco imports which made Glasgow rich, not to mention such peculiarly Scottish statistics as the returns of linen stamped by the Board of Trustees for Fisheries and Manufactures (a body set up in 1727), which are the basic statistical material for the early Scottish industrial revolution. From the problems of minimal and fragmentary material we move into another, but no less fascinating, world.[51]

5.10 Conclusions

The quantitative evidence of English economy and society uncovered in this century has substantially modified the traditional picture, dear to older, political historians, of an imperial, commercial, colonial economy with society to match. Even the selection of figures given in this chapter shows that England did not deviate from the normal European pattern so much as was once thought. Hers was still basically an agrarian economy. Her manufactures (as everywhere in Europe) were still intimately related to the land and its products: woollens, beer, linen, pottery, leather, mining, metal-working – all these processes and those who operated them still had their roots in the soil. Seaborne trade was more with Europe than with Asia, Africa or the Americas. The prices men paid for goods and services, the trends of their incomes and wages and the fluctuating fortunes of economic and social life were all exposed to the same influences as those that affected the rest of Europe.

Divergencies and peculiarities certainly grew after the Restoration as the influence of trade with the extra-European world made itself felt. Out of this came new industries – cotton, calico printing, sugar refining, tobacco cutting and packing. Colonial demand stimulated iron manufacture, metal industries and shipbuilding. London's size and influence stabilized and was even eroded in the seventeenth century as the west coast ports flourished on the profits of the triangular Atlantic trades. The entire economic picture became more rich, more variegated, more balanced. The Netherlands, France and other economies shared in these changes.

A special bonus was provided by the growing production and consumption of coal for domestic and industrial purposes, lifting (but not yet entirely dispersing) the shadow of the timber shortage which fell across every European economy that aspired to development. Another favourable circumstance was the proximity of water transport, inland and coastal. A third was the mixture of terrain and climate that enabled England to develop a mixed agricultural economy and thereby fortified it to some extent against the recurrent depressions that were the scourge of early modern economies everywhere. Other western European states shared some of these advantages: it seems doubtful if any enjoyed as balanced a combination of them as England.

The vicissitudes that are by now a commonplace of demographic history – sixteenth-century growth, seventeenth-century pause and recession, eighteenth-century resumption of growth – were accordingly faced without the traumatic consequences they brought with them in other areas. There was one penalty of urban development that England shared with her continental neighbours. The city grew: the city killed. The Mortality Bills of London remain a grim testimony to this unalterable fact, which was borne in on observers everywhere.

Such facts were recorded and commented on by the English 'political arithmeticians' of the later seventeenth century, those polymaths like Petty, Graunt, King, Davenant and others who used mathematical methods to analyse the economic and social problems of the age – population, national income, taxation policy, the balance of trade, etc. Their works also help to focus the importance of English financial institutions, public and private – the National Debt, the banks, the great companies. In spite of some spectacular catastrophes, it seems reasonable to identify here a unique and decisive relationship between political and financial institutions that brought unusual stability in its train. Capital resources were accumulated, invested, transferred from place to place, activity to activity. In spite of interruptions, confidence grew.

So did a willingness to face the problems of widespread indigence, ignorance and unemployment which England shared with all the European economies. Somehow the great army of paupers and near-paupers, unemployed and underemployed had to be sustained, even though at marginal levels of subsistence. The same problem and varying levels of response were to be found in Italy and the Netherlands. Tudor England had witnessed an extensive growth of private philanthropy. It survived the institutional growth of local poor rates and subsidized 'work-houses' as well as privately maintained orphanages, charity schools and the like where technical instruction was given. Such collaboration of private and public support was parallelled by the acceptance by the landed classes of a major share of the fiscal burdens of the new state represented by the land tax. Yet in time this was to be overshadowed by the growth of indirect taxation which fell upon all consumers.

This was in some respects a semi-developed, in other respects a backward, economy and society, and yet compared with the other countries of Europe it possessed unique dynamism, and it gradually sucked in the economies of its two closest neighbours: Ireland and Scotland. Both countries, in the eighteenth century, became highly commercialized as they were integrated into the British imperial economy. Both began to export unprecedented quantities of agricultural and manufactured goods to London and, through London, to the rest of the world. Ireland and Scotland were noted for their cattle and linen exports; Scotland also had a vast tobacco trade (40 per cent of Scotland's exports by volume and 60 per cent by value in the early 1770s were tobacco). Both countries also experienced rapid urbanization, and until 1750 Ireland's chief towns – Dublin and Cork – were larger than Scotland's – Edinburgh and Glasgow. Finally, both countries participated in the trade to the colonies: Ireland as an important staging post on the route to America; Scotland, especially Clydeside, as an independent centre of Atlantic trade generating demand for home-produced export cargoes. Although the development of the English economy during the early modern period may be seen as a steady evolution, that of the poorer Atlantic economies went through a period of unique discontinuity after the 1690s when they became firmly shackled to their more developed neighbour.

Thus, a highly complex pattern; a society (like our own) often brutal, ignorant, selfish, yet shot through with intelligent aspiration and often rewarded with intermittent measures of material progress.

6   France

6.1 Population

The larger the country, the greater the diversity of economic activity and the more difficult it is to write a synthesis that does justice to the overall trends and developments.[1] France under her Valois and Bourbon kings was large and growing – about 480,000 square kilometres in 1580; about 520,000 square kilometres in 1780 – with a correspondingly expanding population. In 1581 Nicolas Froumenteau, a Treasury official, thought that there were 3,500,000 'hearths' in the France of his day, suggesting a total population of between 16 and 20 millions (depending on whether one takes the average hearth as being 4.5, 5 or 6 people). Perhaps by the middle of the sixteenth century, therefore, some 23 million people lived within the boundaries of France as they were in 1789 (that is, in the areas annexed after 1581 as well as in those covered by Froumenteau).[2] But this is little more than a guess. Only for the last century of the *ancien régime* is it possible to be more precise. Table 6.1 reveals the population recorded in each *généralité* (the basic administrative unit of France) in the 1690s and again in the 1780s. It illustrates the growth of the French population during the eighteenth century in the light of the best documents available for each region. By comparing the figures for the 1690s with those for the 1780s, two facts emerge clearly: first, that there were enormous differences in the demographic performances of different regions; second, that the overall growth was relatively small. It seems clear that the principal gains were registered in the frontier areas devastated by the wars of Louis XIII and his son: the *généralités* of Besançon (Franche-Comté), Dijon (Burgundy), Metz and Nancy (Lorraine), Perpignan (Roussillon), Strasbourg (Alsace) and Valenciennes (French Hainaut). If these areas are excluded, the increase of population in the French 'heartland' was indeed small, thanks mainly to the persistence of the traditional demographic pattern, with its periodic epidemics and famines causing heavy mortality, in several west and centre provinces.

In Table 6.1, the figures in the first column are based upon the data returned by the Intendants of the various provinces to the central government, or upon the estimates by Vauban, corrected where necessary by other data. The second column contains the estimates made by the finance minister Necker in 1780; the third column contains those made by the Chevalier des Pomelles in 1787. Both of the latter employed the same procedure in order to prepare their estimates: they multiplied the number of baptisms entered in the

TABLE 6.1: French demographic growth in the eighteenth century

Généralité	Estimated population size			Change 1690s–1780s %
	1690s	1780	1787	
1. Aix-en-Provence	639,895	754,000	756,508	+18
2. Alençon	585,817	528,500	494,237	−16
3. Amiens	520,175	533,000	534,128	+3
* 4. Auch	(= Montauban)	813,000	887,371	+50
* (Bayonne and Pau)	(241,094)	—	—	—
5. Besançon	340,720	678,000	717,484	+100
* 6. Bordeaux	1,482,304	1,439,000	1,281,409	−13
7. Bourges	291,232	512,000	550,407	+80
8. Caen	600,000 (?)	644,000	625,941	+2
9. Châlons	693,214	812,800	785,528	+15
*10. Dijon	600,000	1,098,821	1,080,000	+80
11. Grenoble	543,585	664,000	690,227	+30
12. Languedoc	1,566,088 •	1,699,000	1,799,520	+15
13. La Rochelle	360,000	479,000	459,869	+30
*14. Lille	500,000	734,600	765,636	+50
15. Limoges	585,000	646,500	668,961	+15
16. Lyon	363,000	633,600	635,813	+75
17. Metz	156,599	349,300	396,349	+150
*18. Montauban	(789,200)	530,200	542,439	+50
19. Moulins	500,000 (?)	633,600	635,813	+30
20. Nancy	300,000 (?)	834,600	923,639	+200
21. Orléans	607,165	709,400	724,565	+20
22. Paris: city	720,000	1,781,700	660,000	+12
country	856,948		1,142,090	
*23. Perpignan	58,041	188,900	116,243	+100
24. Poitiers	616,621	690,500	686,075	+12
25. Rennes	1,900,000 (?)	2,276,000	2,297,205	+20
26. Riom	557,068	681,500	701,421	+27
27. Rouen	656,980	740,000	732,419	+11
28. Soissons	306,500	437,200	447,779	+36
29. Strasbourg	235,000	626,000	654,881	+180
30. Tours	1,066,496	1,253,050	1,309,374	+22
*31. Valenciennes	115,000	265,200	289,342	+150
Total	19,352,000	24,696,000	25,065,000	about +28

Généralités marked with an asterisk underwent slight boundary changes during the eighteenth century. To compensate for this, the figures in column 1 have been adjusted to refer to the *généralité* as it was in the 1780s. For important comments on the figures in column 1, see note 3 on p. 239 below.

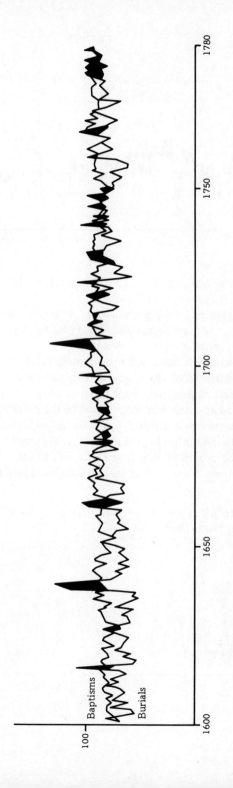

FIGURE 6.1: Baptisms and burials at Le Loroux-Béconnais (Anjou), 1600–1780

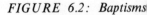

FIGURE 6.2: Baptisms

parish registers over the preceding ten years by 25.75 in order to estimate the number of inhabitants. This coefficient was equivalent to a birth rate of 38.9 per thousand. Although the figures are close enough, it would seem that des Pomelles sometimes had more complete series of data than Necker.[3]

The details of the pattern of demographic performance emerge more clearly from the study of the surviving parish registers of individual communities. Some registers go back to the early sixteenth century in an unbroken series; most of them are continuous at least from the 1670s. Figures 6.1–6.4 are all based on the registers of baptisms and burials kept in selected rural parishes. The graph above shows the evolution of St Aignan-de-Grandlieu, a parish in Brittany not far from Nantes, over three centuries. The general trend, with

FIGURE 6.3: Conceptions and burials at Le Mesnil-Théribus (Ile-de-France), 1700–1800

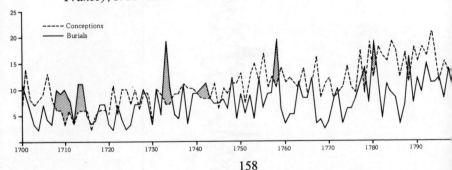

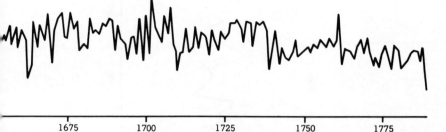

strong increases in the early sixteenth and later seventeenth centuries, seems to have been common to the whole area. The stagnation of the later eighteenth century was also, it seems, typical. It was the same story in Anjou at Le Loroux-Béconnais (Figure 6.1). Both villages lay in areas which, according to Table 6.1, had a low rate of growth in the eighteenth century. By contrast, Figures 6.3 and 6.4 illustrate the so-called 'vital revolution' of eighteenth-century France: a steady increase of births over deaths producing an increase in the net population. The parish register of Le Mesnil-Théribus in the Ile-de-France (Figure 6.3) shows the classic pattern with a net gain every year after 1740 despite some periods of high mortality. In some areas – at Quarouble in Hainaut for instance (Figure 6.4) – the increase began considerably earlier, in about 1720.[4]

The demographic evolution of the main towns of France was quite different from that of the rural parishes illustrated in Figures 6.1–6.4. For example, the population of the city of Bordeaux during the eighteenth century rose and fell in step with the development of the trade with the Antilles, which was largely channelled through the port. The fall in the city's population during the 1790s was caused by the interruption of this trade by the French Revolution. Famines and epidemics scarcely seem to have affected Bordeaux (Figure 6.5), but that was only because the city drew its inhabitants from the entire south-west of France: immigration soon filled the gaps left by the death of the native population.[5]

The population statistics for Paris (Figure 6.6) are particularly interesting because they concern the capital and largest city in the

159

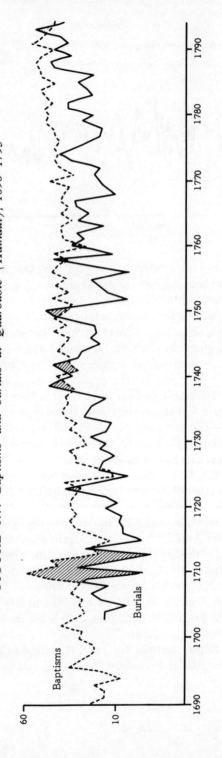

FIGURE 6.4: Baptisms and burials at Quarouble (Hainaut), 1690–1795

FIGURE 6.5: The growth of the population of Bordeaux, 1715–1801

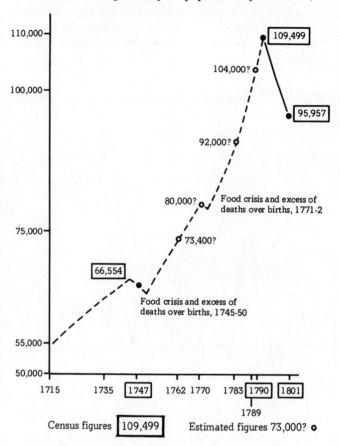

kingdom. But they must be studied with great caution. The number of children baptized included those who had been abandoned and collected from the surrounding countryside and brought in (often on carts) in considerable numbers until the government called a halt (see Figure 6.7). On the other hand, a substantial number of babies, including some foundlings, were sent out to be nursed and brought up in the countryside. Many of them died there, unnoticed in the registers of burials kept in the capital. It is therefore extremely difficult to establish with certainty the 'natural' growth of the population of Paris. Despite the mortality crises, of which the most

161

savage was that caused by the *grand hiver* of 1709–10 (right at the beginning of Figure 6.6), it would seem that there was a slow increase. The total population, swelled by immigration, rose by only between 20 and 30 per cent in the century following 1680: from about 500,000 to 650,000 or 700,000.[6]

FIGURE 6.6: Births, marriages and deaths in Paris, 1709–90 (thousands per year)

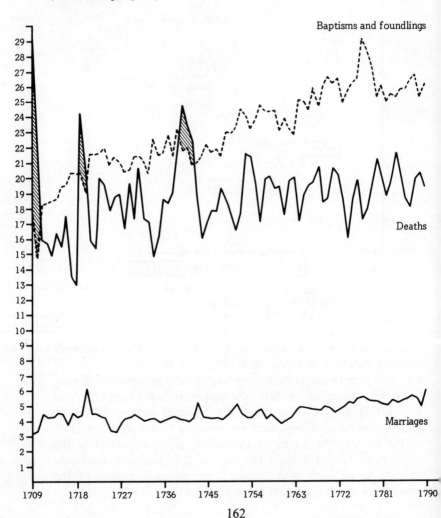

FIGURE 6.7: Foundlings admitted to the Paris Foundlings' Hospital, 1709–90 (thousands per year)

6.2 Agriculture

Thanks to the variety of the soils and climates of France, every region used its land in its own traditional ways; and thanks to the traditional agricultural techniques employed, the pattern of cultivation in some areas retained an almost immutable face throughout the early modern period. Thus, in the eighteenth century, around 80 per cent of the land in the Beauvaisis was arable, 5 per cent was woodland and only 5 per cent waste, common or meadow; in the Bray valley, further south, the figures were 50 per cent, 16 per cent and 26 per cent

TABLE 6.2: Land utilization in Provence: Les Baux, Maussane, Paradou and Mouries, 1584–1744 (in 'cannes' of about 4 square metres)

	Meadow	Arable	Vineyards	Orchard
1584	64	3,560	3,743	273
1627	100	—	4,517	555
1690	93	—	4,804	1,970
1744	90	2,127	6,090	2,324

FIGURE 6.8: Landholding in the north

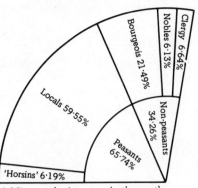

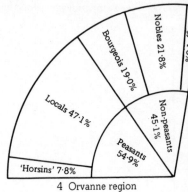

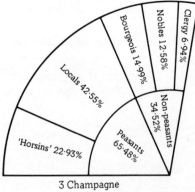

1 Wine-producing areas in the north

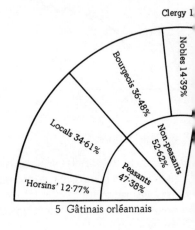

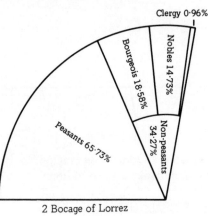

2 Bocage of Lorrez

4 Orvanne region

5 Gâtinais orléannais

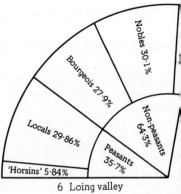

3 Champagne

6 Loing valley

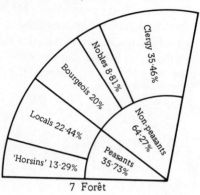

7 Forêt

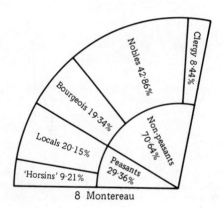

8 Montereau

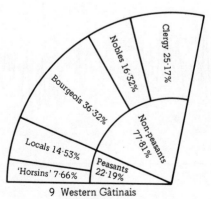

9 Western Gâtinais

respectively. These proportions were strikingly different, but they had remained the same for many generations. However, this was not true of all areas. In Provence, for example (Table 6.2), where we have a series of figures on land utilization that covers two hundred years, the process of bringing new land under cultivation and moving towards greater specialization slowly changed the face of the earth.[7]

FIGURE 6.9: Tithe-yields in Bea

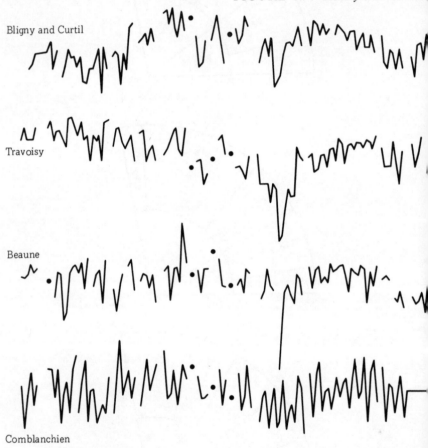

Bligny and Curtil

Travoisy

Beaune

Comblanchien

1500 1510 1520 1530 1540 1550 1560 1570 1580 1590 1600 1610 1620 1630 1640

Note: Measurements in *b.*

Agriculture

In other areas of France, the practice of fallowing was being abandoned in favour of cultivating another crop. In Alsace, in Lorraine and in several mountain areas the potato was widely cultivated in the eighteenth century. In other areas, maize was grown from the seventeenth century. One cannot over-emphasize the diversity of rural life in early modern France. Let us look, by way of

gundy (paid in grain), 1500–1800

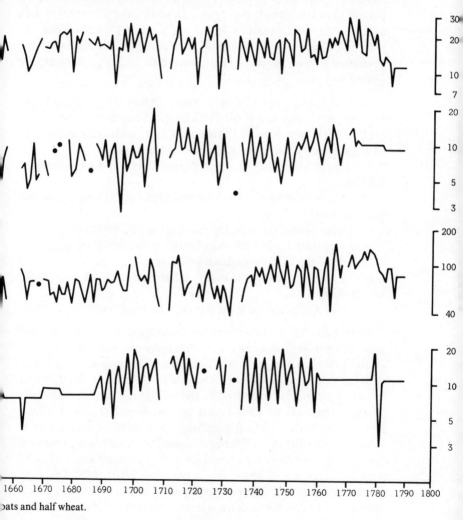

oats and half wheat.

example, at the structure of landowning in the northern Gâtinais, a small yet compact area in central France between Orléans and Fontainebleau, in the late eighteenth century.[8] Taken overall, one could say that the peasants of this area had 45 per cent of its land (and 64 per cent of its income), the bourgeoisie held 26 per cent of its land (and 12 per cent of its income) the nobles 13 per cent (and 11 per cent), the clergy 11 per cent (and 6 per cent), while the state held no land but received 7 per cent of its yield. This is an accurate summation of the pattern of landholding in the region as a whole, and yet to accept such a general picture by itself (as in the end we must) is to overlook the striking differences which, even in a small region, distinguished one community from another. There were nine different variants (see Figure 6.8):

(1) a rich and populous area, much arable (half the land was farmed); predominance of smallholdings of 5 hectares or less;

(2) a fairly populous and fairly rich area, with both arable and pastoral farming; large and medium-size holdings;

(3) a poor and thinly populated area; large and medium-sized holdings;

(4) an area of mediocre land, several types of farming; large and medium-sized holdings;

(5) a wine-producing area, less rich than no. 1; smallholdings;

(6) a very mixed area with some forest tracts; smallholdings;

(7) a poor and thinly populated area; large holdings only;

(8) a fertile area with many inhabitants; good corn-land; smallholdings;

(9) a rich and populous area; intensive farming; fairly large farms.

It is even more hazardous to generalize about agricultural production in early modern times, although one yardstick is the yield of the tithes on the grain produced by each community. Despite possible distortions caused by changes in the rate at which it was levied, or by frauds committed by the collector, a careful evaluation of the tithe receipts does reveal certain broad trends in cereal production. In Burgundy, for instance, the receipts of the chapter of Beaune from 1510 until 1790 clearly reveal the good grain harvests of the early and middle sixteenth and the early seventeenth century, with a sharp drop in the 1580s and 1590s and after 1625. The high productivity of the 1540s was not equalled until the late eighteenth century. In Figure 6.9 we have selected this particular series of tithe returns from the many that have survived because it represents a fairly 'average' evolution.[9]

6.3 Industry

It is possible to present more reliable figures for certain other forms of economic activity. Mining and textile production, for example, were relatively well organized under powerful entrepreneurs whose archives, or whose returns to the local collectors of taxes, have survived relatively intact. Coal mining, for example, has left good records. We know that by 1789 French coal production totalled perhaps 750,000 metric tons annually, of which about 40 per cent came from the mines at Anzin in Hainaut (now in the Département

FIGURE 6.10: Coal production at Anzin (Hainaut), 1744–90 (in thousand metric tons)

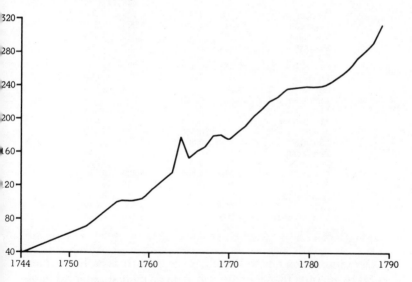

du Nord) (see Figure 6.10). The growth in the quantity of coal extracted from this mine was spectacular, from 25 tons (*sic*) in 1725 to over 300,000 tons by 1789, but French coal mining remained throughout early modern times a small-scale activity. The price of coal remained low and the total value of production, in money, was far below that of any branch of the textile industry; in volume it could hardly match British coal output, which at the end of the eighteenth century was in the region of 10.3 million tons (see p. 124 above).[10]

Information on iron production is far more fragmentary, but incomplete surveys from the late eighteenth century – in 1771 and 1789 – give an idea both of the scale and of the geographical distribution of the industry and its development in the last two decades of the *ancien régime*. Most of the iron was produced in wood-fired furnaces, usually run by small operators. Only a few large companies (Le Creusot, for example) started to use coal. Since the total annual iron production of France in 1789 was probably about 150,000 tons, the output of the regions listed in Table 6.3 represents about two-thirds of the national output.[11]

TABLE 6.3: Iron production in France, 1771 and 1789 (000 lbs)

Généralité	Cast iron		Wrought iron	
	1771	1789	1771	1789
Alençon	12,290	4,000	6,125	2,700
Besançon	33,040	34,140	16,090	19,836
Bordeaux	6,225	15,000	2,575	3,400
Bourges	—	15,175	—	9,494
Caen	—	4,000	—	1,000
Châlons	39,482	39,000	28,731	18,000
Dijon	—	17,000	—	7,000
Grenoble	3,480	3,700	8,220	2,500
Limoges	—	4,150	—	2,513
Metz	—	5,435	—	4,438
Montpellier	—	200	—	5,955
Nancy	—	20,475	—	22,830
Orléans	—	4,600	—	2,440
Perpignan	—	—	—	3,240
Poitiers	—	—	—	2,062
Rennes	9,760	14,800	5,900	6,510
Riom	100	—	35	—
Strasbourg	—	9,200	—	6,272
Tours	5,860	8,255	3,605	5,630
Valenciennes	1,800	800	3,212	4,520

Our information on the French textile industry is both richer and easier to interpret than the surviving data on mining and metallurgy. We have figures for many individual centres such as Amiens (shown in Figure 6.11). From the yield of a cloth tax and the varying numbers of apprentices registered, a picture emerges of rapid growth in woollen textile production in the early sixteenth century, followed by a slump in the 1590s (when Amiens was involved in the religious wars) and then by recovery until the outbreak of war again in 1635. The

FIGURE 6.11: *Woollen manufacture at Amiens, 1525–1700: (a) yield of the farm of the cloth tax at Amiens (in 'livres') and (b) number of apprentice weavers registered at Amiens*

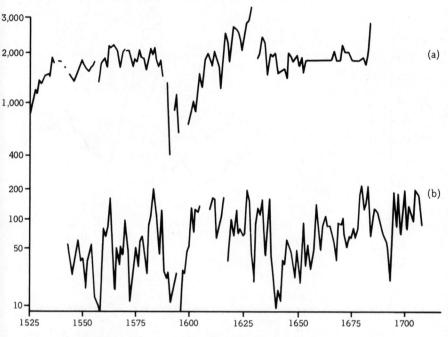

depression lasted until the years of peace and Colbert's reforms after 1660.[12] It must be remembered, when studying the movement of production in a town like Amiens, that there was also an important rural textile industry. Picardy had a well-developed rural industry, but its production is unknown.

TABLE 6.4: *Estimated French woollen production, 1650–1800*

	mid-17th century	early 18th century	late 18th century
No. of pieces of cloth produced	670,540	1,215,000	1,410,000
Total length (in ells)	?	33,500,000	49,000,000
Total size (in sq. ells)	?	19,500,000	33,500,000
No. of businesses involved	34,200	31,500	64,300
Weight of wool used (in tons)	?	39,000	55,000
Value of the product *(in livres tournois)*	19,978,300	78,000,000	140,000,000

FIGURE 6.12: Production of Brittany linen, 1746–89 (in thousand pieces)

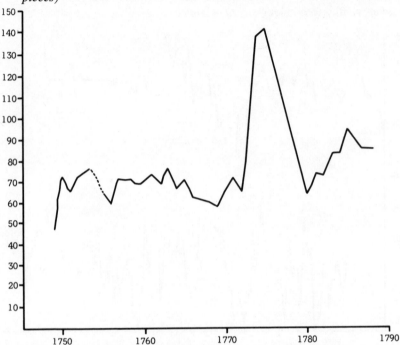

From a survey of all available local figures such as those for Amiens it has been possible to suggest (Table 6.4) some very tentative figures for the total woollen production of early modern France.[13]

There was a more spectacular growth during the eighteenth century in the output of cheaper linen cloth. In both Brittany (Figure 6.12) and Maine (Figure 6.13), production almost doubled between 1740 and 1770, despite the slump caused by the Seven Years' War (1756–63). Brittany linen was exported to Spanish America in considerable quantities, via Cadiz. The sailing of the last fleet, under Don Antonio Ulloa in 1776, is no doubt responsible for the production 'boom' of that year.[14]

6.4 Trade and transport

It is possible to establish with some certainty the pattern of trade at a single port (such as Bordeaux or Marseilles, for which we have

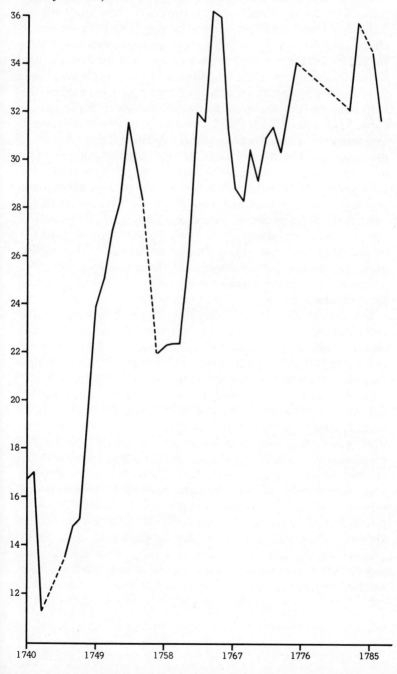

FIGURE 6.13: Linen cloths passed by the Inspectors in Maïne (at Laval, Mayenne and Château Gontier), 1740–86 (in number of pieces, each of 100 ells)

admirable records) or in a single commodity (especially imported ones like spices, sugar or coffee), but it is not so easy to estimate the total volume of French trade, and so establish a national 'balance of trade', until the eighteenth century. From 1716 onwards a regular 'balance of trade' statement was drawn up by a special government office, using the compulsory declarations made by merchants as they entered or left the country, whether or not their merchandise was liable to customs dues. The declarations were sent to the Bureau every three months by the tax farmers at all the major trade centres (the Directions du Commerce at Marseilles, Bayonne, Bordeaux, all ports, St Quentin, Charleville, Lyons and so on). Only Alsace and Lorraine were excluded, and their trade therefore did not feature in the 'balance'. The Bureau made its own estimates of the value of imports and exports. To do this it fixed each year an average price for every article of trade in each area, on the basis of information supplied by local bodies like the customs farmers, the admiralty officials and the chambers of commerce. In theory, the prices used to compile the French balance of trade statistics were variable, although in fact they were not always closely related to market values. Moreover, the same price was used for the same article whether it was an import or an export, which somewhat distorted the true picture of the value of trade.

But despite these reservations, the figures reveal clearly the enormous importance of France's trade with her colonies. It would seem that French exports to the Antilles rose from 2,106,899 *livres tournois* in 1716 to 57,326,217 livres in 1789 (and a further 21 million were sent to Guinea for the slave trade and the 'triangular trade' between Africa, America and Europe). Over the same period, imports from the Antilles rose from 4,484,561 livres to 223,218,505 livres. It is important to note that a large part of these colonial goods were immediately re-exported to the rest of Europe (160,501,428 livres of goods in 1789[15]). The 'deficit' in the trade of France with her colonies, which appears in Table 6.5, is an illusion. It is caused by the government's habit of using the same price for both imports and exports. To take a concrete example: the 57 million livres of merchandise exported to America in 1789, plus the slaves bought in Guinea, were actually sold in the Antilles for a price equal to, or greater than, the 223 million livres of colonial produce imported and registered in the 'balance of trade'. It is therefore necessary to keep separate the trade with Europe and the trade with the colonies (as has been done in Table 6.5). The trade with the United States after 1776 was similar: although the 'balance' showed it as a deficit, in fact it was extremely advantageous for France. As for France's apparent trade surplus with the rest of Europe, research is currently underway to discover how far it was offset by military and diplomatic spending abroad. Perhaps the same is true for Britain's balance of payments in the eighteenth century (p. 125 above).

TABLE 6.5: The geography of French trade in 1776 (in million livres tournois*)*

	Imports	Exports
Germany	8.6	28.9
England	13.2	10.9
Denmark	1.3	3.5
Spain	35.5	44.5
Austrian Netherlands	10.7	22
Geneva	0.1	2.1
Holland	22.1	38.3
Naples	7.2	3
Italy	29.8	24.3
Genoa	3.9	2.9
Venice	0.1	0.1
Levant	28.3	22.2
Russia	4.4	3.2
Baltic	10	37
Sweden	5.2	5.6
Portugal	3.9	4.4
Savoy-Piedmont	5.6	6.2
Swiss Cantons	7.5	7.6
TOTAL OF EUROPEAN TRADE	197.4	266.7
American colonies and islands	136	42
Guinea	—	12.6
East Indies	36.2	6.9
TOTAL OF 'COLONIAL' TRADE	172.2	61.5
GRAND TOTAL	369.6	328.2

There were certain changes made to the methods used to compile the balance of trade figures after 1781. One of them is evident in Table 6.6, covering the years 1787–9: the introduction of the category 'precious metals'. Paradoxically, it increased the apparent trade deficit, since France received more gold and silver (mostly from Spain) than she paid out (to the Levant and the Indies). It is therefore hazardous to compare the figures for the 1780s with those of earlier decades, although to do so (as in Figure 6.14) does illustrate the

FIGURE 6.14: The French balance of trade, 1716–80 (in million livres tournois)

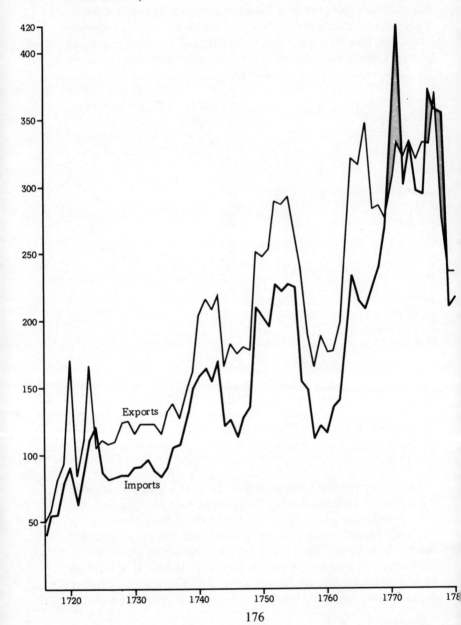

TABLE 6.6: French balance of trade by products, 1787–9 (in million livres tournois)

	1787 Imports	1787 Exports	1788 Imports	1788 Exports	1789 Imports	1789 Exports
Food and drink	204.6	231.8	243.6	252.4	309.3	227.2
Raw materials	194.6	41.5	171.9	42.4	176.1	44.5
Livestock	3.1	1.4	3.1	1.5	2.1	0.9
Crude metals	20.3	6.7	21.5	5.3	18.4	4.1
Manufactured goods	120.3	154	69.6	156.3	62.6	156.5
Drugs and chemicals	6.9	3.3	4.8	3.8	5.6	3.4
Gold and silver	80.8	5.7	60.7	1.1	59.9	1.4
TOTAL	630.8	444.6	575.3	463.1	634.3	438.4

general evolution of France's foreign trade for most of the eighteenth century.[16] This overseas trade was carried by a considerable mercantile fleet. The French merchant navy grew from about 150,000 tons in 1664 and around 240,000 tons in 1686 to about 730,000 tons a century later.[17]

FIGURE 6.15: Total annual value of coinage minted in France, 1493–1725 (in million livres tournois)

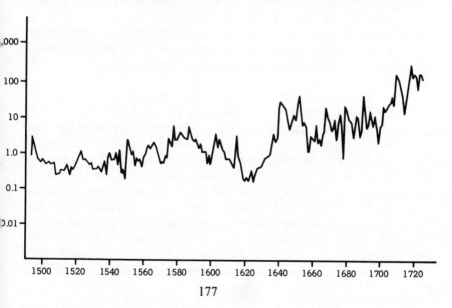

6.5 Currency

The output of the French mint between 1500 and 1725 is known in some detail, thanks to the survival of most of its archives (see Figure 6.15). The figures are interesting, but they reflect the fiscal policies of the Crown (recoinage, the minting of new coins and so on) rather than the overall economic or political situation. Thus the peak in the 1640s was the product of recoinage, not of the *Fronde*, or yet of the war with Spain![18]

6.6 Prices

Since few statistics tell us more about the conditions and the quality of life in a community than the price of basic foodstuffs, there is a case for printing in full the market prices of every major agricultural product in every major town of Europe. Hopefully this will one day be done. In Figure 6.16, by way of example, we have chosen to present the prices of three different cereal crops on three separate markets, one in the east, one in the south and one in the north of France: rye at Grenoble, maize at Toulouse and wheat at Paris. There is a significant unison among the series, especially for wheat and rye, even though the markets were over 300 miles apart, and the concordance goes back to the mid-sixteenth century with its rapid rise in prices. The crises of the 1590s, of 1661–3 and of 1709–10 all show up clearly. The maize sold at Toulouse was a new crop, only introduced to France in the mid-seventeenth century. The series are quinquennial averages calculated from the price of the standard measure of grain expressed in local currency.[19]

The same wealth of statistics and apparently the same co-ordination exists for those other staples of French diet, wine and olive oil. Figure 6.17, just one example among many, charts the behaviour of the price of a *muid* (660 litres) of wine and a *charge* (182 litres) of olive oil at Béziers, at the centre of the region producing *vins courants*. This time the focus is on the price stagnation of the seventeenth century and the strong price rise of the eighteenth century, but the olive tree is less hardy than the vine and the destruction of olive groves on several different occasions led to an increase in the price of oil which broke its close correlation with the price of wine. For this figure we have used a computer analysis which fits a polynomial curve to the data. The computer was programmed to trace a path through

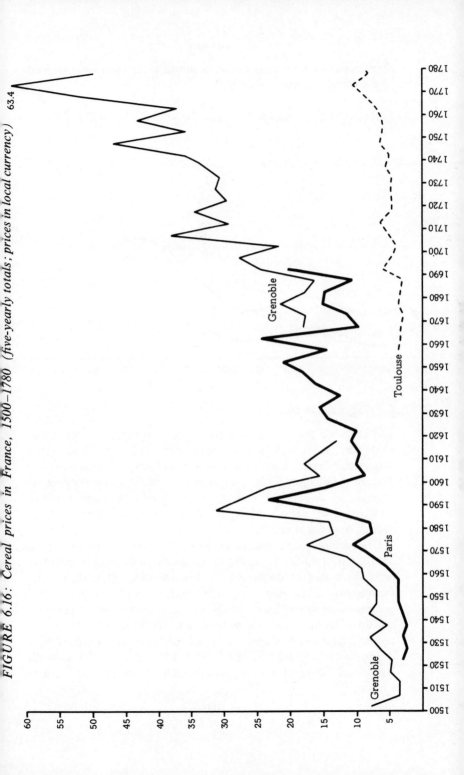

FIGURE 6.16: Cereal prices in France, 1500–1780 (five-yearly totals; prices in local currency)

the data points, producing a more accurate 'form' than that obtained by the use of 'moving averages'.[20]

FIGURE 6.17: Price of olive oil and wine at Béziers, 1588–1790 (in livres tournois)

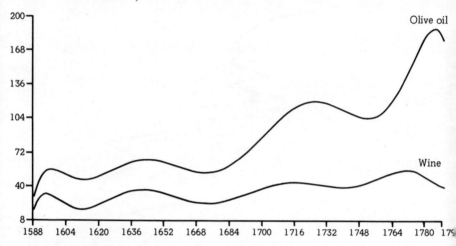

6.7 Wages and incomes

The evidence for wages in early modern France, as with other countries, is far less copious than that for prices. There is a magnificent series of builders' wages from Paris, covering over two centuries (see Figure 6.18); but it is, so far, practically the only one. It reveals, as one might expect, long periods of wage stability punctuated by periods of rapid increase in a vain effort to keep abreast of rising prices.[21]

Evidence on profits and income from property is even harder to obtain, but a vintage example of what can be gleaned from estate account books is contained in Figure 6.19. This shows the fluctuations in the rent charged for certain rural estates by three ecclesiastical institutions during the seventeenth and eighteenth centuries. Despite the wide variations in the Montpellier rents, an upward trend can be detected between 1630 and 1683, followed by a depression of around fifty years. After 1735, however, agricultural land clearly became far more profitable both in northern and central France.[22]

180

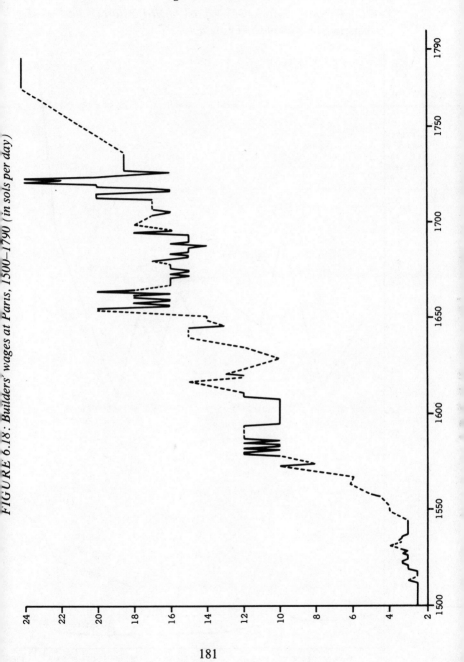

FIGURE 6.18: Builders' wages at Paris, 1500–1790 (in sols per day)

FIGURE 6.19: Leases of certain landed estates, 1605–1785 (annual rent, in thousand livres tournois)

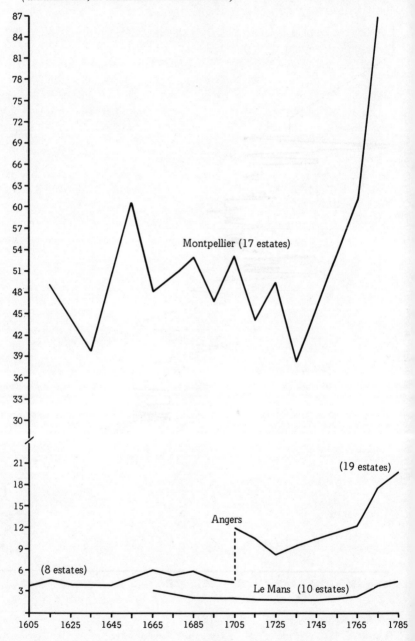

6.8 Wealth and social structure

Real incomes and real wages did not always increase as much as might seem to be the case from nominal figures; they were constantly eroded by rising prices, particularly in the sixteenth century. At Lyon, a large city for which we have excellent records, we can see in Figure 6.20 the steadily worsening situation of day labourers, reaching crisis proportions in the last quarter of the century. Wages alone did not suffice to buy a man his daily bread (Figure 6.21). About one in five inhabitants of Lyon, the second city of France, thus became dependant on poor relief.[23]

FIGURE 6.20: Real wages and the cost of living at Lyon, 1535–1600 (index numbers; 1565–9 = 100)

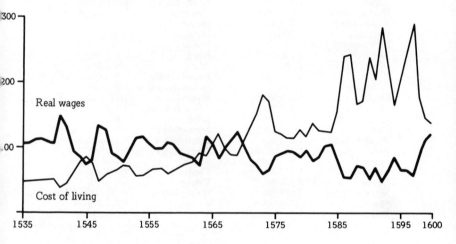

FIGURE 6.21: Real wages expressed in terms of purchasing power for wheat, 1500–1600 (index numbers; 100 = 1565–9)

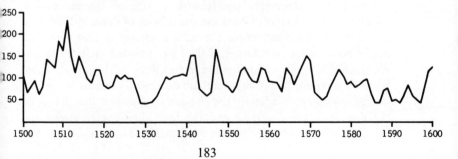

The problem of poverty had scarcely diminished by the end of the *ancien régime*. In 1790 the Committee for Vagrancy of the Constitutent Assembly asked all areas to report on the proportion of poor families among their population. Although not all areas were covered, and although not all areas applied the same criteria to assess poverty, the results of the inquiry were extremely interesting (see Table 6.7). Among other things, they revealed the ubiquity of the poor in all parts of France, with concentrations of up to 20 per cent in some *départements*.[24]

TABLE 6.7: Poverty in France in 1790

Département	Proportion of poor	Département	Proportion of poor
Aisne	1/8–1/9th	Haute-Marne	1/16th
Hautes-Alpes	1/9–1/10th	Mayenne	1/5–1/6th
Basses-Alpes	1/7–1/8th	Meuse	1/15th
Charente	1/16th	Moselle	1/10–1/11th
Charente inférieur	1/13–1/14	Nièvre	1/14–1/15th
Corrèze	1/14th	Nord	1/5–1/6th
Côte-d'Or	1/11th	Oise	1/8–1/9th
Creuse	1/11–1/12th	Pas-de-Calais	1/5–1/6th
Dordogne	1/19th	Hautes-Pyrénées	1/8–1/9th
Doubs	1/7–1/8th	Haute-Loire	1/11–1/12th
Drôme	1/9–1/10th	Saône-et-Loire	1/11th
Eure et Loire	1/7–1/8th	Seine	1/6th
Gers	1/9–1/10th	Seine-et-Marne	1/7–1/8th
Ille-et-Vilaine	1/5–1/6th	Seine-et-Oise	1/12–1/13th
Jura	1/10–1/11th	Deux-Sèvres	1/8–1/9th
Loir et Cher	1/9–1/10th	Somme	1/10–1/11th
Loiret	1/8–1/9th	Vendée	1/7–1/8th
Lozère	1/5–1/6th	Vienne	1/7–1/8th
Maine-et-Loire	1/6–1/7th	Haute-Vienne	1/11–1/12th
Manche	1/6–1/7th	Vosges	1/8–1/9th
Marne	1/11–1/12th	Yonne	1/10–1/11th

But if the poor were numerous, the fact remains that the majority of the population did *not* live on the brink of subsistence.

Figure 6.22 represents the relative wealth of the tax-paying members of the *élection* of Pontoise, north-west of Paris, in 1789. It is based on the tax registers for the *taille* compiled in that year and covers most of the population of the forty parishes included in the *élection*: 3155 heads of families are included; only 213 *gens de néant* (families too poor to pay anything) are omitted. The figure is centred on the *average* tax burden for the *élection*'s population (the line *M* in the middle of the diagram) and the individual contributions are shown as multiples or fractions of *M*. Thus those in area *d*, to the left of *M*, were paying between one-eighth and one-sixteenth of the overall average, *M*, while those in area *D* to the right of *M* were paying between eight and sixteen times the average. The wide gap that separated the rich from the poor of the countryside stands out in this diagram, from the 252 families of day-labourers (*manouvriers*) in category *f* (and the 213 who had even less) up to the one large farmer in category *G*. As one might expect, almost all the day-labourers were below the average while almost all the freeholders (*laboureurs*) were above it.[25]

FIGURE 6.22: Wealth and social structure in Pontoise (Vexin) in 1789

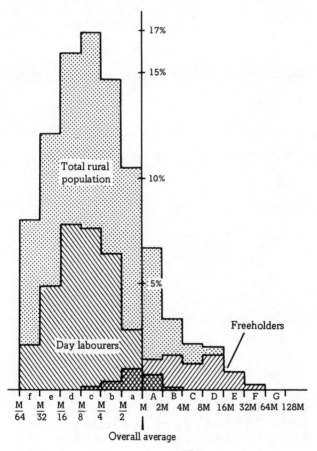

TABLE 6.8: *Personal fortunes of Paris bridegrooms in the eighteenth century*

Wealth in livres tournois	<100	100	200	300	500	1,000	2,000	5,000	10,000	15,000	20,000	30,000	50,000	100,000	200,000	300,000	500,000	Million	Unknown	TOTALS
Day-labourers	1	11	16	58	112	122	78	19	2	1									36	456
Soldiers (not officers)		1	1	1	5	3	5	3	2		2								2	25
Servants	1	2	1	26	56	86	89	42	9	3	2	1							36	354
Artisans			2	3	7	16	15	3		1										47
Unknown status		1	4	10	55	57	35	8	3	1			1						15	190
Employees				2	6	7	8	13	6	2	3	2	1	1					9	61
Masters		2	3	19	48	115	151	91	42	27	21	23	7	1		1			11	560
Merchants				1			5	1	1		2	2	1	4					1	18
Liberal professions			2	2	6		12	10	6	1	5	5	5	5	4				15	78
Judicial officers						4	8	6	10	4	3	9	11	5	2		1		2	65
Military officers			1		1	2	2	5	3	2	2	1	2			1			10	31
'Bourgeois'		1		7	35	39	39	23	11	10	7	12	7	2	3	2	10	2	17	213
Nobles						1	1	2	3	2	4	1	13	7	5	9	11	2	9	67
TOTALS	2	18	30	129	331	457	448	226	98	54	51	55	48	23		14	11	2	163	2165

The spread of wealth within the upper classes in the eighteenth century is illustrated by Table 6.8, derived from the personal fortunes declared by prospective bridegrooms in the city of Paris in their marriage contract. Although the majority estimated their worth at between 500 and 5000 livres, there was a considerable number above this limit and they came from many walks of life (the three day-labourers who valued their assets at over 10,000 livres are interesting!). On the whole, however, it is the formidable financial power of the nobles that stands out.[26]

6.9 Conclusions

The spirit of statistical inquiry was not entirely foreign to the French governments of early modern times. The occasional census was carried out in the sixteenth century, usually as a preliminary to the introduction of a new tax. Under Richelieu and Colbert there were government inquiries into other sectors of economic life, chiefly concerned with shipping and overseas trade. But it was not until the late seventeenth and early eighteenth centuries that major statistical investigations were carried out: totals of textile production compiled by the inspectors of manufactured goods; figures for the balance of trade; later, estimates of harvest yields, price levels, population size, and major surveys of certain key industries (leather, paper, iron and so on). Nevertheless, if the economic historian could count only on the data contained in official inquiries, he would have little to go on, especially for the sixteenth and seventeenth centuries. Fortunately, he can often turn to other sources of information which, although not originally intended to provide statistics, may be made to do so. Parish registers are an obvious example: from the dry daily entries made in each parish of the baptisms, marriages and burials that occurred, entries that were commanded by the government, demographers have been able to compile sophisticated models of the population. The registers yield information on birth and death rates, on contraception, on the social background and place of origin of the bridal couple, on the size of families, even on literacy (because often the couple had either to sign the register or make a mark). Another example of a source that can be made to yield statistics almost in spite of itself is the account books of the towns: because of their dependence upon excise duties and household taxes, we can discover a great deal about patterns of trade and of demand; because of their taxes on production, we can measure output in certain industries.

Of course, one must be prudent. Like the archaeologist, the economic historian of early modern France must always keep his evidence within the context in which it is found. His 'statistics' are not those of the contemporary economist; his economic realities are not those of the twentieth century. When he finds a price rise that stems from harvest failure, he must not mistake it for a consequence of expanding economic activity; when he finds a series of data on industrial output for a town or two, he must not forget that it was probably less important than the production of the rural artisans, whose activity he cannot measure. But the economic historian can still make some useful discoveries. France, a large country in the sixteenth century and larger still in the eighteenth, possessed vast agricultural riches. Even if there appears to have been no great increase in agrarian productivity in the average year, there was a diffusion of new crops – maize, buckwheat, beans, tomatoes, potatoes – and there was some specialization, thanks to the roads and carts that linked regions together: viticulture in some areas, sheep-raising in others. France was rarely forced to import any food from abroad, except in years of wholesale famine. She was large enough and rich enough to be self-sufficient in food.

Because of her size, and because of the vigour of her interregional commerce, it has sometimes been suggested that France did not play any significant role in international trade. This is an error. Directly after the end of the Hundred Years' War, France attracted the attention of the master-merchants of Europe: the Italians. They were interested in both the production and in the demand of their great neighbour. They came to the main cities as financiers and importers, but they also helped to create, with the Crown's blessing, new industries, especially luxury industries like the silk manufacture at Lyons and Tours. After about a century of hesitation, they were imitated by the merchants of Marseilles who, from around 1609, carved themselves an important place in the Levant trade, bringing back the vital raw materials for the manufacture of silk and cotton textiles. The French may have been slow, but they made progress in the end. Likewise, if they failed to take hold of a corner of America for many years, contenting themselves with the fish of Newfoundland and the furs of Canada, they took an active part in the trade between Spain and her colonies in the New World. Cloths from Normandy and Brittany, silks from Lyons, lace from Le Puy were all sent to

Seville and Cadiz, and thence to Spanish America. In 1686, French traders were more heavily involved in the fleets sent to Mexico and Peru than those of any other nation.

The establishment of the first French colonies in the Antilles after 1635 gave a new dimension to French commerce. Cultivation of tobacco, indigo, sugar, cocoa and coffee (in more or less that order) was maintained by the import of Negro slaves and it attracted the attention of more and more French merchants. Colonial goods were exported to northern Europe through Nantes, Rouen and above all Bordeaux, and to Mediterranean Europe through Marseilles. So prosperous did this trade become in the eighteenth century that in 1763 (by the Treaty of Paris) the French abandoned Canada in order to retain Martinique and Guadeloupe. It is even possible that the profits and attractions of colonial commerce masked the decline of other branches of trade – for example, woollens.

Between 1500 and 1800, France appears to have followed faithfully the broad rhythms that affected the rest of western Europe. Her distinguishing features lay in her large population, her undeniable agricultural resources, her well-developed traditional industries and her plantations in the colonies, which supplied most of Europe with tropical produce. The creation of a strong and centralizing state tended to mobilize these resources more effectively and to oblige the population to place a price on their activities in order to pay their taxes. By 1789, these developments had progressed slowly to a point where they created new problems: population growth now threatened to reduce living standards; increased taxes and the traditional fiscal burdens began to become irksome at precisely the moment when a new set of revolutionary ideas were coming into fashion. It was an explosive situation.

7　Germany

Except for price series, which have been preserved from the Middle Ages onwards for many goods and for many areas, the survival of economic 'statistics' from the territories of the former Holy Roman Empire is uneven and fragmentary. The political division of the Empire into separate units and the consequent dispersal of relevant material into many public and private archives, together with the relatively late development of statistical studies (with the Cameralists), has discouraged scholars from making use of those collections that are extant. However, it was not always so. At the beginning of the seventeenth century, the study of *Staatsmerkwürdigkeiten* ('political arithmetic' in England), of which Hermann Conring was the great advocate, was introduced into German universities. Conring and his friends directed their main attention towards the characteristics of a state: its constitution, government, population and financial situation. In 1656 Veit Ludvig von Seckendorf wrote a book, *Teutscher Fürstenstaat*, which used government statistics to delineate the external characteristics of Germany and its principalities. Then came the philosopher Leibnitz, who emphasized the value of statistics for political economy. Somewhat later, in 1740, Johann Peter Süssmilch used the official, tabulated source material of the Prussian state to calculate population growth.[1] After this there was a spate of statistical accounts of the individual states, starting with a two-volume study of Prussia published in 1785–9.[2] The value of these contemporary accounts has been recognized by modern historians and they are now being re-published.[3]

However, these writers only scratched the surface of available material. The complex data that survive from the sixteenth and seventeenth centuries in every major and most minor archives of Germany cry out for attention. The treasury records of many states contain detailed information on population, social structure, housing and livestock as well as on taxation levels, land tenure and interest rates.[4] From 1684 an annual record of births, marriages and deaths was made in electoral Brandenburg, and from 1719 figures giving the size of the total population, based on the parish registers, were compiled first every six months, later (cumulatively) every three years. Comprehensive economic 'statistics' were produced in 1751, 1772 and 1778, giving information on everything from factories (*Generalfabrikentabelle*) to cultivation. Elsewhere, police records can be a valuable source of statistical material. Thus, for example, the police records of the electorate of Mainz, dating from 1725, give information on births, marriages and deaths, on immigration and emigration, normal harvest yields, disasters and so on.[5] All this material, carefully interpreted, is capable of providing much fascinating and important information on the economic and social history of early modern Germany.

7.1 Population and social structure

The population of Germany in the period from 1500 to 1800 can be estimated only approximately: perhaps 15 million inhabitants in 1600 falling to between 10 and 12 million in 1650. By 1700 it is thought that the total population had recovered its level of a century before, rising to around 17 million by 1750.[6] The problem with compiling 'national' figures is that there was no 'nation' in early modern Germany. Instead, centuries of fragmentation had created a loosely connected entity, the Holy Roman Empire, broken up into a large number of independent city-states, secular principalities and ecclesiastical states, ranging from minute 'imperial cities' to states like Brandenburg-Prussia, which was larger than the Dutch Republic. There were around 1000 separate territories. We know in some detail the population of the better organized states, but it is hard to generalize from them to the rest of Germany. However, we can make with some confidence a list of the largest German towns during our period:[7]

  in 1450: Cologne (40,000); Danzig, Lübeck, Nuremberg and Ulm
  (20,000 or more);
  in 1500: Cologne, Nuremberg and Augsburg; Strasbourg, Metz,
  Lübeck, Erfurt, Magdeburg and Danzig (over 20,000);
  in 1600: Nuremberg, Augsburg, Danzig and Hamburg (over
  40,000); Cologne (over 30,000);

in 1700: Berlin and Hamburg (over 60,000); Breslau, Cologne and Danzig (over 40,000);

in 1800: Berlin (172,000); Hamburg (130,000); Breslau, Dresden and Koenigsberg (over 50,000); Cologne (over 40,000).

There were nineteen towns with more than 10,000 inhabitants at the beginning of our period and sixty at its end.[8] To illustrate the limitations and possibilities of the evidence, we have chosen to present, in the first place, crude population data for two provinces – Württemberg (Table 7.1[9]) and Prussia (Table 7.2[10]) – and for four towns – Augsburg, Göttingen, Leipzig and Munich (Figure 7.1[11]).

TABLE 7.1: The population of the Duchy of Württemberg, 1598–1794

1598	414,000	1679	265,000
1622	445,000	1697	284,000
1623	458,000	1707	347,000
1634	415,000	1730	425,000
1639	97,000	1750	467,000
1645	121,000	1754	477,000
1652	166,000	1759	479,000
1669	218,000	1769	476,000
1673	252,000	1794	614,000

It should not be assumed that the growth of a large city like Augsburg or Leipzig was the result of population increase among the native inhabitants. At the city of Breslau in Silesia, for example, there was also a rapid growth in population, from 40,000 in 1745 to 57,000 in

TABLE 7.2: Population growth in the provinces of the Prussian state, 1700–1804

	Magdeburg	Neumark	East Prussia	Pomerania	Silesia	West Prussia
1700	130,000	120,000				
1720			400,000			
1740	186,000	160,000		309,000	1,109,000	
1754		219,000		368,000		
1756					1,162,000	
1765					1,193,000	
1774						356,000
1775			837,000		1,373,000	
1785					1.681,000	
1794					1,794,000	
1800		300,000	931,000	500,000		545,000
1804	309,000				2,000,000	

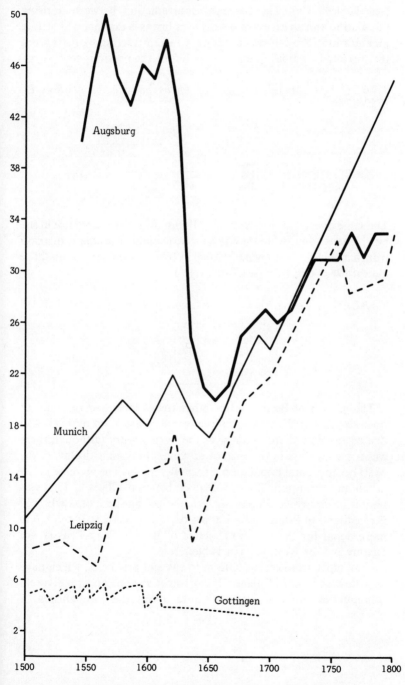

FIGURE 7.1: Population growth in Augsburg, Göttingen, Leipzig and Munich, 1500–1800 (in thousands)

1774 and to 64,500 in 1800; but the number of deaths in the city always exceeded the number of births, often by as much as 20 per cent (see Table 7.3[12]). The apparent contradiction between a rising population and an excess of deaths over births is explained by strong immigration: Breslau was a 'boom' town, attracting workers from the surrounding areas to fill the gaps left by the previous generation.

TABLE 7.3: *Annual averages of births and deaths at Breslau, 1552–1774*

	Average births	Average deaths	Difference
1552–1622	1195	1432	−237 (20 %)
1655–74	889	1021	−132 (15 %)
1705–24	1199	1427	−228 (19 %)
1745–74	1288	1584	−296 (23 %)

The same phenomenon occurred in Berlin, where the rapid rise in the new citizens admitted to the city helps to explain its dramatic increase from a medium-sized town of 10,000 in 1680 to a European capital of almost 198,000 in 1816 (see Table 7.4[13]).

TABLE 7.4: *New citizens admitted annually to Berlin, 1500–1750*

1500–35	23	1709–20	136
1536–70	26	1721–30	148
1571–1619	53	1731–40	236
1620–88	31	1741–50	306
1689–1708	85		

The growth of Berlin and of other towns increased the total of town-dwellers to 27 per cent of the overall population by 1748, and this proportion altered little over the next century (although there was some increase in the eastern provinces and some decline in the west) because rural population also grew rapidly. The increase in the urban and rural population of Prussia between 1700 and 1800 was paralleled elsewhere. In Saxony, population density increased by 37 per cent and in Bohemia by 100 per cent. The increase is charted in more detail for the individual states of Brandenburg–Prussia, for Saxony and for Westphalia in Table 7.5[14].

If we move from census data of towns and provinces, which have provided the basis of Tables 7.1–7.5, to parish registers of individual communities, we can discover more about the mechanisms of

TABLE 7.5: Population density in Germany per square kilometre, 1688–1804

	East Prussia Lithuania	Neumark	West Prussia	Pomerania	Posen	Silesia	Kurmark	Saxony	Westphalia
1688–92	12.6	—	—	—	—	—	16.2	—	—
1698–1702	—	9.2	—	8.2	—	—	—	30.8	—
1712–16	13.2	14.7	—	8.1	—	—	18.1	31.5	51.8
1722–6	15.9	—	—	—	—	—	—	—	—
1733–5	18.7	15.6	17.1	11.7	—	30.1	—	46.3	53.7
1766	—	17.3	—	14.5	—	32.4	24.1	41.8	50.0
1776	—	—	—	—	11.9	—	—	—	—
1784–86	22.8	21.7	17.7	17.2	12.7	45.6	27.8	46.6	54.8
1800–4	24.7	26.3	25.4	20.0	19.4	—	32.4	52.5	54.8

195

TABLE 7.6: Infant mortality at Offenburg: deaths within first year per thousand live births 1751–1800

1751–60	265
1761–70	322
1771–80	337
1781–90	328
1791–1800	441

population change. We can show that infant mortality was high and rising in late eighteenth-century Offenburg (Table 7.6[15]), that average family size in Durlach rose from 4.1 in 1700–25 to 5.8 in 1776–1800, that the crude birth rate in eighteenth century Württemberg fluctuated around 40 per 1000 and that the live births per married couple varied from below 2 in some periods to almost 5 in others (Table 7.7[16]). The trouble with this evidence is that it is incomplete: it refers only to isolated areas and, since the pattern in each one is different, generalization about demographic trends is both hazardous and difficult. But the information is too fascinating to disregard.

TABLE 7.7: Births per 100 married couples, 1600–1800

Munich		Offenburg	
1600–30	395	1631–50	230
1636–45	484	1651–1700	240
1647–50	469	1701–50	490
1651–70	412	*Dresden*	
1671–1700	431	1620–53	346
Durlach		1630–1703	329
1700–10	251	*Augsburg*	
1711–20	231	1571–1622	370
1721–30	187	1623–45	300
1731–40	181	1646–1703	368
1741–50	210		
1751–60	206	*Leipzig*	
1761–70	214	1525–1609	280
1771–80	212	1617–43	295
1781–90	213		
1791–1800	242		

7.2 Agriculture

The archive material available for the compilation of agricultural statistics is very scattered, owing largely to the territorial divisions of Germany in the period between 1500 and 1800. Since legal, political and economic conditions varied from territory to territory, statistical comparisons are often difficult to make. Moreover, the compilation of these statistics is further restricted by the lack of interest in statistical recording at the time, by the incompleteness of such records as do survive and by the fact that most governments did not develop specific policies for agriculture. Some cities, it is true, did evolve an *Agrarpolitik*, but it was limited in extent and restricted to measures to regulate corn production and trading: village communities surrendered their control over the allocation of land to the town, which could then regulate production levels to satisfy its own demands.

TABLE 7.8: Cultivation in Prussia around 1800

	Area in *morgens*	Percentage of total area
Arable land	42,767,914	39.68
Gardens	432,150	0.40
Vineyards	54,050	0.05
Meadows and pasture	20,436,000	18.96
Wooded	25,754,995	23.89

Note: 4 morgens = 1 hectare = 10,000 square metres.

With the development of territorial states, and the gradual loss of the autonomy of the cities, the control of the *Agrarpolitik* passed increasingly to the princes, and was extended by them to their personal lands, administered through their *Hofkammer* or *Rentkammer*. The real changes in agricultural organization only took place after 1740 under the influence of the Physiocrats. The *Kammern* were strengthened and improved, and new officials were appointed to control agriculture, with powers that covered not just the prince's domain but the entire state. This was particularly the case in predominantly agricultural states such as Mainz, with its *Land-Ökonomie-Oberdirektion* from 1765, in Schleswig-Holstein with the *Grössfürstliches General-Landes- und Ökonomieverbesserungsdirektorium* in Kiel after 1768, and in Württemberg with its *Schafzuchtverbesserungsdeputation* after 1783.[17] This growing centralization of government enables us to produce some estimates of the total agricultural output of Germany by the end of the eighteenth century (Table 7.9[18]), and provides an accurate picture of the different types of farming in individual states (Table 7.8)[19]. It was estimated by contemporary specialists that the 11 million hectares (about 27.5 million acres) of German land under cereal cultivation produced about 10 metric quintals of wheat per hectare, about 9 quintals of rye, 8 of barley and somewhat less of oats. In 1800 almost exactly one-third of the soil of Germany (18.2 million hectares out of 54.3 million) was under arable cultivation (see Tables 7.10[20] and 7.11[21]). (Compare the Italian data on page 11.)

TABLE 7.9: Arable production in Germany around 1800

Type of crop	% of cultivated land	% area under cereals	area in 1000 hectares
Total cereals	61.1	100	11,000
Wheat		7.5	825.0
Rye		41.0	4,510.0
Barley		19.0	2,090.0
Oats		25.5	2,805.0
Spelt		4.0	440.0
Buckwheat } Millet		3.0	330.0
Legumes	3.9		708.0
Market gardens	3.8		685.0
Vegetables	2.3		415.0
Potatoes alone	1.5		270.0
Fodder crops, meadow and fallow land	28.9		5,200.0

TABLE 7.10: Livestock in Germany, around 1800

Horses	2,700,000
Cows	10,150,000
Pigs	3,800,000
Sheep	16,190,000
Goats	340,000

TABLE 7.11: Production from cultivated land in Germany in 1800 (in thousand tons)

	Production	As a %
Total production of cultivated land	12,767.6	100
Food and raw materials grown	6,479.3	50.8
Animal fodder	3,965.8	31.0
Seed corn	2,245.2	17.6
Waste	77.2	0.6

Note: Includes 100,000 tons of cereal exported.

198

But despite all these monuments to bureaucratic efficiency, an equally good source of statistics for agriculture are the estate papers of the landholders themselves: these provide information on prices, profits, crops and techniques which are unavailable elsewhere. It is this source that provides the data for Figure 7.2[22] – the growth in arable land on 412 separate estates in the Mittelmark and Uckermark of eastern Germany. It can be seen that by far the most intensive period of arable increase was the sixteenth century. The same phenomenon is reported from other areas: some 40,000 hectares of new land were brought under cultivation in Jeverland, Harlebucht and Leybucht (on the North Sea coast); in Schleswig-Holstein 8000 hectares were reclaimed from the sea; while in Balingen in the Swabian Jura a chronicler reported in 1601: 'In the preceding years of rising prices much rough and stony ground was cleared and planted.'[23]

FIGURE 7.2: Percentage annual growth in agricultural area, 1375–1860

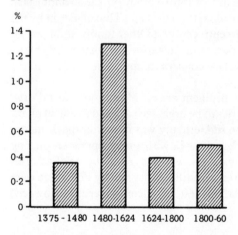

7.3 Mining and industry

The gathering of statistical evidence on industrial production for the period 1500–1800 is exceptionally difficult, mainly because of the dispersal of the relevant records caused by the territorial divisions of Germany. Thus many data on the metal production of the Saar area are in the Staatsarchiv in Saarbrücken, while evidence on the mining in Silesia is in the former Staatsarchiv in Breslau (now Wroclav, Poland). As with agriculture, it was only in the eighteenth century that institutions were created for entire states designed to encourage and control industrial activity: a permanent department of trade (Commercien Deputation) in electoral Saxony from 1735, a department of trade and industry (Handel und Gewerbe) of Prussia was created in 1740, and a mining department (Bergwerks- und Hüttendepartement) in 1768. The archives of these government agencies provide something approaching real 'statistics' on industrial activity. Before the appearance of these central institutions we have to rely on the records of towns and princes interested chiefly in trade regulation and trade taxation: they tell us a great deal about the number of masters and apprentices, about immigrant workers and about toll receipts, but little about actual production. For that, we need to consult the papers of the entrepreneurs themselves. The Fuggerarchiv, for example, housed at Dillingen on the Danube, is the most important private archive in Germany for the economic historian, containing a wealth of information on the metallurgical and mining concerns in Slovakia, the Tyrol and Thuringia run by the Fugger family from the fifteenth century. Other family archives can also provide interesting data, for instance the papers of many Nuremberg patrician families concern mining enterprises in the Mansfeld area of Saxony.

Here, however, another problem arises. Mining and metallurgy were among the few industries to be organized around a central plant. Most industrial production in Germany was based on the domestic 'outwork' system (the *Verlagssystem*), with an entrepreneur 'putting out' the raw material to workers who stayed at home. Factories began to appear only in the eighteenth century and by 1790 there were about 1450 of them (perhaps 60 of them government-owned) distributed as follows:

Habsburg lands	280	(of these, 140 were in Lower Austria)
Bohemia	90	
Brandenburg–Prussia	(220)	(of these, 120 were in the 'middle provinces')
Silesia	(30)	
Ansbach–Bayreuth	40	
Westphalia	30	
	200	

Saxony	170
Bavaria/Upper Palatinate	(150)
Jülich and Berg	40
Lower Palatinate	40
Hanover	(20)

The figures in brackets are estimates, and all figures exclude mines, quarries and brickworks. Unfortunately, the copious records that these factories produced rarely begin before the end of the period covered by this volume. It is another source that fails us, but against this loss we may set a gain: industrial history may be illuminated by contemporary textbooks on technology – such as Georg Agricola's *De re metallica* (1554) – or by written or pictorial descriptions of various occupations – such as Jobst Ammann's *Handwerkdarstellungen* (1578).[24]

Given the extensive nature of the mining and industrial activity of early modern Germany, it seems logical to examine the data on each branch of production individually.

Silver production

A complete survey of silver production in central Europe before 1618 was provided in a well-known article published by Professor J. U. Nef in 1941.[25] Further information that has come to light subsequently has merely confirmed Nef's overall pattern of rising production until about 1550, then gradual decline. Thus the Marienberg mines in Saxony reached a peak of production between 1541 and 1556 (total output in the latter year was over 25,000 marks) while the Saigerhütten in Thüringia achieved a similar peak (an average of 30,000 marks annually) between 1525 and 1550, as Figure 7.3[26] shows.

According to Soetbeer's vintage but reliable study, the total annual production of German silver fell from a peak of 360 tons in the 1540s to a low of 120 tons during the Thirty Years' War, but it recovered to a level of around 504 tons annually between 1721 and 1740 (1 metric ton is 1000 kilograms). The records of the Marienberg mines, discovered many years after Soetbeer wrote, do not entirely correspond to this broad picture: except for the decade 1709–19, production remained very low until the 1770s. Even then, the 'peak' years saw a total production of only 4000 marks – barely a sixth of the 1556 figure.[27]

FIGURE 7.3: Thüringian silver production, 1506–1622 (in thousand marks of silver)

Copper and brass production

The mining of copper rose considerably during the sixteenth century. In the Mansfelt region, the most important area of German production, it reached 2000 tons a year; in the Tyrol and Carpathian mines it reached 1700 tons; and in Bohemia it reached 2500 tons. Unfortunately we do not have enough figures to present either the overall trend during the sixteenth century or the overall production of German copper in the seventeenth and eighteenth centuries. However, we can make up the latter deficiency to some extent from the known figures of brass production, since its manufacture was necessarily dependent on the supply of copper. The brass-making centres were situated near the deposits of zinc ore, another essential ingredient: in the Lower Rhine area, especially around Aachen, in Silesia and in the Tyrol. Thus in 1559, 30,000 *zentner* (110 pounds) of brass were produced by 100 furnaces in and about Aachen; in 1648 35,000 zentner were produced by 115 furnaces, mostly in Aachen and Stolberg. By the 1690s annual production had risen to 40,000 zentner, and output continued to rise until 1726, when 200 furnaces were active in Stolberg alone, producing 60,000 Zentner. This total was down to 135 furnaces and 40,000 zentner by 1783 but had recovered to 196 and 60,000 respectively twenty years later.[28]

Iron production

The output of iron, like that of copper, increased steadily in the course of the sixteenth century, stabilizing and then declining for most of the next hundred years, after which production again began to increase. Tables 7.12[29] and 7.13[30] give a rough idea of the increase.

TABLE 7.12: Iron production in Germany, 1500–1750 (in tons per year)

Region	c. 1500	c. 1750
Steiermark	10,000	16,000
Prussia		15,000
Silesia		15,000
Schmalkalden	5,000	6,750
Harz		5,550
Nassau–Siegen	3,000	4,100
Upper Palatinate	10,000	1,000

We can trace the decline and fall of production in the Upper Palatinate in some detail: it provides an example of an economic decay which clearly predated the Thirty Years' War but which was intensified during the period of conflict. Even by 1850 the iron production of the province was lower than it had been in 1609, although it almost tripled between 1665 and 1802. The recovery towards the end of the eighteenth century is noticeable, but it cannot compare with the growth of iron production in the Ruhr area, on the right bank of the Rhine: the territories of Mark and Berg alone, which had 451 forges between them in the 1750s, had 652 in 1800, and there were 43 in the Siegerland and 83 more in the duchy of Westphalia.[31]

TABLE 7.13: Iron production in the Upper Palatinate, 1609–1802

	No. of forges	Total production of iron (in Zentner)	Average annual production per forge	Total annual coal and wood requirements (in Festmeters)
1609	182	172,000	950	310,000
1618	60	48,000	800	100,800
1665	29	17,000	600	35,700
1783	40	28,000	700	58,000
1802	51	45,000	900	94,500

Note: 1 *Festmeter* = 1 cubic meter of solid wood.

Textile production

Textiles of all sorts were produced in the Holy Roman Empire: woollen cloth was manufactured in most towns (in the teeth of competition from the English and Dutch 'new draperies' marketed by companies like the *Zeughandlungskompanie* of Calw); linen was made in Swabia, Lower Saxony, Hesse and Silesia; cotton goods were produced from the eighteenth century chiefly in Saxony; silks were made in Cologne, and later in Krefeld, Berlin and elsewhere. The problem with such diversity is that it makes the compilation of total production figures almost impossible. Thus we know that in 1796 the territories of Minden and Ravensberg in Westphalia had 4969 looms worked by 5379 weavers, but that tells us nothing of how important this was in terms of the production of all Germany. It is very disappointing.[32]

Salt production

By contrast, because salt was produced in only a few areas – Halle, Stassfurt, Schönebeck, Reichenhall, Schwäbisch-Hall, and above all Lüneburg – the output figures of individual centres are more meaningful. Figure 7.4[33] reproduces the annual volume of the salt exported from Lüneburg as measured by the excise duty and *Scheffelgeld* (an additional salt tax) levied. Both are expressed in *Wispel* (1 Wispel of tax for every 12.5 hectolitres of salt produced) with an equivalent in metric tons added on the right. The high output of around 37,000 tons of salt annually, which was maintained between 1550 and 1620, was never recovered after the Thirty Years' War and production steadily declined until the end of our period.

7.4 Trade and transport

Archival material on this subject is abundant: the sites of the great fairs (Leipzig, Frankfurt-am-Main), the towns situated at commercial crossroads (Magdeburg, Cologne, Augsburg, Nuremberg), main trading centres, ports – all have their archives containing business records, port registers, ship's manifests and so on. Some ports established special agencies to control maritime trade, such as the Admiralität in Hamburg, which was founded in 1623 to organize convoys and control the harbour; its archives are extensive and important. Later on the major principalities also created special

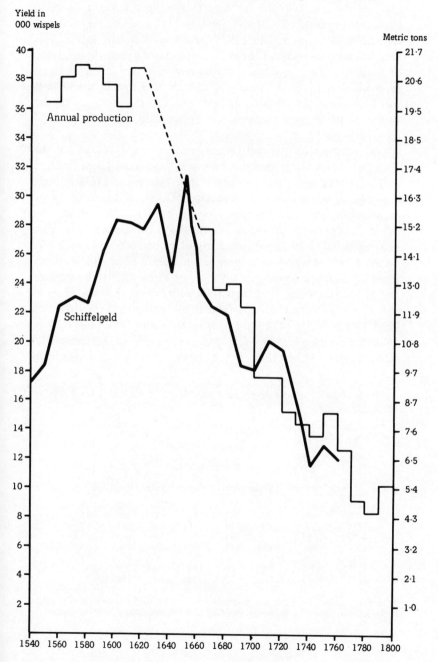

FIGURE 7.4: Production of the Lüneburg saltworks, 1550–1800

institutions to regulate trade (this was, of course, the age of mercantilism): in 1689 the Geheime Hofkammer was established in Prussia to organize all tolls and trade; in 1747 something similar was created in Bavaria, and in 1753 in Austria.[34] By the side of this archival material there are the manuals prepared by merchants, some of them extremely ambitious, containing information useful to all those involved in trade. These grew so numerous that by the 1790s it was found desirable to issue bibliographies of the literature on the subject – the largest compendium (printed in 1796) listed 1274 separate items.[35]

One reason why the toll records are so rich a source for the economic historian is because Germany's political fragmentation had created an incredible number of tariff barriers. To take a single example, we may consider the accounts of Gottfried Kleeditz, a barge captain from Pirna on the Elbe near the borders of Bohemia, who made four return journeys in 1671–4 to Hamburg. It was, geographically, a straightforward trip of around 300 miles each way on the Elbe, taking about a month, but Kleeditz had to stop thirty times on each journey to pay tolls – from Pirna itself to Lauenburg just above Hamburg. And these tolls were heavy: they added up to 986 *Thaler* going to Hamburg (and 1020 coming back) in 1671, 905 (and 574) in 1672, 1434 (and 655) in 1673 and 1096 (and 627) in 1674.[36] Crushing burdens like this were a serious disincentive to internal trade. At best they caused changes of a load in transit from

TABLE 7.14: Volume of goods transported in Bavaria, 1766–99 (in thousand Zentner)

		Water transport			Land transport		
	Total goods trans-ported	Total	Liable to full duty	Wholly or partly duty-free	Total	Liable to full duty	Wholly or partly duty-free
1766	466	265	251	14	201	190	11
1770	404	209	193	16	195	180	15
1775	381	209	196	13	172	162	10
1780	325	75	65	10	250	215	35
1785	356	133	118	15	223	198	25
1790	354	97	76	30	257	180	77
1795*	489	249	56	193	1,240	280	960
1799	443	113	79	24	330	250	80

*The heavy traffic of this year was no doubt connected with the movement of baggage trains and provisions for the armies involved in the Franco–Austrian War.

river to land carriage in order to minimize tolls to pay; on the whole it proved cheaper to transport goods by road, and a study of transportation in Bavaria in the later eighteenth century (see Table 7.14[37]) shows a steady shift from water to land carriage (although no doubt this shift owed something to improved methods of transport and better roads).

TABLE 7.15: Estimated carrying capacity of selected merchant fleets, 1470–1670 (in metric tons)

Country	c. 1470	c. 1570	c. 1670
Germany	60,000	110,000	104,000
Netherlands	60,000	232,000	568,000
England	?	42,000	94,000
Scotland	?	10,000	10,000
France	?	80,000	80,000

Of course, ships were also used for external trade and, despite her relatively small coastline, the German mercantile fleet was powerful until the early seventeenth century. In the late fifteenth century, when the Hanseatic League was still at the height of its power, the total carrying capacity of the German trade fleet was about 60,000 metric tons (20,000 engaged in trade with France and the Iberian peninsula, 20,000 engaged in the Baltic and the rest trading around the North Sea, to Iceland and to Norway).[38] By 1570 the total capacity had risen to around 110,000 tons (28,000 at Emden, 16,000 at Lübeck, 13,500 at Hamburg), but this was the peak: during the Thirty Years' War it fell, and even in 1670 had not quite recovered its former level – the total capacity was around 104,000 tons (42,000 at Hamburg, 18,000 at Lübeck). The significant fact, however, was that while Germany's merchant fleet stood still, those of most of her rivals did not (see Table 7.15[39]). The steady erosion of the position of the Hanse

TABLE 7.16: Baltic trade: Germany and her competitors in the sixteenth century

	Annual average number of ships entering Baltic				
	Hamburg	Bremen	Lübeck	Netherlands	All countries
1539–48	153	97	39	619	1,279
1562–9	150	52	81	2,256	3,365
1574–83	28	66	171	2,266	4,462
1584–93	105	59	150	2,768	5,179
1594–1603	97	89	146	3,024	5,241

in European seaborne trade is evident in the number of ships entering the Baltic, as Table 7.16[40] makes clear.

Once again, it was not that the German towns declined; they were simply unable to expand as fast as their competitors. It was only the decline of the Dutch Republic and the colonial wars of France and England that allowed the Hanse towns, Hamburg in particular, to recover. The French conquest of Holland in 1795 was particularly beneficial to Hamburg – as Figure 7.5 reveals. The expanding fleet was used increasingly in trade with France (thanks to a commercial treaty in 1769): by 1790 20 per cent of all sugar and 45 per cent of all coffee exported by the French colonies was handled by Hamburg. There was also increased trade with Great Britain (mainly London) during the wars with America and France.[41]

FIGURE 7.5: The size of Hamburg's trading fleet, 1765–1842

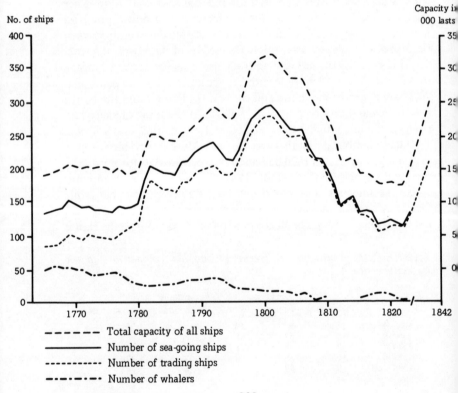

7.5 Currency and finance

Given the fragmentation of Germany, with almost 300 territories entitled to issue their own money, it is totally impossible to estimate the quantity of currency circulating in the country. There were even three different monetary areas – those of the thaler, the gulden and the mark. The one thing that we can say with certainty is that the value of all currencies was falling throughout our period. Table 7.17[42] makes this clear as regards the Cologne silver mark – 234 grammes of silver – which was the basis of the German monetary system until 1857.

TABLE 7.17: Purchasing power of a Cologne silver mark in rye, 1399–1782

Year	Value in bushels	Year	Value in bushels
1399	34	1615	16
1432	40	1668	12
1508	74	1694	13
1536	42	1715	16
1556	28	1739	17
1568	22	1750	17
1588	19	1768	15
		1782	13

The same problem complicates any investigation of public finance: the archives each of the 294 *Reichsstände* must be plundered in order to provide a complete picture. Of course each area was different, few having a centralized treasury, most preferring a multiplicity of revenue bodies with separate accounts. Even in the most centralized states the ruler normally regarded public income as his own, and he levied a number of 'feudal' taxes; in Brandenburg–Prussia the ruler had a *Kammer* to handle his private income and a *Hofrentei* to administer public funds. And Brandenburg was unusually well organized. In 1563, for the first time, the Elector made use of statistics to organize a new distribution of taxation in the state and to justify increases in taxes on trade, moveable goods and luxury articles. The earliest surviving treasury accounts date from 1601 for the *Kammer* and from 1608 for the *Hofrentei*. These indicate an income of around 50,000 thalers annually for the former and around 100,000 for the latter in the years before the outbreak of the Thirty Years' War. During the war, and especially after 1627 and Wallenstein's advance to the Baltic, the Elector's revenues dropped to under half these figures – in 1638–9 his income from all sources was only 36,000 thalers – but under the Great Elector and his successors there was a dramatic recovery. Income leapt from 59,000 thalers in 1643–4 to 268,000 in 1652–3, 824,000 in 1661–2 and 3.2 million in 1688–9. The long-term development is shown in Figure 7.6.[43] Needless to say, the great increase in revenue was caused by the military endeavours of the Hohenzollerns. The Seven Years' War (1756–63) in particular imposed an enormous strain on the financial resources of Brandenburg–Prussia, almost as great as the cost of fighting France forty years later (and rather less successfully). Frederick II's total income in 1756–7 leapt from 11 million thalers to 18 million, and fell back to 12 million only after 1763.

FIGURE 7.6: Total income of Brandenburg–Prussia, 1650–1800 (in million thalers)

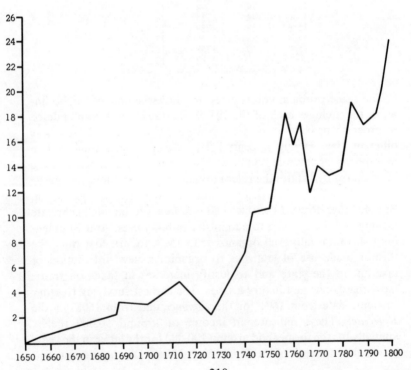

The financial evolution of a less ambitious state such as Bavaria was entirely different (see Figure 7.7[44]). It will be observed that, between 1650 and 1750, expenditure regularly exceeded income. This was a feature common to most states of the Empire (and the recurrent deficits help to explain the attraction of mercantilist ideas to eighteenth-century rulers). The Bavarian state debt – owed to foreign potentates, bankers, Jews, monasteries and public officials – amounted to 20 million florins in 1720, 27 million in 1726 and 34 million in 1749. After this peak – representing over eight years' income – there was an improvement and the debt was reduced to 22.5 million in 1778 and 15 million in 1798.[45] The debt, and the rise in state spending, inevitably caused an increase in taxation. By the 1780s, the incidence of taxation for the 900,000 or so inhabitants of the state of Bavaria worked out at over 3 florins per head, or perhaps 15 florins a family, every year. As we shall see, in relation to most people's wages

FIGURE 7.7: Income and expenditure in Bavaria, 1510–1800 (in million florins)

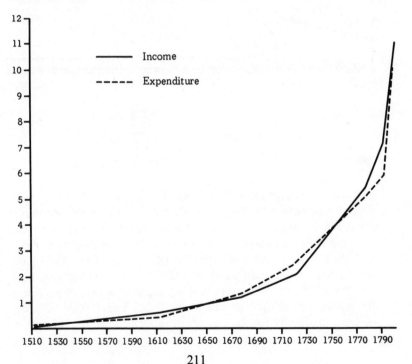

this was a serious burden. It was much the same in other states, large and small, although there is some evidence that, relatively, taxation was heaviest in the later seventeenth century. Unfortunately, the archives of ordinary taxpayers seldom survive, but they are extremely valuable when they are preserved. A small farm at Lutter in Brunswick, for example (see Figure 7.8[46]), with 18.6 hectares (about 46 acres) of farm land, paid almost 50 thalers of tax every year in the 1700s, but by the 1790s it was paying only 30 thalers (and inflation had reduced the value even of that).

FIGURE 7.8: The tax burden in Brunswick, 1660–1806 (in thalers)

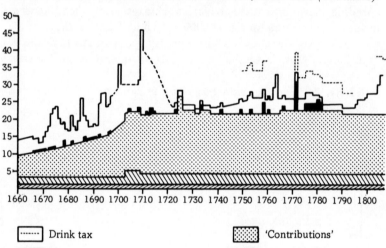

It is unfortunate that the fiscal records of the major German states do not exist before 1600. For knowledge of the evolution of public finance in the sixteenth century we have to turn to municipal records. The imperial cities played an important role in the Empire anyway, and their budgets are interesting in themselves. The yield of the wealth tax (*Vermögenssteuer*) imposed by the city of Augsburg between 1475 and 1724 reveals a sharp increase in the tax burden in the century before the outbreak of the Thirty Years' War, a century of great prosperity for the city: even though the actual number of citizens wealthy enough to be assessed for the tax rose little, the

212

wealth of many of them – led no doubt by the Fuggers – increased dramatically (see Figure 7.9[47]).

FIGURE 7.9: Revenue from the wealth tax of Augsburg (in thousand florins), 1475–1724, with the number of taxpayers

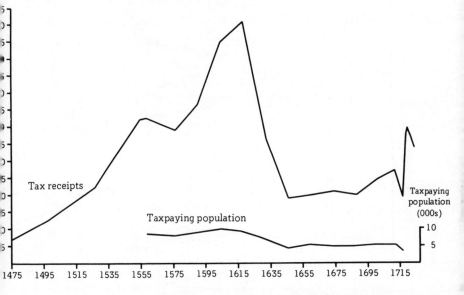

The financial history of another great trading town of south Germany, Nuremberg, tells a slightly different story (Figure 7.10[48]). Although the steep rise of public expenditure in the sixteenth century is clear, the increase is dwarfed by the military emergencies of the next two hundred years: the crises of 1621–2 (when Protestant Nuremberg was threatened in turn by the armies of Tilly, Mansfelt and 'the mad Halberstadter'), 1629–34 (with a siege, a brutal sack and the duel between Wallenstein and Gustavus Adolphus) and 1646–8 (the indemnities payable to the troops at the end of the war) stand out. The city paid dearly again during Louis xiv's wars, but the next emergency comparable with 1621–2 did not occur until the Seven Years' War (1756–63).

But war was only one item of expenditure for towns: its incidence was dramatic but (happily for most towns) infrequent. The budgets of two cities, Hanover and Munich, taken at fifty-year intervals, reveal the profile of urban finance in early modern Germany (Tables

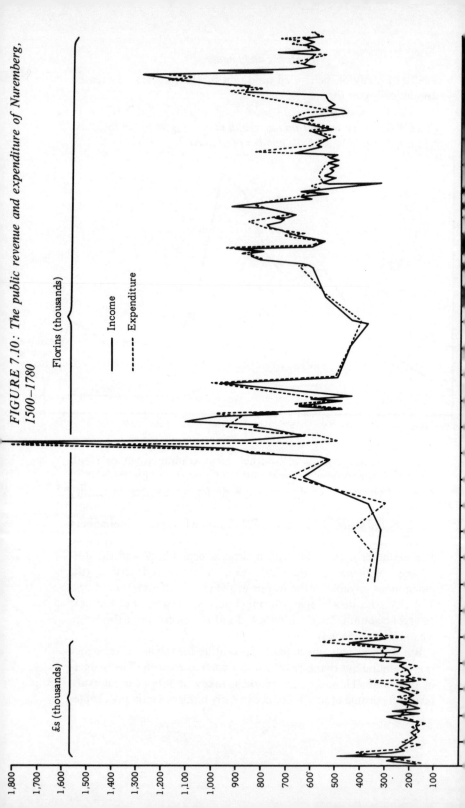

FIGURE 7.10: The public revenue and expenditure of Nuremberg, 1500–1780

7.18[49] and 7.19). The salient features in both towns are the increasing costs of administration (it doubled in Munich and tripled in Hanover between 1650 and 1800), the absence of heavy military spending and (until 1700) of public works, and the dependence on indirect taxation

TABLE 7.18: Principal items of income and expenditure in Hanover–Altstadt, 1650–1800 (in thalers)

INCOME	1650	1700	1750	1800
Excise, tolls and common taxes	4,679	4,967	7,502	8,290
Direct taxation	3,672	4,624	4,539	5,197
Fines and dues	2,191	3,542	5,434	7,276
Wealth tax	705	750	4,174	6,305
Total income (includes *all* sources)	16,255	19,937	23,641	34,589
EXPENDITURE				
Civic administration and salaries	4,431	5,594	7,483	12,791
Debt interest and repayment	10,315	13,557	8,617	6,791
Defence	43	131	61	161
Building (including wages)	595	—	5,710	12,661
Social services	22	22	177	269
Total expenditure (includes *all* items)	15,582	17,529	22,046	32,687

TABLE 7.19: Principal items of income and expenditure in Munich, 1550–1800 (in florins)

INCOME	1550	1600	1650	1700	1750	1800
Tolls, excise indirect taxes	6,951	13,320	8,622	17,287	19,716	41,768
Loans and bonds	1,449	1,845	9,631	9,498	14,419	69,772
Direct taxes	3,127	7,962	7,433	9,131	20,023	32,772
Fines and legal dues	1,655	6,636	4,256	3,177	8,471	9,667
Lottery tax, special taxes	—	—	—	—	21,695	55,207
Total income (all sources)	14,258	35,374	31,800	40,601	88,593	101,397
EXPENDITURE						
Civic admin. and salaries	8,898	10,240	10,558	14,843	29,721	20,668
Debt interest and repayment	1,481	4,662	1,581	4,768	8,547	81,925
Defence	146	85	388	423	671	3,750
Buildings	4,187	4,127	5,043	6,539	19,913	36,400
Social services	1,647	1,957	417	3,652	5,576	15,344
Total expenditure (all items)	21,301	26,804	26,080	43,767	96,025	187,544

for the largest single item of income. There were also differences, the principal one being the extent to which Munich depended upon loans for current revenue: in common with many German cities, she was deep in debt by the later eighteenth century.

7.6 Prices and wages

Any study of prices and wages in the Empire is complicated by the large number of currencies and the frequent changes in their values.

FIGURE 7.11: Cereal prices at Leipzig, 1560–1800 (in denaren per Dresden Scheffel)

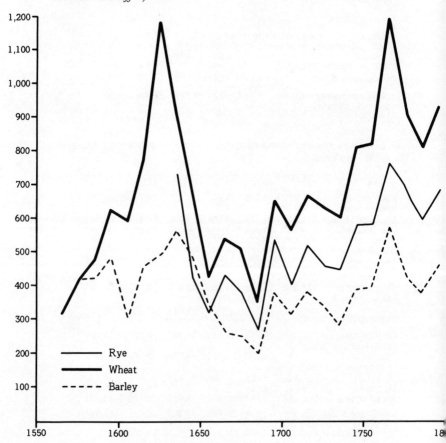

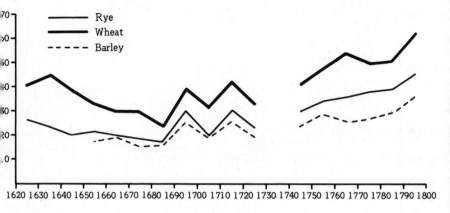

FIGURE 7.12: *Cereal prices at Berlin, 1624–1800 (in silver grosschen per Brandenburg Scheffel)*

Price and wage series expressed in local currencies can only show nominal fluctuations; to separate real changes in prices and wages from changes in the value of money, we have to express our data in the relative silver content of the various currencies.[50] Even having done this, there are still problems. The longest continuous series of prices are those paid for various commodities by monasteries, town authorities and other institutions; they, however, always bought in bulk whenever the goods were cheapest – what they paid was unrepresentative of local prices, as surviving short-run merchants' accounts show. Wages too, are suspect since, owing to the close paternal relationship between employer and employee, wages formed only part of the total remuneration for work. The salaries of the better paid were more 'modern' in this respect, but they were normally negotiated by each individual and were thus not representative of a whole class of employees. Finally, there was no wage parity between various areas in early modern Germany.

There is little doubt, however, about the overall trends: prices rose fast in the sixteenth century. Martin Luther preached sermons against inflation and blamed it on usury; Nicholas Copernicus wrote about inflation and blamed it on the inflow of foreign bullion. He saw a part of the problem, but there is no guarantee that subsequent commentators, from the seventeenth century onwards, have explained away the fascinating 'price revolution' any better.[51]

Figures 7.11[52], 7.12[53] and 7.13[54] indicate that, despite the

FIGURE 7.13: Cereal prices and population at Munich, 1500–1800 (index numbers)

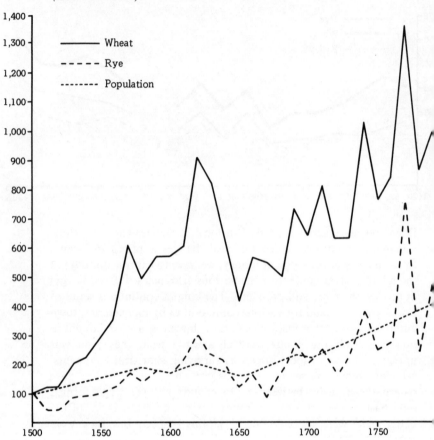

Note: Population in 1500 was *c.* 10,800.

enormous size of Germany, fluctuations in the price of grain followed much the same rhythm in the north (Berlin), east (Leipzig) and south (Munich) of the country. Similar data exist for other areas.[55] All the series have one peak between 1625 and 1635, caused by the devastation of war which destroyed harvests and created acute overpopulation, and a second between 1765 and 1775. The Munich graph (Figure 7.13) suggests that population movement was closely connected with cereal prices, especially with rye, the staple ingredient of the bread of the poor. Demographic growth was associated with rising grain prices, demographic decline with the reverse.[56]

These fluctuations in prices, above all in food prices, were matters of vital importance to the majority of the population, who worked for fixed wages and who saw the value of their remuneration being steadily eroded. The schoolmasters of Munich, who were paid 32 florins a year in the 1520s and 40 florins a year in the 1540s, saw their wages rise to 100 florins by the end of the century, but what was this threefold increase compared with the almost sixfold rise in the price of a wheaten loaf?[57] As Figures 7.14[58] and 7.15[59] show, it took over a century for wages to catch up with prices: it was only during the Thirty Years' War, no doubt because of the shortage of manpower, that wages surged upwards. After 1735 a new phase of

FIGURE 7.14: Summertime wages at Augsburg, 1500–1800 (in denaren)

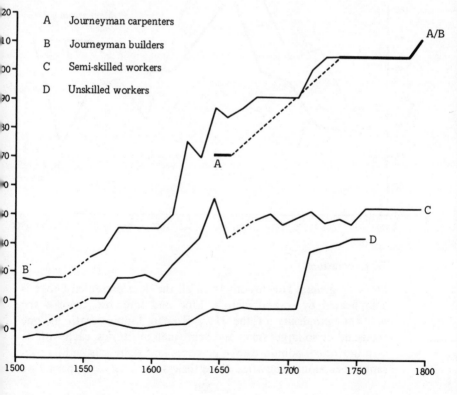

A Journeyman carpenters

B Journeyman builders

C Semi-skilled workers

D Unskilled workers

inflation set in, and wages again lagged far behind, as shown by Table 7.16[60] – based on a similar Leipzig source to the preceding one.

FIGURE 7.15: Women's wages and cereal prices at Leipzig, 1570–1700 (in denaren)

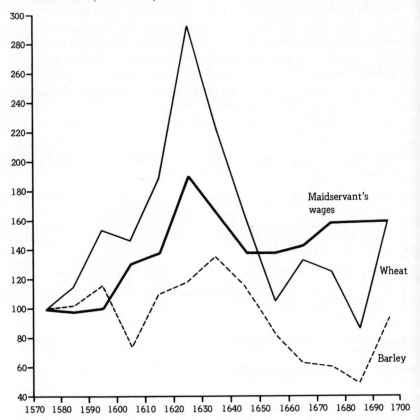

7.7 Conclusions

Drawing general conclusions from all the data presented above is complicated by several factors. First and foremost, there is the political complexity of the Holy Roman Empire, with its one thousand or so large, small and very small territories, each with its own individual administrative practices and standards and its own range of economic activities. Nevertheless, for most of the period we

220

FIGURE 7.16: Women's wages and cereal prices at Leipzig, 1700–1800 (index numbers)

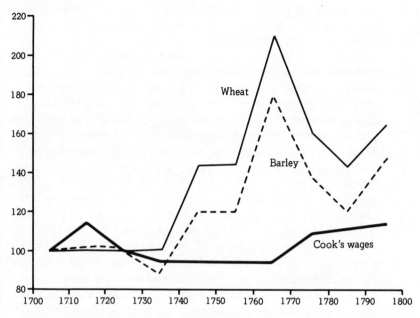

can distinguish four broad regions within the Empire which possessed a common economic structure which transcended the frontiers of the political territories: the Rhine valley in the west; the coastal areas from Friesland to Prussia in the north; 'High Germany', with textile and metallurgical industries and its international trading concerns, in the south; and central east Germany, with a mining and metallurgical industry of growing importance. After the trauma and destruction of the Thirty Years' War, this economic pattern began to change, mainly as a result of the mercantilist policies pursued by the larger states like Brandenburg, Austria and Bavaria, which tried to establish autonomous regions of their own. But there was still no 'national' German economy, and we therefore have to interpret all the statistical data we find in a special way: they can be safely applied only to the area from which they originate. German economic historians thus face unusual difficulty in making broad generalizations. Admittedly, the source material is abundant, especially for the seventeenth and eighteenth centuries, but each set of data is no more than a single piece of a jigsaw puzzle: it makes sense only when placed beside the other pieces. Information from one place only becomes of broader significance when placed beside similar pieces from other areas within the same broad economic regions mentioned above.

We have to admit that, by this criterion, research done on German economic history so far is insufficient to enable us to draw conclusions of a general character. Most of the statistics embodied in our graphs are illustrations of developments; they do not represent in any accurate sense the overall economic development of any of the countries comprehended in the political system of the Holy Roman Empire. They can be used to support only the vaguest generalizations. Up to the Thirty Years' War, economic activity was increasing rapidly, with new land brought into cultivation, rising population and increased production in almost all sectors. Then came the war, which ended expansion in all, or almost all areas, and the recession which it caused was prolonged by the influx of competitive goods from western Europe, by the exhaustion of many mines, by the shortage of fuel and other technological handicaps and by the high incidence of taxes on trade, tolls and customs dues. Recovery seems to have begun only in about 1740, aided by a new awareness of economic realities among the various territorial governments, and by the general upswing in the European economy which is noted in each of the chapters in this book.

Table of Weights and Measures

Units of measurement used only once or twice in tables or figures are explained in their context. Except in the chapter on the British Isles, 'ton' refers to metric tonnes.

	British standard
1 ell (French)	45 inches
1 metre	1.09 yards
1 hectare (10,000 square metres)	2.47 acres
1 kilometre	0.62 miles
1 square kilometre	0.39 square miles
1 litre	1.75 pints
1 hectolitre (100 litres)	21.9 gallons
1 bushel	8 gallons
1 fanega	12 gallons
1 kilogram	2.2 lbs
1 arroba	25 lbs
1 quarter	28 lbs
1 quintal	100 lbs
1 metric quintal (100 kilograms)	220 lbs
1 zentner (50 kilograms)	110 lbs
1 metric ton (1,000 kilograms)	0.98 tons
1 last (2,000 kilograms)	1.97 tons

Notes and References

PREFACE
1 The *World Economic History*, published by Weidenfeld & Nicolson and under the general editorship of Charles Wilson, already includes the following volumes: Ralph Davis, *The Rise of the Atlantic Economies* (1973); D.K.Fieldhouse, *Economics and Empire, 1830–1914* (1973); Georges Duby, *The Early Growth of the European Economy: Warriors and Peasants from the Seventh to the Twelfth Century* (1974) and Hermann Kellenbenz, *The Rise of the European Economy* (1976).

2. These are the terms used in the recent suggestive book of I. Wallerstein, *The modern world-system. Capitalist agriculture and the origins of the European world-economy in the sixteenth century* (London, New York 1974).

3. J.H.Clapham, 'Economic history as a discipline', in *Encyclopaedia of the social sciences* (New York 1929).

4. For many details of sources and invaluable commentary see Carlo Cipolla, *Before the industrial revolution: European society and economy 1000–1700* (New York 1976), pp. 225–6 and *passim*.

5. See G.N.Clark, *Guide to English commercial statistics 1696–1782.* (London 1939) and C.Wilson, *England's apprenticeship* (London 1965), *passim*.

6. Cipolla, op. cit., pp. 86–7 is the source of these examples.

7. For the problem of interpreting the customs evidence see G.N.Clark, op. cit. For studies of shipping statistics see the various works by Professor Ralph Davis; also L.A.Harper, *The English navigation laws* (New York 1939). Numerous publications by Professor B.H.Slicher van Bath in the series of monographs of the Department of Agrarian History at Wageningen University, the Netherlands, throw light on the methods of extracting evidence about agricultural productivity from figures of seed sown and crops harvested. For an excellent bibliography and exploration of the various types of quantitative evidence see Cipolla, op. cit., especially pp. 228–314.

8. E.J.Hamilton, *American treasure and the price revolution in Spain, 1501–1650* (Cambridge, Massachusetts 1934).

9. It is interesting to note that the 1650s and the 1690s stand out as decades of economic disaster in the data for almost every country represented below, a coincidence that strongly supports a climatic interpretation. See the recent remarks of H.Lamb, 'The development of climate, man's history and the future', Inaugural lecture, University of East Anglia,

1975; and J.D.Post, 'Meteorological historiography', *Journal of Interdisciplinary History*, 3 (1973), pp. 721–32.

CHAPTER 1 ITALY

1. The principal source for Tables 1.1 and 1.2 and for Figure 1.1 is K.J.Beloch, *Bevölkerungsgeschichte Italiens* (3 vols.) (Berlin 1937–61), supplemented by my own research.
2. Taken from R.Mols, 'Population in Europe', in C.M.Cipolla (ed) *The Fontana Economic History of Europe,* (London 1974), II pp. 49–50.
3. The sources for Figure 1.2 are as follows: D.Beltrami, *Storia della popolazione di Venezia dalla fine del secolo XVI alla caduta della repubblica* (Padua 1954), p. 144; A.Bellettini, *La popolazione di Bologna dal secolo XV all' unificazione italiana* (Bologna 1961), pp. 88–96; A.Zuccagni Orlandini, *Ricerche statistiche sul granducato di Toscana* (Florence 1848), I, pp. 419–473; O.Casagrandi, *La popolazione, le nascite, le morti nel duecentennio 1702–1903 a Roma* (Rome 1903), pp. 6–9; C.Petraccone, *Napoli dal '500 all' '800* (Naples 1974), pp. 31 and 149; 'Le nascite a Bari dall'inizio del XVI secolo all'unificazione del regno d'Italia', *Studi di demografia*, 8 (1971), pp. 68–86; F.Maggiore-Perni, *La popolazione di Sicilia e di Palermo dal X al XVIII secolo* (Palermo 1892), pp. 545–7; for Genoa I used the results, as yet unpublished, of my own researches.
4. The sources for Tables 1.4 and 1.5 are as follows: G.Doria, *Uomini e terre di un borgo collinare dal XVI al XVIII secolo* (Milan 1968: about the village of Montaldeo), p. 29; S. Pugliese, *Due secoli di vita agricola. Produzione e valore dei terreni, contratti agrari, salari e prezzi nel Vercellese nei secoli XVIII e XIX* (Turin 1908), pp. 90–4; G.L.Basini, *L'uomo e il pane. Risorse, consumi e carenze alimentari della popolazione modenese nel Cinque e Seicento* (Milan 1970), p. 140; Ministero di Agricoltura, *Monografia della città di Roma e della campagna romana* (Rome 1881), I, pp. 334–7; G.Parenti, *Prezzi e mercato del grano a Siena, 1546–1765* (Florence 1942), p. 118; A.Lepre, *Feudi e masserie. Problemi della società meridionale nel 600 e nel 700* (Naples 1973), pp. 138–9; M.Aymard, 'Rese e profitti agricoli in Sicilia, 1640–1760', *Quaderni storici*, 14 (1970), p. 423; A. De Maddalena, 'Il mondo rurale italiano nel Cinque e Seicento', *Rivista storica italiana*, 76 (1964), p. 425; C. de Cupis, *Le vicende dell' agricoltura e della pastorizia nell' Agro romano* (Rome 1911), p. 341.
5. Source: G.Doria, *op. cit.*, pp. 133–4.
6. Sources: D.Sella, *Commerci e industrie a Venezia nel secolo XVII* (Venice, Rome 1961), pp. 117–18 (Venetian pieces of cloth measured from 34 to 38 metres in length); A. de Maddalena, 'L'industria tessile a Mantova nel '500 e all' inizio del '600', in *Studi in onore di Amintore Fanfani* (Milan 1962), IV, p. 652 (Mantuan pieces measured 32 metres); M.Carmona, 'Sull' economia toscana del '500 e del '600', *Archivio storico italiano*, 120 (1962), pp. 38 and 44; R.Romano, 'A Florence au XVIIe siècle. Industries textiles et conjoncture', *Annales E.S.C.*, 7

(1952), p. 511; B. Caizzi, *Industria e commercio della repubblica veneta nel XVIII secolo* (Milan 1965), pp. 50 and 59.

7. Source: M. Aymard, 'Commerce et production de la soie sicilienne aux XVIe et XVIIe siècles', *Mélanges d'archéologie et d'histoire de l' Ecole française de Rome*, 77 (1965), table 5.

8. Source: R. Romano, 'Documenti e prime considerazioni intorno alla "Balance du Commerce" della Francia dal 1716 al 1780', in *Studi in onore di Armando Sapori* (Milan 1957), II, pp. 1282–92.

9. Source: R. Romano, 'Per una valutazione della flotta mercantile europea alla fine del secolo XVIII', in *Studi in onore di Amintore Fanfani* (Milan 1962), V, pp. 584–6. Sources of other figures on Italian states' merchant fleets: M. Baruchello, *Livorno e il suo porto. Origini, caratteristiche e vicende dei traffici livornesi* (Leghorn 1932), pp. 468–9; M. Calegari, 'Navi e barche a Genova tra il XV e XVI secolo', *Guerra e commercio nell' evoluzione della marina genovese tra XV e XVII secolo* (Genoa 1970), p. 26; E. Grendi, 'Traffico portuale, naviglio mercantile e consolati genovesi nel Cinquecento', *Rivista storica italiana*, 80 (1968), p. 612; R. Romano, 'La marine marchande vénitienne au XVIe siècle', in *Les sources de l'histoire maritime en Europe, du Moyen Age au XVIIIe siècle* (Paris 1962), p. 34; Sella, op. cit., pp. 104–5 and 109; U. Tucci, 'La marina mercantile veneziana nel Settecento', *Bollettino dell' Istituto di storia della società e dello stato veneziano* (1960), II, pp. 169 and 192–3.

10. For Naples cf. L. de Rosa, 'Navi, merci, nazionalità, itinerari in un porto dell'età pre-industriale. Il porto di Napoli nel 1760', in *Studi sul Settecento italiano* (Naples 1968), pp. 331–91. For the movement of the port of Genoa cf. E. Grendi, op. cit., p. 637; E. Grendi, 'I Nordici e il traffico del porto di Genova, 1590–1666', *Rivista storica italiana*, 83 (1971), pp. 65–6; L. Bulferetti, 'Il regresso del commercio di Genova nel periodo napoleonico', in *Studi in onore di Armando Sapori* (Milan 1957), II, p. 1372, and H.-T. Niephaus, *Genuas Seehandel von 1745–1848. Die Entwicklung der Handelsbeziehungen zur Iberischen Halbinsel, zu West- und Nordeuropa sowie den Ueberseegebieten* (Cologne, Vienna 1975), pp. 31–108. One could also provide a similar trend for the port of Livorno (Leghorn), taken from F. Braudel and R. Romano, *Navires et marchandises à l'entrée du port de Livourne, 1547–1611* (Paris 1951); P. Scrosoppi, 'Il porto di Livorno e gli inizi dell'attività inglese nel Mediterraneo', *Bollettino storico livornese*, 1 (1937), p. 380; and G. Sonnino, *Saggio sulle industrie, marina e commercio sotto i primi due Lorenesi, 1737–1790* (Cortona 1909), pp. 128 and 132–3. For Venice the overall movement of port activity is charted by F. C. Lane, 'La marine marchande et le trafic maritime de Venise à travers les siècles', in *Les sources de l'histoire maritime en Europe du Moyen Age au XVIIIe siècle* (Paris 1962), pp. 16, 20–1 and 28–9.

11. The gold doubloon, or double escudo, had 6.20 grams of pure gold; the large silver ducat just under 31 grams of pure silver. Their fluctuating value has been taken from: F. Argelati, *De monetis Italiae variorum illustrium virorum dissertationes* (Milan 1750), II, *passim*; C. M. Cipolla, *Mouvements monétaires dans l'état de Milan (1580–1700)* (Paris 1952),

pp. 65–7; J.G. da Silva, *Banque et crédit en Italie au XVIIᵉ siècle* (Paris 1969), I, pp. 342–3; A. de Maddalena, *Prezzi e aspetti di mercato in Milano durante il secolo XVII* (Milan 1949), pp. 149–53.

12. Source for Figure 1.8 and Table 1.7: G.Felloni, *Gli investimenti finanziari genovesi in Europa tra il Seicento e la Restaurazione* (Milan 1971), pp. 32–54, 345 and 434.

13. Sources: L.Bianchini, *Della storia delle finanze del regno di Napoli* (Naples 1835), III, p. 293; G. Felloni, op. cit., pp. 112–13, 144, 167, 184–5, 196, 208–9, 287, 301 and 328–30. For earlier periods we have only the highly suspect figures (or rather, guesses) of foreign ambassadors. The 'guesstimates' of Venetian ambassadors, for what they are worth, are printed in F.Pino-Branca, *La vita economica degli stati italiani nei secoli XVI, XVII e XVIII secondo le relazioni degli ambasciatori veneti* (Catania 1938).

14. Source: G.Parenti, *Prime ricerche sulla rivoluzione dei prezzi in Firenze* (Florence 1939), appendix 1.

15. Sources for Figures 1.9 and 10: for Genoa – G. Calò, *Indagine sulla dinamica dei prezzi in Genova durante il secolo XVII* (Genoa 1958) and M. Carrara-Cagni, *I prezzi sul mercato di Genova nel secolo XVIII* (Genoa 1958); for Modena – G.L.Basini, *L'uomo e il pane* (Milan 1970), pp. 155–6; for Naples – N.F.Faraglia, *Storia dei prezzi in Napoli dal 1131 al 1860* (Naples 1878), pp. 211–12 and 296–8, and R.Romano, *Prezzi, salari e servizi a Napoli nel secolo XVIII* (Milan 1965); for Siena – G.Parenti, *Prezzi e mercato del grano a Siena, 1546–1765* (Florence 1942), pp. 27–8. Long price series have also been produced for Bassano (G.Lombardini, *Pane e denaro a Bassano tra il 1501 ed il 1799* (Venice 1963) pp. 58–65), for Pavia (D.Zanetti, *Problemi alimentari di una economia preindustriale* (Turin 1964) pp. 155–9), for Catania (A.Petino, 'Primi assaggi sulla "rivoluzione dei prezzi" in Sicilia', in *Studi in onore di Gino Luzzatto* (Milan 1950), II, pp. 207–9); and for many other places too numerous to mention.

16. Sources: Monferrat – G.Doria, *Uomini e terre*, p. 427; Vercellese – S.Pugliese, *Due secoli di vita agricola … nel Vercellese* (Turin 1908), appendix, pp. 23–8; Milan – D.Sella, *Salari e lavoro nell' edilizia lombarda durante il secolo XVII* (Pavia 1968), pp. 94, 103–4 and 106–10, and A. de Maddalena, *Prezzi e mercedi a Milano dal 1701 al 1860* (Milan 1974), p. 419; Modena – G.L.Basini, *L'uomo e il pane* (Milan 1970), p. 169; Genoa – G.Sivori, 'I salari della manodopera edilizia a Genova nel secolo XVII' (unpublished manuscript study; I am very grateful to Dr Sivori for permission to use her material); Florence–Parenti, op. cit., pp. 201 and 205–6; Naples – G.Coniglio, 'La rivoluzione dei prezzi nella città di Napoli nei secoli XVI et XVII', in *Atti della riunione scientifica della Società italiana di statistica* (Rome 1950), pp. 234–5, and R. Romano, op. cit., pp. 49–52. Other series of wages are printed in A.Fanfani, *Storia del lavoro in Italia dalla fine del secolo XV agli inizi del XVIII* (Milan 1959), pp. 311–46, and L. del Pane, *Storia del lavoro in Italia dagli inizi del secolo XVIII al 1815* (Milan 1958), pp. 200–19.

17. Sources in notes 15 and 16 above; cf. also G.Vigo, 'Real wages of the

working class in Italy: building workers' wages (14th to 18th century)',
Journal of European Economic History, 3 (1974), pp. 396–9.

18. The principal sources for the percentages of nobility are as follows:
Genoa – M. Nicora, 'La nobiltà genovese dal 1528 al 1700', in
Miscellanea storica ligure, II (1961), pp. 270–1, and G. Felloni, *Gli
investimenti finanziari genovesi* (Milan 1971), p. 473; Venice –
D. Beltrami, *Forze di lavoro e proprietà fondiaria nelle campagne venete
dei secoli XVII e XVIII* (Venice, Rome 1961), p. 41; Florence –
R. B. Lithfield, 'Caratteristiche demografiche delle famiglie patrizie
fiorentine dal sedicesimo al diciannovesimo secolo', in *Saggi di
demografia storica,* II (1969), p. 21; Piedmont–del Pane, op. cit., p. 119,
and M. Ricciarda Duglio, 'Alfabetismo e società a Torino nel secolo
XVIII', in *Quaderni Storici,* 17 (1971), p. 504; Naples – C. Petraccone,
Napoli dal '500 all' '800 (Naples 1974), pp. 64–5; Castellamare di Stabia
– G. De Meo, *Saggi di statistica economica e demografica sull' Italia
meridionale nei secoli XVII e XVIII* (Rome 1962), p. 92; Bronte –
G. Lo Giudice, *Comunità rurali della Sicilia moderna. Bronte
(1747–1853)* (Catania 1969), pp. 86–8.

19. Source: K. J. Beloch, *Bevölkerungsgeschichte Italiens* (Berlin and Leipzig
1937), I, pp. 73–84.

20. Sources: for Piedmont: L. Einaudi, *La Finanza sabauda all' aprirsi del
secolo XVIII e durante la guerra di successione spagnuola* (Turin 1908),
p. 64; G. Prato, *La vita economica in Piemonte* (Turin 1908), pp. 62 and
187. For Lombardy: S. Pugliese, *Condizioni economiche e finanziarie
della Lombardia* (Turin 1924), pp. 72–3. For Milan: M. Romani, 'Note
sul patrimonio edilizio milanese intorno alla meta del Settecento', in
Studi in onore di Armando Sapori (Milan 1957), II, p. 1311. For the
Veneto: D. Beltrami, *Forze di lavoro e proprietà fondiaria* (Venice, Rome
1961), pp. 123 and 142–5. For the Bolognese: R. Zangheri, *Prime
ricerche sulla distribuzione della proprietà fondiaria nella pianura
bolognese (1789–1835)* (Bologna 1957), pp. 87 and 91. For Ravenna:
G. Porisini, *La proprietà terriera nel commune di Ravenna dalla metà del
secolo XVI ai giorni nostri* (Milan 1963), pp. 23, 27, 31, 35 and 39. For
the Roman plain: M. Raffaeli Cammarota, '1770: la divisione della
proprietà terriera nell' agro romano', *Clio* (1971), 2, pp. 303–28. For
Calopezzati: F. Assante, 'Calopezzati: proprietà fondiaria e classi rurali
in un commune della Calabria (1740–1886)', *Annali dell' Istituto di storia
economica e sociale dell' Università di Napoli,* 4 (1965), p. 153.

21. Sources: L. de Rosa, *Studi sugli arrendamenti del regno di Napoli. Aspetti
della distribuzione della ricchezza mobiliare nel Mezzogiorno con-
tinentale, 1649–1806* (Naples 1958), pp. 266–331; L. Einaudi, *La finanza
sabauda all' aprirsi del secolo XVIII* (Turin 1908), p. 273; G. Felloni, *Gli
investimenti finanziari genovesi* (Milan 1971), pp. 114–15, 145, 151, 176
and 334.

22. Sources: Genoa – my researches and E. Grendi, *Introduzione alla storia
moderna della repubblica di Genova* (Genoa 1973), pp. 76–7; Modena –
G. L. Basini, *L'uomo e il pane. Risorse, consumi e carenze alimentari della
popolazione modenese nel Cinque e Seicento* (Milan 1970), p. 81; Milan –

C.M.Cipolla, *Storia economica dell' Europa pre-industriale* (Bologna 1974), p. 38; Venice – D.Beltrami, *Storia della popolazione di Venezia dalla fine del secolo XVI alla caduta della repubblica* (Padua 1954), p. 204; Piedmont – G.Prato, 'Censimenti e popolazione in Piemonte nei secoli XVI, XVII e XVIII', *Rivista italiana di sociologia*, 10 (1906), pp. 367–9, and *La vita economica in Piemonte a mezzo il secolo XVIII* (Turin 1908), pp. 330–1; Bologna – N.La Marca, *Saggio di una ricerca storico-economica sull' industria e l' artigianato a Roma dal 1750 al 1849* (Padua 1969), p. 21, and A. Bellettini, *La popolazione di Bologna dal secolo XV all' unificazione italiana* (Bologna 1961), p. 74.

CHAPTER 2 SPAIN

1. Sources: J. Nadal, *La población española, siglos XVI a XX* (Barcelona 1966), chapters 2 and 3; A.Domínguez Ortiz, *The Golden Age of Spain, 1516–1659* (London 1971), pp. 173–6; J.Vicens Vives (ed.), *Historia de España y America social y económica*, 2nd ed. (Madrid 1971), III, pp. 3–23 and 207–22; F.Ruíz Martín, 'La población española al comienzo de los tiempos modernos', *Cuadernos de Historia*, I (1968), pp. 189–202; A. Domínguez Ortiz, *La sociedad española en el siglo XVIII* (Madrid 1955), chapter 1; M.Livi-Bacci, 'Fertility and nuptuality changes in Spain from the late 18th to the early 20th century', *Population Studies*, 22 (1968), pp. 83–102 and 211–34; E. Fernández de Pinedo, *Crecimiento económico y transformaciones sociales del País Vasco, 1100–1850* (Madrid 1974), pp. 20 and 87.

2. D.R.Ringrose, 'The impact of a new capital city: Madrid, Toledo and New Castile, 1560–1660', *Journal of Economic History*, 33 (1973), pp. 761–91.

3. Sources: Livi-Bacci, op. cit.; A. Dominguez Ortiz, *La sociedad española en el siglo XVIII*, pp. 60ff.

4. From M.Weisser, 'The decline of Castile revisited: the case of Toledo', *Journal of European Economic History*, 2 (1973), p. 622.

5. From J.G.Casey, 'Moriscos and the depopulation of Valencia', *Past and Present*, 50 (1971), p. 28.

6. Sources: Simancas – B.Bennassar, *Valladolid au siècle d'Or. Une ville de Castille et sa campagne au XVIe siècle* (Paris, The Hague 1967), p. 200; Catalonia– P.Vilar, *La Catalogne dans l'Espagne moderne* (Paris 1964), III, appendix 84.

7. M.del Carmen González Muñoz, *La población de Talavera de la Reina (siglos XVI–XX)*. *Estudio socio-demográfico* (Toledo 1974), pp. 109, 196 and 281. Compare the findings of P.Laslett and K.Oosterveen, 'Long-term trends in bastardy in England, 1561–1960', *Population Studies*, 27 (1973); D.Levine and K.Wrightson, 'The social context of illegitimacy in early modern England', *Journal of Interdisciplinary History*, 6 (1976).

8. Sources: P.Ponsot, 'En Andalousie occidentale. Les fluctuations de la production du blé sous l'Ancien Régime', in J.Goy and E.Le Roy Ladurie (eds), *Les fluctuations du produit de la dîme. Conjoncture décimale et domaniale de la fin du Moyen Age au 18e siècle* (Paris 1972), graph 46;

M. Weisser, *Peasants of the Montes. The roots of rural rebellion in Spain* (Chicago 1976), p. 68. For some further series see G. Anes Alvárez and J. P. Le Flem, 'Las crisis del siglo XVII: producctión agricola, precios e ingresos en tierras de Segovia', *Moneda y Crédito*, 93 (1965).

9. Spain's total corn production was thus 88.5 million bushels or about 11 million quarters; this should be compared with the 18 or so million quarters produced by England at the same period (cf. Table 5.7 below). Figures from the *Censo de Frutos y Manufacturas* of 1797 in J.Vicens Vives (ed.), *Historia de España y America social y económica*, 2nd ed. (Madrid 1971), IV, p. 131.

10. Source: J.P.Le Flem, 'Las cuentas de la Mesta (1510–1709)', *Moneda y Crédito*, 121 (1972), pp. 23–104, and J.Klein, *The Mesta*, 2nd ed. (Washington 1964).

11. Source: F.Ruiz Martín, 'Un testimonio literario sobre las manufacturas de panos en Segovia por 1625', in *Homenaje al Profesor Alarcos* (Valladolid 1967), II, pp. 1–21.

12. Source: H. and P.Chaunu, *Seville et l'Atlantique, 1504–1650,* (Paris 1957), VII, 50–1. For serious criticisms of some of the foundations upon which this enormous study is built cf. E. Otte in *Moneda y Crédito*, 88 (1960) and W.Brulez in *Revue belge de philologie et d'histoire*, 42 (1964), pp. 568–92.

13. Table from Vicens Vives, op. cit., III, p. 282.

14. Source: Vicens Vives, op. cit., IV, p. 157, based on the same source (French) as Figure 4.17 and Table 5.6.

15. Source: ibid., p. 153. For a little information on the mules and carts that carried this trade cf. D.R.Ringrose, 'The government and the carters in Spain, 1476–1700', *Economic History Review*, 22 (1969), pp. 45–57; and J.Tudela, 'La cabaña real de carreteros', in *Homenaje a Don Ramon Carande y Tovar*, (Madrid 1963), I, pp. 155–75.

16. E.J.Hamilton, *American Treasure and the Price Revolution in Spain, 1501–1650* (Cambridge, Massachusetts 1934), p. 35.

17. But see M. Morineau, 'Des métaux précieux americains au XVIIe et XVIIIe siècles et de leur influence', *Bulletin de la Société d'Histoire Moderne*, 1976, pp. 17–33 (e.g. graph at p. 21).

18. Source: Vicens Vives, op. cit., III, p. 47.

19. Sources: A.Domínguez Ortiz, *Política y hacienda de Felipe IV* (Madrid 1960), *passim*; F.Ruiz Martín, 'Las finanzas españolas durante el reinado de Felipe II', *Cuadernos de Historia*, 2 (1968), pp. 109–73; A.Castillo, 'Los juros de Castilla: apogeo y fin de un instrumento de crédito', *Hispania*, 23 (1963), pp. 43–70.

20. Source: G.Parker, 'War and economic change: the economic costs of the Dutch Revolt', in J.M.Winter (ed.), *War and economic development* (Cambridge 1975), p. 56, with extra data from H.Pohl, 'Zur Bedeutung Antwerpens als Kreditplatz im beginnenden 17. Jahrhundert', in *Die Stadt in der europäischen Geschichte. Festschrift Edith Ennen* (Bonn 1972), pp. 667–86.

21. Source: Kamen, *The War of Succession in Spain* (London 1969), p. 23.

22. Source: J.Vicens Vives, *An economic history of Spain* (Princeton 1969),

pp. 378 and 380.
23. Source for Figures 2.15, 2.16 and 2.17: E.J.Hamilton, *War and prices in Spain, 1650–1800* (Cambridge, Massachusetts 1947), pp. 176, 184 and 215.
24. Source: Nadal, op. cit., p. 44.
25. Information from: Domínguez Ortiz, *La sociedad española en el siglo XVIII, passim*; Domínguez Ortiz, *La sociedad española en el siglo XVII*, (Madrid 1970), II, *passim*; A.Molinié-Bertrand, 'Le clergé du royaume de Castille à la fin du XVIe siècle. Approche cartographique', *Revue d'histoire économique et sociale*, 51 (1973), pp. 5–53; F.Ruiz Martín, 'Demografía eclesiástica hasta el siglo XIX', in *Diccionario de Historia Eclesiástica de España*, (Madrid 1972), I, pp. 682–733.
26. Q.Aldea, 'La economía de las iglesias locales en la Edad Media y Moderna', *Atti della VI settimana di studi del Istituto Internazionale di Storia Economica Francesco Datini* (forthcoming).
27. Information from J.H.Elliott, *Imperial Spain, 1469–1716* (London 1963), p. 101, and the memorial of Pedro Nuñez de Salcedo printed in *Boletín de la Real Academia de la Historia*, 73 (1918), pp. 470–91.
28. N.Salomon, *Les campagnes de la Nouvelle Castille à la fin du XVIe siècle d'après les 'Relaciones topográficas'* (Paris 1964), pp. 257–79; and M.Livi-Bacci, op. cit. Source for Figure 2.19: R.Herr, *The eighteenth-century revolution in Spain* (Princeton 1958), map 1.

CHAPTER 3 PORTUGAL

1. F.Mauro, *Le Portugal et l'Atlantique au XVIIe siècle (1570–1670). Etude économique* (Paris 1960), pp. 296–7 and 333.
2. ibid., p. 379.
3. ibid., pp. 518–19.
4. V. Rau, 'Rumos e vicissitudes do comercio do sal português nos séculos XIV a XVIII', *Revista da Faculdade de Letras de Lisboa*, 3rd series 7 (1963), pp. 1–27.
5. V.Magalhães Godinho, *L'économie de l'Empire portugais aux XVe et XVIe siècles* (Paris 1969), pp. 701–5. After 1500 the 'brazil wood' used for dye-making began to arrive in increasing quantities from Brazil, giving its name to the 'Land of the Holy Cross' discovered and christened by Cabral.
6. P.Chaunu, *Conquête et exploitation des nouveaux mondes (XVIe siècle)* (Paris 1969), pp. 321–3.
7. Mauro, op. cit., p. 516.
8. Lisbon, Arquivo Nacional da Torre do Tombo, *Ministerio do Reino*, maço 397 (cited by J.de Macedo, *A situação económica no tempo de Pombal* (Porto 1951), pp. 293–4).
9. V.Rau, *Subsídios para o estudo do movimento dos portos de Faro e Lisboa durante o século XVII* (Lisbon 1954), pp. 256–9.
10. H.E.S.Fisher, *The Portugal trade. A study of Anglo-Portuguese commerce, 1700–1770* (London 1971), p. 15, based on the ledgers of the English customs and excise office.

11. Mauro, op. cit., pp. 494–5, and Rau, op. cit., *passim.*
12. C.R.Boxer, *The Portuguese seaborne empire, 1415–1825* (London 1969), p. 379.
13. See Magalhães Godinho, op. cit., p. 432.
14. Mauro, op. cit., p. 522.
15. V.Magalhães Godinho, *Prix et monnaie au Portugal 1750–1850* (Paris 1955), pp. 202–3.
16. Mauro, op. cit., pp. 520–2.
17. V.Magalhães Godinho, *Prix et monnaie,* pp. 76–7 and 81–3.

CHAPTER 4 LOW COUNTRIES

1. Sources: A.Cosemans, *De bevolking van Brabant in de XVIIe en XVIIIe eeuw* (Brussels 1939); J.Cuvelier, *Les dénombrements de foyers en Brabant (XIVe–XVIe siècle)* (Brussels 1912); M.A.Arnould, *Les dénombrements de foyers dans le comté de Hainaut (XIVe–XVIe siècle)* (Brussels 1956); J.Grob and J.Vannérus, *Dénombrements des feux des duché de Luxembourg et comté de Chiny* (Brussels 1921), I; J.de Smet, 'Dénombrements des foyers en Flandre en 1469', *Bulletin de la Commission Royale d'Histoire,* 99 (1935), pp. 105–50. J.A.Faber, H.K.Roessingh, B.H.Slicher van Bath, A.M.van der Woude and H.J.van Xanten, 'Population changes and economic developments in the Netherlands: a historical survey', *A.A.G.Bijdragen,* 12 (1965), pp. 47–110; J.A. van Houtte, *Economische en sociale geschiedenis van de Lage Landen* (Zeist, Antwerp 1964); J.de Vries, *The Dutch rural economy 1500–1700* (New Haven, London 1974); E.Hélin *La démographie de Liège aux XVIIe et XVIIIe siècles* (Brussels 1963).
2. A.M. van der Woude, 'Variations in the size and structure of the household in the United Provinces of the Netherlands in the 17th and 18th century', in P.Laslett and R.Wall (eds), *Household and Family in Past Time* (Cambridge 1972), pp. 299–318.
3. Sources: the studies of Faber and collaborators, van Houtte and de Vries used for Table 4.1, plus: R. Boumans, 'Le dépeuplement d'Anvers 1575–1600', *Revue du Nord,* 29 (1947), pp. 181–93; F.Blockmans, 'De bevolkingscijfers', in *Antwerpen in de XVIIIe eeuw* (Antwerp 1952), pp. 395–412; J.Verbeemen, 'Bruxelles en 1755', *Bijdragen tot de Geschiedenis,* 45 (1962), pp. 203–33; 46 (1963), pp. 65–133; J.Verbeemen, 'L'évolution démographique d'une ville wallonne: Mons (1283–1766)', *L'Intermédiaire des généalogistes,* 55 (1955), pp. 23–5.
4. From A.Wyffels, 'De omvang en de evolutie van het Brugse bevolkingscijfer in de XVIIe en XVIIIe eeuw', *Revue belge de philologie et d'histoire,* 36 (1958), pp. 1243–74; H. van Werveke, *'De curve van het Gentse bevolkingscijfer in de 17e en 18e eeuw* (Brussels 1948); J. de Brouwer, *Demografische evolutie van het Land van Aalst 1570–1800* (Brussels 1968); A. de Vos, 'Dertig jaar bevolkingsevolutie te Evergem (1571–1601), *Handelingen der Maatschappij voor Geschiedenis en Oudheidkunde te Gent,* 14 (1960), pp. 117–29; A. de Vos, 'De' bevolkingsevolutie van Evergem ... 17e en 18e eeuw', *Appeltjes van het Meetjesland,* 8 (1957), pp. 5–76; J.Verbeemen, 'De demografische

evolutie van Mechelen (1370–1800)', *Handelingen van de Koninklijke Kring voor Oudheidkunde, Letteren en Kunst van Mechelen*, 57 (1953), pp. 63–97.

5. From de Vries, op. cit., p. 83.

6. For two examples from the end of the eighteenth century, see J. Verbeemen, 'Mechelen in 1796', *Handelingen van de Koninklijke Kring voor Oudheidkunde, Letteren en Kunst van Mechelen*, 58 (1954), pp. 135–79, and P. Deprez, 'De bevolking van Evergem, Knesselare, Ronsele en Zomergem in het licht van de volkstellingen van 1796/1798', in *Vijf bijdragen tot lokale demografie, 17e–19e eeuw* (Brussels 1963), pp. 151–93.

7. de Vries, op. cit., p. 162. In 1803 Dutch cheese exports totalled 18.7 million pounds (ibid., p. 168); B. H. Slicher van Bath, 'Yield ratios, 810–1820', *A.A.G. Bijdragen*, 10 (1963), pp. 3–264.

8. From B. H. Slicher van Bath, *Een samenleving onder spanning. Geschiedenis van het platteland van Overijssel* (Assen 1957).

9. A. M. van der Woude, *Het Noorderkwartier* (Wageningen; A. A. G. Bijdragen 1972), III, p. 811 (on whales); M. Simon Thomas, *Onze IJslandsvaarders in de 17e en 18e eeuw* (Amsterdam 1935) (on cod-fishing); H. Wätjen, 'Zur Statistik der Holländischen Heringsfischerei im 17. und 18. Jahrhundert', *Hansische Geschichtsblätter*, 16 (1910), pp. 129–85, and H. A. H. Kranenburg, *De zeevisserij van Holland in den tijd der Republiek* (Paris, Amsterdam 1946) (on herring).

10. E. Coornaert, *Un centre industriel d'autrefois. La draperie-sayetterie d'Hondschoote (XVIe–XVIIIe siècles)* (Paris 1930), based on tables at end.

11. From J. Bastin, 'De Gentse lijnwaadmarkt en linnenhandel in de 17e eeuw', *Handelingen der Maatschappij voor Geschiedenis en Oudheidkunde te Gent*, 21 (1967), pp. 131–62.

12. A total of 9859 men were registered as new burgesses in Leiden over this period; many of them probably came with their families (who did not have to be registered) and there were probably many more who came and never paid to be registered.

13. N. W. Posthumus, *De Geschiedenis van de Leidsche Lakenindustrie* (The Hague 1908–39), 3 vols.

14. P. Moureaux, *Les comptes d'une société charbonnière à la fin de l'Ancien Régime* (Brussels 1969).

15. H. Hasquin, *Une mutation: le 'pays de Charleroi' aux XVIIe et XVIIIe siècles* (Brussels 1971).

16. Based on W. Brulez, 'Le commerce international des Pays-Bas au XVIe siècle: essai d'appréciation quantitative', *Revue belge de philologie et d'histoire*, 46 (1968), pp. 1205–21; W. Brulez, 'De economische kaart van de Nederlanden in de 16e eeuw volgens Guicciardini', *Tijdschrift voor Geschiedenis*, 83 (1970), pp. 352–7. W. Brulez, 'De handelsbalans der Nederlanden in het midden van de 16e eeuw', *Bijdragen voor de Geschiedenis der Nederlanden*, 21 (1966–7), pp. 278–310.

17. J. A. Goris, *Etude sur les colonies marchandes méridionales (Portugais, Espagnols, Italiens) à Anvers de 1488 à 1567* (Louvain 1925), pp. 330–4.

18. H. van der Wee, *The growth of the Antwerp market* (The Hague 1963), I, 514–17.

19. From M. Morineau, 'La balance du commerce Franco-Néerlandais et le resserrement économique des Provinces-Unies du XVIIIe siècle', *Economische-Historisch Jaarboek*, 30 (1965), pp. 170–235.

20. H. Pavelka, 'Englands Wirtschaftsbeziehungen zu den Habsburgischen Niederlanden im 18. Jahrhundert', in *Mélanges offerts à G. Jacquemyns* (Brussels 1968), pp. 531–49.

21. The trend for Amsterdam, shown in Figure 4.8, in fact follows closely the number of ships which we know to have used the port – around 3000 every year 1660–90, 3200 annually 1690–1710, falling steadily to 2300 annually in the 1740s. Cf. W. F. H. Oldewelt, 'De scheepvaartstatistiek van Amsterdam in de 17e en 18e eeuw', *Jaarboek Amstelodamum*, 45 (1953), pp. 114–51.

22. From H. E. Becht, *Statistische gegevens betreffende den handelsomzet van de Republiek der Vereenigde Nederlanden gedurende de 17e eeuw (1579–1715)* (The Hague 1908); J. C. Westermann, 'Statistische gegevens over den handel van Amsterdam in de 17e eeuw', *Tijdschrift voor Geschiedenis*, 61 (1948), pp. 3–15; J. de Vries, *De economische achteruitgang der Republiek in de 18e eeuw* (Amsterdam 1959).

23. From W. S. Unger, 'De Sonttabellen', *Tijdschrift voor Geschiedenis*, 41 (1926), pp. 137–55, and 71 (1958), pp. 147–205; A. E. Christensen, *Dutch trade to the Baltic about 1600* (Copenhagen, The Hague 1941); J. A. Faber, 'Het probleem van de dalende graanaanvoer uit de Oostzeelanden in de 2e helft van de 17e eeuw', *A.A.G. Bijdragen*, 9 (1963), pp. 3–28.

24. W. Vogel, 'Beiträge zur Statistik der deutschen Seeschiffahrt im 17. und 18. Jahrhundert', *Hansische Geschichtsblätter*, 58 (1932), pp. 78–151.

25. D. S. van Zuiden, *Bijdrage tot de kennis van de Hollandsch-Russische relaties in de 16e–18e eeuw* (Amsterdam 1911); S. van Brakel, 'Statistische en andere gegevens betreffende onze handel en scheepvaart op Rusland gedurende de 18e eeuw', *Bijdragen en Mededelingen van het Historisch Genootschap*, 34 (1913), pp. 350–404.

26. From W. S. Unger, 'Bijdragen tot de geschiedenis van de Nederlandse slavenhandel', *Economisch-Historisch Jaarboek*, 28 (1961), pp. 3–148.

27. From V. Janssens, *Het geldwezen der Oostenrijkse Nederlanden* (Brussels 1957), pp. 300–5.

28. From van der Wee, op. cit., p. 527; R. van Uytven, *Stadsfinanciën en stadseconomie te Leuven van de XIIe tot het einde der XVIe eeuw* (Brussels 1961), pp. 199–200.

29. Posthumus, op. cit.; W. F. H. Oldewelt, 'Twee eeuwen Amsterdamse faillissementen en het verloop van de conjunctuur (1636 tot 1838)', *Tijdschrift voor Geschiedenis*, 75 (1962), pp. 421–35.

30. From N. W. Posthumus, *Inquiry into the history of prices in Holland* (Leiden 1946–65), 2 vols; C. Verlinden, J. Craeybeckx and collaborators, *Dokumenten voor de Geschiedenis van prijzen en lonen in Vlaanderen en Brabant, XVe–XVIIIe eeuw* (Bruges 1959–73), 4 vols.

31. From P. Deprez, 'De Boeren' in *Flandria Nostra* (Brussels 1957), I,

p. 147; van der Wee, op. cit., pp. 479–82.

32. From E. Scholliers, 'Un indice du loyer: les loyers anversois de 1500 à 1873', in *Studi in onore di Amintore Fanfani* (Milan 1962), V, pp. 593–617; D. van Ryssel, *De Gentse huishuren tussen 1500 en 1795. Bijdrage tot de kennis van de konjunktuur van de stad* (Brussels 1967).

33. From Verlinden and collaborators, op. cit., II, pp. 354–461 and 1057–230; van der Wee, op. cit., pp. 460–3; M. van de Mosselaer, 'De levensstandaard van de Arbeiders in de XVIe eeuw. Een lonenstudie voor Mechelen' (unpublished M A thesis – *licentieverhandeling* – University of Louvain 1968).

34. H.K. Roessingh, 'Beroep en bedrijf op de Veluwe in het midden van de 18e eeuw', *A.A.G.Bijdragen*, 13 (1965), pp. 181–274; J. Verbeemen, 'Bruxelles en 1755', *Bijdragen tot de Geschiedenis*, 45 (1962), pp. 203–33; J. Verbeemen, 'Antwerpen in 1755', *Bijdragen tot de Geschiedenis*, 40 (1957), pp. 27–63; Slicher van Bath, op. cit., pp. 154–64; J. Verbeemen, 'Mechelen in 1796', *Handelingen van de Koninklijke Kring voor Oudheidkunde, Letteren en Kunst van Mechelen*, 58 (1954), pp. 135–79.

35. L. Vanaverbeke, *Peiling naar de bezitsstruktuur van de Gentse bevolking omstreeks 1738* (Brussels 1969), I.

36. P. Deprez, 'De boeren', in *Flandria Nostra* (Brussels 1957), I, pp. 123–65; Slicher van Bath, op. cit., p. 631; L. van Buyten, 'Grondbezit en grondwaarde in Brabant en Mechelen, volgens de onteigeningen voor de aanleg der verkeerswegen in de 18e eeuw', *Bijdragen voor de Geschiedenis der Nederlanden*, 18 (1963), pp. 91–124; I. Delatte, *Les classes rurales dans la principauté de Liège au XVIIIe siècle* (Paris, Liège 1945), p. 70.

37. J. Cuvelier, *Les dénombrements de foyers en Brabant (XIVe–XVIe siècles)* (Brussels 1912); J. Verbeemen, 'Antwerpen in 1755' and 'Bruxelles en 1755' (cf. note 36); van Uytven, op. cit.; H.J. van Xanten and A.M. van der Woude, 'Het hoofdgeld en de bevolking van de Meijerij van 's Hertogenbosch omstreeks 1700', *A.A.G.Bijdragen*, 13 (1965), pp. 3–96; Slicher van Bath, op. cit., p. 334.

38. E. Scholliers, *Loonarbeid en honger: de levensstandaard in de XVe en XVIe eeuw te Antwerpen* (Antwerp 1960), pp. 158–67; E. Engel, *Die Lebenskosten belgischer Arbeiter familien früher und jetzt* (Dresden 1895); *Annuaire statistique de poche* (Royaume de Belgique, Ministère des affaires économiques, 1970), p. 170.

CHAPTER 5 BRITISH ISLES

1. J. Cornwall, 'English population in the early 16th century', *Economic History Review*, 23 (1970); J. Rickman, 'Estimated population of England and Wales', *Great Britain: Population enumeration abstract*, 22 (1843); P. Deane and W.A. Cole, *British Economic Growth, 1688–1959* (Cambridge 1963), pp. 5–6, 288. Cornwall's figures, which refer only to England, have been increased by 10 per cent to make them comparable with the rest of the series which relates to England and Wales. The population of Wales alone has been estimated at about 225,000 in 1550, about 340,000 in 1670, and about 500,000 in 1801. Cf. L. Owen, 'The population of Wales in the 16th and 17th centuries', *Transactions of the*

Honourable Society of Cymmrodorion, Session 1959.

2. Rickman, op. cit., and Deane and Cole, op. cit., p. 288.

3. From the forthcoming book of R.S.Schofield and E.A.Wrigley, *Population trends in early modern England: an aggregative analysis from the mid-16th to the early 19th century* (London, forthcoming). It should be understood that not all the 404 parishes were registering continuously throughout the three centuries. The methods used to identify and correct the deficiencies will be described in the book. The effect of some of the corrective measures is reflected in the graph but others have yet to be incorporated.

4. Deane and Cole, op. cit., p. 127.

5. C.H.Hull (ed.), *The economic writings of Sir William Petty*, (Cambridge 1899), II, p. 468 and *passim*.

6. Gregory King, *Natural and political observations and conclusions upon the state and condition of England* (1696) and C.Davenant, *An estimate of the live stock of England and Wales in 1688*, adapted by Lord Ernle, *English farming past and present*, 6th ed. (London 1961), pp. 501–3.

7. See J. Thirsk (ed.), *The agrarian history of England and Wales* (Cambridge 1967), IV, p. 4.

8. Deane and Cole, op. cit., p. 72, based on the 'Report of the Select Committee on Waste Lands', *House of Commons Reports*, 9 (1795), pp. 202–3.

9. B.H.Slicher van Bath, 'Yield Ratios, 810–1820', *A.A.G.Bijdragen*, 9 (1963), p. 117. Critics have observed that the base for these ratios is in some cases rather narrow, but used with discretion they provide a useful idea of the orders of magnitude.

10. W.H.R.Curtler, *Enclosure and redistribution of our land* (Oxford 1920), p. 148; Deane and Cole, op. cit., p. 65.

11. Tables 5.8 and 5.9 are taken from Deane and Cole, op. cit., pp. 51 and 78.

12. P.Deane, 'The output of the British Woollen Industry in the 18th century', *Journal of Economic History*, 17 (1957), pp. 211–20.

13. J.U.Nef, *The rise of the British coal industry* (London 1932), p. 20.

14. G.Schanz, *Englische Handelspolitik gegen Ende des Mittelalters* (Leipzig 1881), II, pp. 30–6; A.Friis, *Alderman Cockayne's project and the cloth trade* (Copenhagen, London 1927), p. 421; E.Misselden, *The circle of commerce* (London 1623), pp. 121f. and 128f.; R.Davis, 'English foreign trade, 1660–1700', *Economic History Review,* 7 (1954); L.A.Harper, *The English navigation laws* (New York 1939), p. 305.

15. R.Davis, op. cit.

16. Figure 5.2 and Table 5.14 are taken from Deane and Cole, op. cit., pp. 29 and 46, based in turn upon E.B.Schumpeter, *Overseas trade statistics, 1697–1808* (Oxford 1960), pp. 15–18.

17. R.Davis, 'English foreign trade, 1700–1774', *Economic History Review*, 15 (1962), p. 108.

18. J.D.Gould, *The Great Debasement: currency and the economy in mid-Tudor England* (Oxford 1970), p. 120; F.J.Fisher, 'London's export trade in the early seventeenth century', *Economic History Review*, 3

(1950); B.E.Supple, *Commercial crisis and change in England, 1600–1642* (Cambridge 1959), appendix A.

19. Harper, op. cit., p. 339.
20. R.Davis, *The rise of the English merchant shipping industry* (London 1962), p. 17.
21. The source for Table 5.18 and Figure 5.4 is the same as for Table 5.17.
22. Sir John Sinclair, *History of the Public Revenue of the British Empire*, (London 1789), III, p. 50. For the output of the London Mint, cf. Sir John Craig, *The Mint* (London 1953).
23. E.L.Hargreaves, *The national debt* (London 1930), p. 291.
24. P.G.M.Dickson, *The financial revolution in England 1688–1756* (Oxford 1967), p. 10.
25. J.Sinclair, op. cit., (London 1789), III, p. 61; see C.Wilson, *Anglo-Dutch commerce and finance* (Cambridge 1940).
26. M.P.Ashley, *Financial and commercial policy under the Cromwellian Protectorate*, 2nd ed. (London 1962), p. 48.
27. S.Dowell, *A history of taxes and taxation in England* (London 1888), II, p. 63.
28. W.R.Ward, *The English land tax* (London 1953), pp. 8–9.
29. W.R.Scott, *The constitution and finance of English, Scottish and Irish joint stock companies to 1720* (Cambridge 1910), I, pp. 335–6.
30. ibid., p. 350; Table 5.27 comes from the same source.
31. See Dickson, op. cit., p. 139.
32. L.S.Pressnell, *Country banking in the Industrial Revolution* (Oxford 1956); D.M.Joslin, 'London private bankers 1720–85', *Economic History Review*, 7 (1954); R.E.Cameron, *Banking in the early stages of industrialization* (New York 1967) pp. 60–99 (on Scottish banking).
33. E.H.Phelps Brown and S.V.Hopkins, 'Seven centuries of the prices of consumables, compared with builders' wage rates', *Economica*, 23 (1956). (The index scale is logarithmic, not arithmetical.)
34. J.Thirsk (ed.), *The agrarian history of England and Wales* (Cambridge 1967), IV, pp. 862–3.
35. Based on Gregory King, *Two tracts*, ed. G.E.Barnett (London 1936). There is an interesting analysis of the subsidy rolls of early Tudor England with a view to establishing the 'wealth and social structure' of the country: J.Sheail, 'The distribution of taxable population and wealth in England during the early 16th century', *Institute of British Geographers' Transactions*, 55 (1972), pp. 111–26.
36. P.Laslett and R. Wall, *Household and family in past time* (Cambridge 1972), p. 137.
37. Adapted from Gregory King's *Observations* by Deane and Cole, op. cit., p. 2.
38. G.Donaldson, *Mary Queen of Scots* (London 1974), p. 68, and J.M.Brown, 'Taming the Magnates?', in G.Menzies *The Scottish Nation* (London 1972), pp. 46–59.
39. J.G.Kyd (ed.), *Scottish Population Statistics including Webster's Analysis of Population 1755*, Scottish History Society publication no. 44, third series (Edinburgh 1952); Sir John Sinclair, *Analysis of the*

Statistical Account of Scotland (1825), quoted in R.H.Campbell and J.B.A.Dow (eds), *Source Book of Scottish Economic and Social History* (Oxford 1968), p. 2. I am extremely grateful to Professor Christopher Smout of the Department of Economic History in the University of Edinburgh for his kindness in discussing with me the Scottish historical demography project in his department. The results will be published by Cambridge University Press as M.Flinn (ed.), *Scottish Population History from the Seventeenth Century to the 1930s*.

40. *vide* G.Donaldson, 'Sources for Scottish Agrarian History before the Eighteenth Century', *Agricultural History Review*, 8 (1960), pp. 82–90.

41. T.C.Smout and A.Fenton, 'Scottish Agriculture before the Improvers – an Exploration', *Agricultural History Review*, 13 (1965), p. 76. The 'boll' here = 140 pounds avoirdupois. For bolls and other traditional Scottish units of measurement *vide* J.M.Henderson, *Scottish Reckonings of Time, Money, Weights and Measures*, Historical Association of Scotland publication, new series no. 4 (1926).

42. Figure 5.7 from R. Mitchison, 'The Movements of Scottish Corn Prices in the Seventeenth and Eighteenth Centuries', *Economic History Review*, 2nd Series, 18 (1965), pp. 281 and 284.

43. Historical Manuscripts Commission, *Report on the Manuscripts of the Earl of Mar and Kellie* (London 1904), pp. 70–4.

44. T.C.Smout, 'Lead-mining in Scotland, 1650–1850', in P.L.Payne (ed.), *Studies in Scottish Business History* (London 1967), pp. 103–35.

45. *vide* 'The compt off the deutis resavit at the stapell port of Campheir for the Minister be me David Drummond', printed as Document No. 119 in M.P.Rooseboom, *The Scottish Staple in the Netherlands* (The Hague 1910), pp. CXLII–CXLV. For the general history of the Staple, Rooseboom should be supplemented by J.Davidson and A.Gray, *The Scottish Staple at Veere* (London 1909).

46. R.Douglas, 'Coal-mining in Fife in the second half of the eighteenth century', in G.W.S.Barrow (ed.), *The Scottish Tradition: Essays in honour of Ronald Gordon Cant* (Edinburgh 1974), p. 213.

47. S.G.E.Lythe, 'Scottish Trade with the Baltic 1550–1650', in J.K.Eastham (ed.) *Economic Essays in Commemoration of The Dundee School of Economics 1931–1955* (Dundee 1955), p. 64. For general background to Scottish overseas trade, *vide* S.G.E.Lythe, *The Economy of Scotland 1550–1625* (Edinburgh, London 1960) and T.M.Devine and S.G.E.Lythe, 'The Economy of Scotland under James VI', *Scottish Historical Review*, 50 (1971), p. 101.

48. F.Roberts and I.M.M.Macphail, *Dumbarton Common Good Accounts 1614–1660* (Dumbarton 1972), appendix B, pp. 260–73; L.B.Taylor (ed.), *Aberdeen Shore Work Accounts 1596–1670* (Aberdeen 1972).

49. G.Donaldson (ed.), *Accounts of the Collectors of Thirds of Benefices 1561–1572*, Scottish History Society, publication no. 42, third series (Edinburgh 1949); and D.E.Easson, *Medieval Religious Houses: Scotland* (London 1957).

50. T.C.Smout, *Scottish Trade on the Eve of Union 1660–1707* (Edinburgh, London 1963), appendix 1, Table 1, pp. 282–4.

51. For the major post-1707 statistical series *vide* the statistical appendices to H. Hamilton, *An Economic History of Scotland in the Eighteenth Century* (Oxford 1963).

CHAPTER 6 FRANCE

1. It is worth noting at the outset three recent publications which present valuable data on modern economic history: B.Gille, *Les sources statistiques de l'histoire de France: des Enquêtes du XVIIe siècle à 1870* (Paris 1964); F.Braudel and C.E.Labrousse, *Histoire économique et sociale de la France* (vol. 2 – Paris 1970; vol. 1 – Paris 1976); J. Marczewski (ed.), *Histoire quantitative de l'économie française* (vols 1 and 2 (Paris 1961) and vol. 8 (Paris 1968) contain data relating to our period; future volumes will no doubt contain more).

2. Nicholas Froumenteau, *Le secret des finances de France* (Paris 1581).

3. Source: M.Morineau, *Les faux-semblants d'un démarrage économique: agriculture et démographie en France au XVIIIe siècle* (Paris 1971), pp. 294–5, with several modifications proposed by J. Dupâquier in his review of the book in *Annales E.S.C.*, 27 (1972), pp. 80–4, and by myself, 'Note sur le peuplement de la généralité de Moulins', in *Hommage à Marcel Reinhard* (Paris 1972), pp. 475–503.

4. J.Delumeau (ed.), *Histoire de la Bretagne* (Toulouse 1969), pp. 257–7 for St Aignan (cf. also A. Croix, *Nantes et le pays nantais au XVIe siècle* (Paris 1975), *passim*); F.LeBrun, *Les hommes et la mort en Anjou aux 17e et 18e siècles* (Paris, The Hague 1971), pull-out table, for Le Loroux; J.Ganiage, *Trois villages de l'Ile de France, Etude démographique* (Paris 1963), p. 102, for Le Mesnil; and M. Morineau, *Les faux-semblants*, pull-out table, for Quarouble.

5. Source: C. Higounet (ed.), *Histoire de Bordeaux*, (Bordeaux 1968), V, pull-out graph.

6. The source for Figures 6.6 and 6.7 is P.Charlot and J.Dupâquier, 'Mouvement annuel de la population de la Ville de Paris de 1670 à 1821', *Annales de Démographie Historique*, 3 (1967), pp. 512–14.

7. Source: R.Baehrel, *Une croissance: la Basse Provence rurale (fin du XVIe siècle – 1789)* (Paris 1961), I, p. 648. For the picture around Beauvais cf. P.Goubert, *Beauvais et le Beauvaisis de 1600 à 1730. Contribution à l'histoire sociale de la France au 17e siècle* (Paris 1960), pp. 94 and 112.

8. Data from J.Dupâquier, *La propriété et l'exploitation foncières à la fin de l'Ancien Régime dans le Gâtinais septentrional* (Paris 1956).

9. Source: A.Silbert, 'La production de céréales à Beaune d'après les Dîmes, 16e–18e siècle', in J. Goy and E.Le Roy Ladurie (eds), *Les fluctuations du produit de la Dîme* (Paris, The Hague 1972), pp. 142–3.

10. Source: M.Rouff, *Les mines de charbon en France au 18e siècle: 1744–1791* (Paris 1922), p. 424 (based on Michel and Rénouard, *Histoire d'un centre ouvrier: Anzin* (Paris 1891)).

11. Source: B.Gille, *Les origines de la grande industrie métallurgique en France* (Paris 1947), pp. 168–9.

12. Source: P.Deyon, 'Variations de la production textile aux 16e et 17e siècles', *Annales E.S.C.*, 18 (1963), pp. 948–9; cf. also P. Deyon, *Amiens,*

capitale provinciale: étude sur la société urbaine au 17e siècle (Paris 1967).

13. Source: T.J.Markovitch, 'L'industrie lainière française au début du XVIIIe siècle', *Revue d'histoire économique et sociale*, 46 (1968), pp. 573–4.

14. Sources for figures 6.12 and 6.13: J.Tanguy, 'La production et le commerce des toiles "Bretagne" du 16e au 18e siècle. Premiers résultats', in *Actes du Congrès National des Sociétés Savantes. Rennes 1966, période moderne* (Paris 1969), p. 126; F.Dornic, *L'industrie textile dans le Maine et ses débouchés internationaux, 1650–1815* (Le Mans 1955), p. 218.

15. Source: documents from the Archives Nationales in Paris, published by R.Romano, 'Documenti e prime considerazioni intorno alla "Balance du Commerce" della Francia dal 1716 al 1780', in *Studi in onore di Armando Sapori*, 2 (Milan 1957), p. 1274. It should be noted that the favourable balance takes no account of the rates of currency exchange between France and her neighbours, which were almost always *un*favourable and therefore reduced the value of French exports while increasing the price of her imports.

16. The source for Table 6.5 is the same as for Figure 6.14. The source for Table 6.6 is P. Chaptal, *De l'industrie française* (Paris 1819), I, pp. 150–1, but this author appears to have had access to the same 'Etats de la Balance du Commerce' used by Professor Romano.

17. M.Morineau, *Deux recensements de la marine française de commerce sous le règne de Louis XIV* (forthcoming). R.Romano, 'Per una valutazione della flotta mercantile europee alla fine del secolo XVIII', in *Studi in onore di Amintore Fanfani* (Milan 1962), IV, p. 589. Cf. also Table 7.15 below.

18. Source: F.Spooner, *The international economy and monetary movements in France, 1493–1725* (Cambridge Massachusetts 1972), p. 302.

19. Source for Figure 6.16: Grenoble – H.Hauser (ed.), *Recherches et documents sur l'histoire des prix en France de 1500 à 1800* (Paris 1936), pp. 371–6, based on the annual average price calculated and recorded by the Chambre des Comptes of Dauphiné; Toulouse – G. and G.Frêche, *Les prix des grains, des vins et des légumes à Toulouse, 1486–1868* (Paris 1967), pp. 88–90, based on the *mercuriale* (market prices) of the city (maize, called 'millet d'Espagne' was first quoted on the Toulouse *mercuriale* in 1639 and appeared regularly after 1655); Paris – M.Baulant and J.Meuvret, *Prix des céréales extraits de la mercuriale de Paris* (Paris 1960), I, p. 243; (Paris 1962), II, p. 135.

20. Source: E. Le Roy Ladurie, *Les Paysans de Languedoc* (Paris 1966), I, pp. 823–5. In the polynomial graph, the computer chooses the path through the data points which minimizes the sum of the squares of the distances from the points to the curve (the method of 'least squares'). With this method it is necessary to specify in advance the number of deviations that are to appear in the curve; each increase in the number of deviations improves the accuracy of the curve. In this graph, only nine deviations were used.

21. Sources: M. Baulant, 'Les salaires du bâtiment à Paris (1400–1726)', *Annales E.S.C.*, 29 (1971), pp. 463–84; Y.Durand, 'Recherches sur les

salaires des maçons à Paris au 18e siècle', *Revue d'histoire économique et sociale*, 44 (1966), pp. 468–80.

22. Source: D.Zolla, 'Les variations du revenu et du prix des terres en France au XVIIe et au XVIIIe siècle', *Annales de l'Ecole des Sciences politiques* (année 1893), pp. 299–326, 439–61 and 686–705; (année 1894), pp. 194–216 and 417–32.

23. Source for Figures 6.20 and 6.21: R.Gascon, *Grand commerce et vie urbaine au XVIe siècle*, pp. 402–4.

24. Prepared by the author from the 'Rapport du Comité de Mendicité' to the French Constituent Assembly in 1790. It should be noted that not every *département* applied the same criteria in assessing the level of poverty.

25. Source: J. Dupâquier, 'Structures sociales et cahiers de doléances: l'exemple du Vexin français', *Annales historiques de la révolution française* (année 1968), p. 439.

26. A.Daumard and F.Furet, *Structures et relations sociales à Paris au XVIIIe siècle* (Paris 1961), p. 19.

CHAPTER 7 GERMANY

(For sources on German economic history see above all the introduction to the *Handbuch der deutschen Wirtschafts- und Sozialgeschichte*, ed. H. Aubin and W. Zorn, (Stuttgart 1971), pp. 1–10 and 383–5.)

1. H.Zehrfeld, *Conrings Staatenkunde* (Berlin 1926) and E.Wolf, *Grosse Rechtsdenker der deutsche Geistesgeschichte* (Tübingen 1961) on Conring; V.L. von Seckendorf, *Teutscher Fürstenstaat* (Frankfurt 1656); J.P.Süssmilch, *Die göttliche Ordnung in den Veränderungen des menschlichen Geschlechts, aus der Geburt, dem Tode und der Fortpflanzung desselben erwiesen* (Berlin 1741), 2 vols.

2. J.F.Goldbeck, *Vollständige Topographie des Königreichs Preussen* (1785 and 1789, 2 vols); (reprinted Hamburg 1966).

3. A.Günther, *Geschichte der älteren bayerischen Statistik* (Beiträge zur Statistik des Königreiches Bayern, vol. 77, Munich 1910); J.Vincke, 'Die Besiedlung des Osnabrücker Landes bis zum Ausgang des Mittelalters', in *Osnabrücker Mitteilungen*, 49 (1947), pp. 58ff; M.Schaab, 'Die Anfänge einer Landesstatistik im Herzogtum Württemberg, in den Badischen Markgrafschaften und in der Kurpfalz', *Zeitschrift für Württembergische Landesgeschichte*, 26 (1967), pp. 89–112.

4. One example: W.Deeters, *Quellen zur Hof- und Familienforschung im Niedersächsischen Staatsarchiv in Stade* (Veröffentlichung der Niedersächsischen Archivverwaltung), 24 (1968).

5. Staatsarchiv Würzburg, *Mainzer Polizeiakt*, 2236/I–IV; Aschaffenburger Archivreste, 4/VIII, nr. 1.

6. *Bevölkerungs-Ploetz*, 3 (Würzburg), p. 46 (the figures refer to Germany as its boundaries were in 1937).

7. E.Keyser, *Bevölkerungsgeschichte Deutschlands*, 2nd ed. (Leipzig 1941), p. 376.

8. The 60 were not evenly distributed: 11 were in Prussia, 9 in ecclesiastical territory, 5 in Bavaria, 3 in Saxony and so on.

9. Sources: K. von Inama Sternegg and R. Häpke, 'Bevölkerungswesen', in *Handwörterbuch der Staatswissenschaft*, 1st ed. p. 435, 3rd ed. p. 885 and 4th ed. p. 673.

10. Source: E. Keyser, *Bevölkerungsgeschichte*, pp. 362 ff. and *Handwörterbuch der Staatswissenschaft*, 1st ed. p. 435.

11. Sources: M.J. Elsas, *Umriss einer Geschichte der Preise und Löhne in Deutschland vom ausgehenden Mittelalter bis zum Beginn des neunzehnten Jahrhunderts*, I, (Leiden 1936), p. 79 (for Augsburg and Munich), 2B (Leiden 1949), p. 85 (for Leipzig); and W. Kronshage, *Die Bevölkerung Göttingens. Ein demographischer Beitrag zur Sozial- und Wirtschaftsgeschichte vom 14. bis 17. Jahrhundert* (Göttingen 1960), p. 395 (table 7a).

12. Source: Keyser, op. cit., p. 381.

13. Source ibid., pp. 376ff.; Keyser also provides information on the origins of the new citizens.

14. Source: *Handwörterbuch der Staatswissenschaft*, 1st ed. pp. 435ff.

15. Source: P. Mombert, *Bevölkerungslehre* (Grundrisse zum Studium der Nationalökonomie), 15 (1929), p. 129.

16 Source: ibid., pp. 120–1. Demographic studies are not as well developed in Germany as they are in, for example, France and England. This is because genealogical and population studies were patronized by the Nazis. Since 1945 the subject has been in 'disgrace', and the situation is only now beginning to change.

17. W. Abel made an evaluation and summary of the sources in a pioneering work: *Geschichte der deutschen Landwirtschaft* (Berlin 1963; 2nd ed. 1967). Cf. also F. Lütge, *Geschichte der deutschen Agrarverfassung vom frühen Mittelalter bis zum 19. Jahrhundert* (Berlin 1963; 2nd ed. 1967).

18. The estimates in Table 7.10 are the average of three made in the early nineteenth century (by Mucke in 1815, by Rybark in 1815 and by Finck von Finckenstein). They are all printed by E. Bittermann, *Die Landwirtschaftliche Produktion in Deutschland 1800–1950* (Halle 1956), pp. 17, 19, 31.

19. Source: G. Hassel, 'Vollständige und neueste Erdbeschreibung der Preussischen Monarchie und des Freistaates Krakau', in A.C. von Gaspari, G. Hassel and J.G. Fr. Cannabich (eds), *Vollständiges Handbuch der neuesten Erdbeschreibung* (Weimar 1819), I, III.

20. Bittermann, op. cit., p. 421.

21. ibid., p. 82.

22. Source: S. Korth, 'Die Entstehung und Entwicklung der ostdeutschen Grossgrundbesitzes' (University of Göttingen doctoral dissertation, 1952; unpublished typescript).

23. Cf. W. Abel, *Geschichte der deutschen Landwirtschaft*, pp. 141ff., and *Agrarkrisen und Agrarkonjunktur* (Stuttgart 1966), p. 102; cf. also W. Kuhn, *Geschichte der deutschen Ostsiedlung in der Neuzeit* (Cologne, Graz, 1955–7), 2 vols.

24. The source material for mining and industry is little known and less

used. A summary of most important literature on the subject is available in H. Kellenbenz, 'Les industries dans l'Europe moderne (1500–1750)', in *L'industrialisation en Europe* (Paris 1972), pp. 75–114. Cf. also the general studies of H. Aubin and W. Zorn (eds), *Handbuch der deutschen Wirtschafts und Sozialgeschichte* (1971), I, pp. 335–57, 414–64 and 531–73; F. Hartung, *Deutsche Verfassungsgeschichte vom 15. Jahrhundert bis zur Gegenwart*, 6th ed. (Stuttgart 1950) and F. Facius, *Wirtschaft und Staat. Die Entwicklung der staatlichen Wirtschaftsverwaltung in Deutschland vom 17. Jahrhundert bis 1945* (Boppard-am-Rhein 1959).

25. J. U. Nef, 'Silver production in central Europe, 1450–1618', *Journal of Political Economy*, 49 (1941), pp. 575–91.

26. Source: E. Westermann, *Das Eislebener Garkupfer und seine Bedeutung für den europäischen Kupfermarkt* (1460–1560; Cologne 1971), p. 287.

27. See W. Bogsch, *Der Marienberger Bergbau in der ersten Hälfte des 16. Jahrhunderts* (Schwarzenberg 1933); W. Bogsch, *Der Marienberger Bergbau seit der zweiten Hälfte des 16. Jahrhunderts* (Cologne, Graz 1966), p. 182.

28. Cf. R. Stahlschmidt, 'Das Messinggewerbe im spätmittelalterlichen Nürnberg', *Mitteilungen des Vereins für Geschichte der Stadt Nürnberg*, 57 (1970), pp. 127ff; K. Schleicher, 'Geschichte der Stolberger Messing Industrie unter besonderer Berücksichtigung ihrer technischen Entwicklung' (University of Cologne doctoral dissertation, 1958); H. Kellenbenz, 'Die Wirtschaft des Aachener Baumes', in C. Bruckner (ed.), *Zur Wirtschaftsgeschichte des Regierungsbezirkes Aachen* (Aachen 1967), pp. 472ff; A. Schulte, *Die Entwicklung der gewerblichen Wirtschaft in Rheinland-Westfalen* (Cologne 1959), p. 38.

29. Source: H. Niedermayer, *Die Eisenindustrie der Oberpfalz in geschichtlicher und handelspolitischer Beziehung unter besonderer Berücksichtigung der Roheisenerzeugung* (Regensburg 1912), pp. 74f.; Cf. also R. Sprandel, *Das Eisengewerbe im Mittelalter* (Stuttgart 1968); W. Zorn, 'Gewerbe und Handel', in H. Aubin and W. Zorn (eds), *Handbuch der deutschen Wirtschafts- und Sozialgeschichte* (Stuttgart 1971), I, p. 543 and F. M. Ress, 'Geschichte und wirtschaftliche Bedeutung der oberpfälzischen Eisenindustrie von den Anfängen bis zur Zeit des 30 jährigen Krieges', *Verhandlungen des Historischen Vereins von Oberpfalz und Regensburg*, 91 (1950).

30. E. Schremmer, *Die Wirtschaft Bayerns* (Munich 1970), p. 327.

31. Schulte, op. cit., pp. 26 and 34ff.

32. E. Schmitz, *Leinengewerbe und Leinenhandel in Nordwestdeutschland* (Cologne 1967), p. 117.

33. Source: H. Witthöft, 'Struktur und Kapazität der Lüneburger Saline seit dem 12. Jahrhundert', *Vierteljahrschrift für Sozial- und Wirtschaftsgeschichte.*, 63 (1976), pp. 1ff.

34. Cf. the studies of Hartung and Facius mentioned in note 24 above. Cf. also J. Schildhauer, 'Hafenzollregister des Ostseebereiches als Quellen zur hansischen Geschichte', *Hansische Geschichtsblätter*, 86 (1968), pp. 63–76, and *Inventare hansischer Archive* (Berlin 1896–1913), 3 vols. For inland areas the data are still in the archives.

35. J.C.Schedel, *Neuestes Handbuch der Literatur und Bibliographie für Kaufleute oder Anleitung zur merkantilischen Bücherkunde* (1796). Another bibliography by J.S.Gruber appeared in 1794 with 928 numbers.

36. Source: K.Blaschke, 'Elbschiffahrt und Elbzölle im 17, Jahrhundert', *Hansische Geschichtsblätter*, 82 (1964), pp. 49–50.

37. Source: E.Schremmer, *Die Wirtschaft Bayerns. Vom hohen Mittelalter bis zum Beginn der Industrialisierung* (Munich 1970), p. 659.

38. W.Vogel, 'Zur Grösse der europäischen Handelsflotten im 15., 16. und 17. Jahrhundert. Ein historisch-statistischer Versuch', in *Festschrift Dietrich Schäfer* (Jena 1915), p. 280.

39. Cf. the data on shipping in the chapters on England (p.129 above) and France (p. 177). These figures are from Vogel again, op. cit., p. 301.

40. Source: E.Wiskemann, *Hamburg und die Welthandelspolitik von den Anfängen bis zur Gegenwart* (Hamburg 1929), p. 61.

41. Source: W.Kresse, *Materialien zur Entwicklungsgeschichte der Hamburger Handelsflotte, 1765–1823* (Hamburg 1966), pp. 64–5.

42. Source: O.Behre, *Geschichte der Statistik in Brandenburg-Preussen bis zur Gründung des Königlichen Statistischen Bureaus* (Berlin 1905), p. 265.

43. Sources: ibid., pp. 77, 82, 91f., 101–8; R.Koser, 'Der preussische Staatsschatz von 1740 bis 1756', in O. Hintze (ed.), *Forschungen zur brandenburgischen und preussischen Geschichte* (Leipzig 1891), IV, pp. 64ff., 447 and 471–2; and A.F.Riedel, *Der Brandenburgisch-Preussische Staatshaushalt in den beiden letzten Jahrhunderten* (Berlin 1866), pp. 20ff.

44. Source: L.Hoffmann, *Geschichte der direkten Steuern in Bayern vom Ende des XIII. bis zum Beginn des XIX. Jahrhunderts* (Leipzig 1883), pp. 77, 101–2, 137ff, and 217–18.

45. E.Schremmer, *Die Wirtschaft Bayerns*, p. 262. For the development of the state debt in Prussia cf. L.Krug, *Geschichte der Preussischen Staatsschulden* (Breslau 1861).

46. Source: W.Achilles, 'Die steuerliche Belastung der braunschweigischen Landwirtschaft und ihr Beitrag zu den Staatseinnahmen im 17. und 18. Jahrhundert', *Quellen und Darstellungen zur Geschichte Niedersachsens*, 82 (1972), pp. 148 and 167.

47. Source: J.Hartung, 'Die augsburgische Vermögenssteuer und die Entwicklung der Besitzverhältnisse im 16. Jahrhundert', in G.Schmollers *Jahrbuch für Gesetzgebung, Verwaltung und Volkswirtschaft im deutschen Reich*, 19 (1895), pp. 867–83, and 'Die direkten Steuern'. More sources see Herbert Hassinger, 'Politische Kräfte und Wirtschaft 1350–1800', in Hermann Aubin and Wolfgang Zorn (eds), *Handbuch der Deutschen Wirtschafts- und Sozialgeschichte* (Stuttgart 1971), I, pp. 646s; J.Rosen, 'Der Staatshaushalt Basels von 1360–1535', in H.Kellenbenz (ed.) *Öffentliche Finanzen und privates Kapital im späten Mittelalter und in der ersten Hälfte des 19. Jahrhunderts* (Stuttgart 1971), pp. 24–38; Hermann Kellenbenz, 'Die öffentlichen Finanzen im Reich von der Mitte des 17. bis ins 19. Jahrhundert', in *Finances publiques d'Ancien Régime – Finances publiques contemporaines, Colloque International Spa 16–19–IX, 1971* (Pro Civitate, Collection

Histoire No. 34, Brussels 1972), pp. 133–57.
48. Source: P.Sander, *Die reichsstädtische Haushaltung Nürnbergs 1431–1640* (Leipzig 1902), pp. 780ff.
49. Source for Tables 7.18 and 19: H.Mauersberg, *Wirtschaft- und Sozialgeschichte zentraleuropäischer Städte in neuerer Zeit* (Göttingen 1960), p. 451.
50. According to M.J.Elsas (*Umriss einer Geschichte der Preise und Löhne*, 2B, p. 88) the devaluation in the major moneys of account in Germany was as follows: *the Augsburg Rechnungspfennig* dropped 30.7 per cent between 1509 and 1600, the Frankfurt *Pfund Heller* dropped 11.8 per cent (1500–98), the Leipzig *Meissnischer Gulden* 1.3 per cent (1565–1600) the Speyer *Rechnungs Pfund* 25 per cent (1521–1600) and the Würzburg *Rechnungs Gulden* 13.4 per cent (1506–1600). It should be emphasized that this was not just a German phenomenon: cf. F.Redlich, 'Die deutsche Inflation des frühen 17. Jahrhunderts in der zeitgenössischen Literatur: die Kipper und Wipper', in *Forschungen zur internationalen Sozial- und Wirtschaftsgeschichte* (Cologne, Vienna 1972), VI, pp. 11–13.
51. The basic study on prices in Germany was done by M.J.Elsas (cf. note 11 above: vol. 1 1936, vol. 2A 1940, vol. 2B 1949). Since then there are the important studies of W.Abel, *Agrarkrisen und Agrarkonjunktur* 2nd ed. (Stuttgart 1966) and *Geschichte der deutschen Landwirtschaft vom frühen Mittelalter bis zum 19. Jahrhundert*, 2nd ed. (Stuttgart 1967). Cf. also W.Abel, *Landwirtschaft 1500–1648* and *Landwirtschaft 1648–1800* in *Handbuch der deutschen Wirtschafts- und Sozialgeschichte*, I (Stuttgart 1971), pp. 386–413 and 495–530.
52. For Cologne see: Franz Irsigler, 'Getreide- und Brotpreise, Brotgewicht und Getreideverbrauch in Köln vom Spätmittelalter bis zum Ende des Ancien Régime', in *Zwei Jahrtausend Kölner Wirtschaft*, I, (Cologne 1975), pp. 519–39.
53. Source: 'Getreidepreise in Berlin seit 1624', *Vierteljahrshefte zur Statistik des deutschen Reichs*, 44 (1935), pp. 308–21.
54. Source: Elsas, op. cit., I, pp. 560–5. It should be noted the figures are taken from the records of the Heilig-Geist Hospital; had we taken the figures in the municipal accounts (printed by Elsas, op. cit., pp. 540–5) the pattern would have been slightly different. The hospital records were chosen because they were more complete, even though they probably represented real market trends rather less well.
55. E.g. E.Waschinsky, *Währung, Preisentwicklung und Kaufkraft des Geldes in Schleswig-Holstein von 1226 bis 1864* (Neumünster 1952), I, p. 249.
56. Source: Irsigler, op. cit., vol. IIB, pp. 121–3.
57. Elsas, op. cit., vol. IIA, p. 626.
58. ibid., vol. I, pp. 714f., 731–6.
59. ibid., vol. IIA, pp. 597f.
60. ibid., vol. IIA, pp. 299f., 2B, pp. 121–3.

Index

246